Yoga Mama's Buddha Sandals:
Mayans Zapatistas, and Silly Little White Girls

Donna Stewart

ISBN-13:
978-0692738719

ISBN-10:
0692738711

"My books are like water. Those of the great geniuses like wine. (Fortunately) Everybody drinks water."
Mark Twain

Contents

Chapter I: Mayans, Zapatistas, and Silly Little White Girls

"Travel is fatal to prejudice, bigotry, and narrow-mindedness, and many of our people need it sorely on these accounts. Broad, wholesome, charitable views of men and things cannot be acquired by vegetating in one little corner of the earth all one's lifetime."
Mark Twain

Little white girls don't go to the depths of Mexican jungles alone, in the middle of a revolution, without knowing how to speak Spanish. That would be stupid, right? I might end up as a headline: American Girl Disappears in the Jungles of Chiapas. I might be robbed, raped, murdered or kidnapped—according to my mother, all of her friends, and several articles I found online. I could be bitten by poisonous snakes or attacked by roving bands of rabid monkeys. I could pay too much for souvenirs, develop vicious hangovers or diabolical intestinal distresses. I could trip over my own feet and stub my toes.

Not that any of those things couldn't happen, but when, exactly, did Americans go from being pioneering adventurers to cowering within our borders, afraid to go out of cell phone range? Sure Americans were no longer the most popular, or sometimes even welcome, tourists, on the planet, but I was two years out of college and it was high time I fulfilled a childhood dream or two. And, yes, I'd definitely seen too many movies. Particularly all of the Indiana Jones movies.

I probably shouldn't even say this out loud, but during my childhood, I'd actually developed an Indiana Jones...*thing*. When I was a little girl, my family and I lived on a little farm near Memphis, Tennessee. My parents had dreamed of returning to a rural existence where people lived off the land and the good old fashioned fruits of their own sweaty labor. We weren't luddites, but we didn't have both feet in the modern world either.

We did have a T.V., but whatever we watched on it underwent strict scrutiny. Somehow the *Raiders of the Lost Ark* movie passed through the thin margins and I watched it over and over and over again. I can still recite half the words in the movie (to the absolute annoyance of anyone who watches it with me).

I fell head over heels for Indiana Jones, and his desert-to-jungle trekking lifestyle. I dreamed I'd grow up and either marry Indiana Jones, or become him…as a her. I had a real leather bullwhip I'd bought at a flea market with my own allowance and I spent my days in the pine forests behind our farmhouse swinging from tree to tree, from limbs higher than my mother would have wanted to know about. I came home almost everyday smelling of pine, with sap and pine needles stuck in my hair. I dragged neighborhood friends through muddy Tennessee backwaters and made our Barbie dolls dodge giant, runaway boulders in *their* ball gowns.

This trip was for her, that sweet little farm girl who'd had a Southern drawl so thick and twangy no one but her family could understand a word she said. Now that she was all growed-up and had smoothed her words to sound more like Boston than Baton Rouge, she was ready to start ticking off exotic locations.

Dr. Jones probably would have been better prepared than I was for my first traverse outside of my native country. Considering I was actually a research writer—it's literally what I did for a living—my preparation deficits could be baffling. I did so little it's amazing I even managed to make my flight. In my defense, this was during the honeymoon phase at my first real job out of college, and I was so engrossed in my work it consumed most of my energy. I had also been pretty distracted by a boy, and then the sudden end of a relationship with him. But neither of those events are the real reasons for my paltry preparation. But it gets this story started.

I didn't grow up to become or marry Indiana Jones. I'll explain why later, but I didn't. That being what it was, I still wanted to see the mysterious, ancient ruins I'd pretended to explore in the thick woods behind our farmhouse. I decided I'd start with the Seven Wonders of the World, but when I went online to find the list and pick my first destination, I found that there were several lists of various types of wonders of the world. Ancient Wonders, places dubbed so by the B.C. Greeks, the only one of which still somewhat standing are The Pyramids of Giza; Modern Wonders, which include such destinations as the Panama Canal; Natural Wonders, which include the Grand Canyon, etcetera.

Then there are several far more informal lists of world wonders which are subject to inexplicable change or outright disappearance. I found Palenque, in the Mexican state of Chiapas, on one of those lists, discovered it was relatively close, ergo affordable air fare-wise, and was surrounded by jungle. Rugged, exotic and affordable. Muy Bien.

Palenque was said to be the most exquisite example of ancient Mayan construction in Mexico and the place where the first Mayan mummy was discovered. Grand palaces and pyramids covered with mysterious engravings, hieroglyphics, and tenaciously-spirited vines were surrounded by jungles teaming with howler monkeys, jaguars and trillions of birds, bugs and butterflies. The people living around the ruins still lived basically agrarian lives, as of yet relatively unpolluted by Western Civilization. It was exactly the place I'd dreamed of seeing since I was a girl. I picked my destination within ten minutes of beginning my search. Voila. Good or bad, it's the usual time frame I like to take making decisions. No dilly dally. No hem-haw.

I did do *some* additional research, like what kind of plants and animals I might see; Some possible interpretations for Mayan hieroglyphics; how to order a beer and find a bathroom. I scanned 'The Tree,' (travel icon *Lonely Planet's* travel forum), looking for tips and top-secret travel treasures.

But it didn't occur to me to research what it might be like to go from the tiny, Colorado mountain town where I lived to cities and cultures distinctly different from mine, where, perhaps, no one even spoke my language; nor about any ongoing political or social unrest. I was always hearing about folks coming or going to Cancun and, with the exception of sometimes spending a few days laid low because of something called Montezuma's Revenge, they always seemed to have a grand time. I knew where I was going wouldn't be exactly like Cancun, but how much different could it be just a little further south of the main gringo trail? I actually thought I'd be safer because where I was going was so remote, I thought there'd be less chance of issues with drug dealers or hardened city criminals.

Still, I knew it wasn't going to be Cancun. I knew I'd need to beef up my immunizations, get American Express traveler's checks (in the apparently high likelihood I would be robbed or have my pockets picked), and carry lots of iodine tablets for purifying the hell out of any water I planned to consume. It's not that other countries are germier than the U.S. But we tend to build up tolerances to the boogers in our own backyards. That being the case, I also knew I should stay away from any food not completely cooked or that I couldn't peel and eat myself, so I planned to bring a box of tuna fish packets and some crackers. Just in case.

I also knew it would be incredibly hot. A passage from one travel book gave this particularly vivid description: "It's always sweltering hot in Palenque, and there's hardly ever any breeze." I shared that passage with my two friends, Chesney and Michelle, who were joining me on this adventure. I was worried they might have unreal expectations about our trip, because they kept talking about the beach and the beach was a bit of a haul from where I planned to go.

I wanted them to be clear that this wasn't going to be a spring break of draping ourselves over lounge chairs and sipping margaritas from frosty, salt-rimmed glasses. That's never been my thing anyway. At least, not for more than a day.

Don't get me wrong. I can tie one on like only the daughter of a raging alcoholic can, but, mindful of the hereditics of alcoholism, I do it once in a blue moon.

This trip was to be about Adventure (note the capital A)! It was about trekking through jungles, covered in sweaty grit and carrying heavy backpacks to camp under the jungle canopy listening to sounds I'd only heard in action movies and *National Geographic* specials. We'd be three, courageous women traveling to the most remote part of Mexico to see one of the Seven Ancient Wonders of the World (or so I thought), a Mayan marvel, a UNESCO World Heritage Site, and maybe even stumbling on our own discoveries, Indiana Jones style. It would be thrilling, I assured them.

Chesney backed out first, within days of my sharing the "sweltering hot" passage, while Michelle waited several months to just before our departure date to tell me she wouldn't be swatting skeeters in the jungle with me. When she learned I planned to go even if it was alone, she did offer, however, to pick me up if I flew into L.A. from Durango, then take me back to the airport the next morning to fly out for Mexico and pick me up again from the airport when I returned to the U.S..

"You know that's Zapatista country, right?" she said while we were getting pedicures, my first ever and Michelle's treat, the day before my flight.

"Yes, but that was almost a decade ago." I answered, realizing she probably had done more practical research than I had…which was why she was backing out. "I've been reading up on *Lonely Planet's* Thorn Tree forum and almost everyone says it's perfectly safe, as long as you're not out in the middle of the night."

"I read that, too," she said, "but I'm pretty sure they said 'at night.' Actually, I'm pretty sure that post said, in Villahermosa, don't walk around after sunset. Always take a cab even if only a few blocks."

"Sounds like a good way to sell taxi rides," I joked, leaning back into the automated fists of my massage chair.

She gave me a chastising look that suggested I hadn't done my homework and 'what was I thinking?' At least, that's what I felt like she was saying, and part of me knew that if it was, she might be right. I probably should have done more research, but I guess I just didn't want to.

Besides, I'd talked to a friend who had been there and he said it was fantastic. True, I met that friend back when we were both rootless adolescents living out of tents and cars in the National Forests above Durango, Colorado, with a bunch of other wild, misfit kids, so perhaps a questioning of the source might have been in order. But my friend, Wes, had always seemed grounded, even back then.

We'd spent our days hiking, mountain biking, reading the big books on spirituality and the greats of literature, and writing poetry, after which time I went to college and he became a drug dealer. Yes, somehow he still seemed to have it together, but perhaps that was only in comparison with myself and our fellow wood-dwelling peeps. He still seemed the same sweet, smart guy and he'd actually been to Palenque, if you can believe it. He told me the Zapatistas were honorable and had adopted a nonviolent approach for the most part.

Michelle was more skeptical.

In 1994, the Zapatistas of Chiapas and surrounding areas had captured the world's attention when they declared war on the Mexican government, taking over five towns in the province of Chiapas. The actual siege itself lasted only twelve days and cost the lives of 200 people, mostly Zapatistas, before then President Carlos Salinas de Gortari called for a cease-fire to discuss peace. The talks failed and the conflict transitioned to more of a civil resistance campaign that continues today.

Occasionally there are still skirmishes and shots fired, though usually only between military groups and Zapatistas. Though, rumors do come back with travelers who claim they, or someone they know, was robbed or pressed for cash by gangs claiming to represent Zapatistan interests— *TripAdvisor* has quite a few—but almost no one is ever actually hurt. Almost.

I really only had vague memories about it. Hadn't there been something about them wearing masks? At the time, I had been too young and caught up in my own drama to really pay attention, and anyway, that was ages ago. There hadn't been any trouble for years, as far as I knew.

"Have you seen this?" Michelle asked, a wall of brown curls obscuring her face as she leaned over, reached into her purse and pulled out a stack of papers folded in half.

I took the papers and flipped them open. At the top of the first page was a U.S. Department of State seal and the heading 'MEXICO TRAVEL WARNING.' Michelle pursed her lips together and raised an eyebrow over one of her sharp, blue eyes.

Our day of luxurious indulgence, I suddenly realized, was all a plan to talk me out of getting on that plane the next morning. I took a deep breath to remind myself she was only looking out for me. She snatched the pages back and began to read aloud:

"The U.S. Department of State warns U.S. citizens about the risk of traveling to certain places in Mexico due to threats to safety and security posed by organized criminal groups in the country. U.S. citizens have been the victims of violent crimes, such as kidnapping, carjacking, and robbery by organized criminal groups in various Mexican states." she finished, handing the paper back angrily. "THAT! You read *that*?" she asked, raising her voice with both eyebrows, causing other pedicure patrons to momentarily drop their *People* magazines in their laps and look our way.

"Yes, I read that," I said, reassuringly, "but if you scan down further you'll see where it says 'millions of U.S. citizens travel to Mexico yearly quite safely.' Most of the people who get killed were involved in risky behavior, like buying drugs. I don't do drugs. I'll be fine." I smiled reassuringly, as the man working on my feet buffed away at my Colorado-calloused heels. The pungent smell of many open bottles of fingernail polish and something strong enough to kill foot fungus filled the air around us. Stone Temple Pilots played through the overhead speakers, barely perceptible over the sounds of chatter, scrubbing and clinking of metal tools against glass bottles.

She sighed, looking down at the gentleman painting her toenails, so intent on his task he was oblivious to our conversation, "I feel guilty that I backed out on you, that maybe if I'd backed out sooner, you wouldn't have bought tickets and wouldn't feel obligated to go," she said quietly.

I reached over and put my hand on her arm, "Michelle, I don't feel obligated to go. I feel ecstatic! This is the kind of trip I've been dreaming about since I saw *Raiders of the Lost Ark* as a kid. It's going to be such an amazing adventure!" I reassured her.

She rolled her eyes, exasperated, "Look at you"

"What?" I said, indignantly.

"Your curly blond hair. Your blue eyes. Your tiny frame. You look like a shaggy little Barbie doll, for Christ's sake!" she barked. "You'll stick out like a sore thumb. Criminals will see you coming for miles!"

I shrugged, "I've read plenty of stories about other women who travel alone. Sure it's a little riskier, but I know that going in, so I already plan to be careful. And I've taken a PPF (Purely Platonic Friendships) oath for the trip, meaning no romance. So that should eliminate a whole other level of danger. I'll be fine!" I didn't mention that, yea, I was a little miffed she backed out practically at the last minute, but I wasn't lying about being excited for my trip. It was long overdue.

I'd graduated from college two years before, a feat that had taken five years and included a brutal schedule while living well below the poverty line (by American standards) despite sometimes working two jobs, sometimes going months without a day off.

Somehow I graduated with honors, then landed a job as a research associate for an executive education firm specializing in reminding corporate executives how to play nice with others. Part of my job included helping the CEO research, write, and edit books to help distinguish his company from a growing number of competing firms. It was a fascinating, but demanding job, and I burned the midnight oil more than once in the line of duty.

That could be another reason why I didn't go overboard on research for my own trip, but it's not. The truth is, I didn't want to know everything about where I was going. I needed a freefall adventure. I wanted to be surprised, to not know what was coming each and every day. As the adage goes, "Careful what you ask for…"

Chapter 2: The Back Story

"It was the best of times, it was the worst of times, it was the age of wisdom, it was the age of foolishness, it was the epoch of belief, it was the epoch of incredulity, it was the season of Light, it was the season of Darkness, it was the spring of hope, it was the winter of despair, we had everything before us, we had nothing before us...In short, the period was—much like the present period."
Charles Dickens, A Tale of Two Cities

Warning: This chapter might be kind of a downer. You can skip it for now if you want but it's the soil from which I sprang, the one that would cause a girl to do the kinds of things you're about to read about. I'm betting at some point you're going to go, 'Wait. Why would? How could? What?'

Maybe I'm just the way God sent me. Or maybe I was molded and forged. I don't really know myself, but this is where I come from: I've been on my own since the age of 16. Thirteen, if I got really technical.

My parents had always had some issues, but they became true anti-parents when they had themselves a brutal divorce when I was twelve. For us, the divorce process included such shenanigans as one of them setting fire to our barn (it's still not clear who), slashing of car tires, breaking windows, nails in driveways...that sort of thing. My sister and I went from living under constant, stifling supervision, to all hell breaking loose and hours of daylight where, suddenly, no one was watching at all.

For the first time ever our mother, who now had to work, wasn't overseeing our every move, our every music or book selection, our every friendship, with a well-intentioned, but hyper-critical eye.

Ahhhhhhhh. We grew heady from the aroma of free air. At first, our slowly-going-mad father further opened freedom's gates, letting us smoke cigarettes, drink alcohol and party with our friends when we were at his apartment. Until he got custody of us. Then he still let us smoke cigarettes, drink and party with our friends, but on some days, he'd inexplicably beat us up for it. He'd drawn my sister and I to live with him when he started telling us lies about how our mother had been having an affair and the vicious things he'd said was saying that it would take me decades to know she hadn't said.

When given the choice of which parent we wanted to live, I had originally chosen my mother without hesitation, despite her strict, intolerant, Southern Baptist parenting style, serious control issues, and a biblically-sanctioned right to beat her children. I chose to live with her because, while she wasn't an openly affectionate person, I at least knew she loved me, and that her extreme strictness came from a fear of what she thought the world could do to me if I didn't watch out.

My father I'd hardly known. He was a very handsome man with dark, defined eyebrows, a strong jaw, sharp nose and intense eyes. His thick head of wavy black hair was kept swept back but was almost always mussed. Women loved him though his manner was gruff and sometimes cruel. He'd always kind of scared me when he was home, which wasn't very often. He usually worked the 3 to 11 shift at the cellulose plant and left most of the child rearing to my mother. Turns out that had been a really good thing.

My sister, who is a few years older and whose hormones were having a really hard time with the extreme shelter of our mother's love, chose to live with our father immediately and covertly made the move while she was supposed to be in school. My mother was crushed both by her decision as well as her deception. Realizing the level of planning and secrecy that had been involved in such a move, I was stunned.

Despite the fact that she never seemed to like me, I idolized my sister. Combine that with my father's lies, and the destructive skirmishes between my father and mother, and my sister was the only one who still seemed to be who I thought she was. So when she went to live with my father, I decided to follow shortly after.

Besides, there was more freedom over there, I thought, and it was pretty suffocating living under my mother's uber-protective wing. I became intoxicated by the additional freedom I experienced at my father's apartment, and the adventures that came with it. The apartments where he lived were full of latch-key kids who banded together and ran wild. Coming from a rural world where there were hardly any other children around most of my life, this was very exciting! Living with dear old dad, however, turned into a nightmare I don't plan to spend too much time dwelling on.

Daddy was a war veteran with Post Traumatic Stress Disorder. I'm almost certain it was he who set our barn on fire. I think this because, according to one of my uncles, he used to torture small animals before he ever went to war, indicating a predisposition for psychosis that was further inflamed by the experiences of war and the introduction to drugs and alcohol. There had been baby chickens locked in a hutch in the barn at the time and my mother would never have burned a barn with any animals inside.

Besides, a few weeks after the fire, I was walking around the charred, acrid ruins of our barn when I found my grandfather's, (my Father's Father's), tool box in the tall grass of our back pasture. For as long as I could remember it had been stored under the back awning, wound in cob webs, and shaded with a thick coat of dust and mouse droppings. Someone had drug it out into the pasture before the barn was set alight. Which suggests the arsonist was probably my Father. Though, I remember my mother smelling like gasoline when she picked me up from my grandparents that night. Who knows? Anyhoo.

Where my mother believed that you 'spare the rod and spoil the child,' my father thought there was no child-rearing problem that couldn't be solved with a belt and some horrifying, boot-camp-like mental abuse. Turned out he was a monster who, I think, had really tried his best for many years not to be.

There was a constant battle being waged within him between the good man he wanted to be and a horde of demons he could barely keep in check. You could see it in his eyes, especially towards the end. A cold shell barely concealed the storm within. My mother had married him too quickly to see that side of him though, and being the devout Southern Baptist she was, tried everything she could to hold up the "til death do you part' promise she'd made at the altar. She kept it for 15 years. To this day I don't know what finally caused her to divorce him.

Whatever he had been before, after the divorce he slowly started to lose the ability to control his demons at all and year by year he grew steadily worse. When I moved in with him so I could be with my sister, she suddenly moved out, or was kicked out, still not sure which, and I found myself living alone with a man I had good reason to fear. Bad stuff happened.

Which brings me to my big sister who has hated me since I emerged from the womb to strain the already meager rations of human affection available in our household. For years I struggled to understand her hatred. As a young child, I always thought it was something I had done. That for some reason I didn't understand, I must be an awful creature whom my family was stuck with and I was lucky they kept.

Until my parent's divorce. Then the world ceased being what it was and every belief had to be re-examined, including whether I deserved my sister's, or anyone's, animosity or abuse.

Years later she finally told me that she had thought Mom and Dad were reading me stories in my room without her when we were kids, that I was secretly being smuggled cuddles. Where she got that idea I don't know, but it wasn't true. Nevertheless, she used these delusions to justify a lifelong grudge and bullying. Maybe I would have been the same way if I had been the older one, I don't know. Cognitively, I know she was having her own struggles and trying to cope as best she could figure out…but it sure sucked to be me.

She beat up on me throughout childhood. Maybe all big sisters or brothers do, but sometimes this got pretty serious. Such notable moments included dislocating my elbow by slinging me onto the metal pole of our rusty old swing set; shoving me face-first down on the sharp edge of a bass boat seat where I split open my forehead and had to get stitches; and pushing me down on an open dresser drawer, where my cheek got caught on the corner, ripped open and also required stitches. Accidents? Probably the lasting damage part. The worst were the times when I'd somehow managed to make a friend and she'd come along and bully me unmercifully in front of them or tell them things that made them not like me. Utterly humiliated, I'd just crawl away somewhere to play by myself.

She did this until I was twelve years old. At twelve she was beating up on me and whether it was the ignition of pubertal hormones or a new found confidence gained from surviving the crazy behavior of my parent's vindictive divorce, but I was just done with that. Being older and bigger boned than I, she was always able to overpower me easily, but though she still outweighed me, I somehow managed to pick her up, run across the room with her and slam her against the wall screaming, "NOOOOOOOOO!" She never touched me again. She has also barely spoken to me since.

Something happened that day. My self-esteem had been crushed for so much of my life, I'd simply taken everything as if I deserved no better. But when my sister shoved me that last time she ever would, some part of me rose up and said, "No. I don't deserve this." Actually, it said, "NOOOOOOOOOOOOOOO!" SLAM! In that moment I began to change.

I'd been a kicked cur who crept back to her abuser, head low, tail wagging timidly, begging for a scrap of love. That stopped. An ember of self-esteem that had long been smoldering, flared up and I fought to protect the meager spark.

I fought classmates who had previously made fun of the shy little girl with her eyes cast to the ground. I fought teachers who picked on me. I fought against all real or perceived slights. And I fought my Father, quietly in my own mind, when he made me sit for hours in the middle of the night while he told me what a piece of shit I was and how no one would ever care about me but him. I would sit on our nubby beige couch with my eyes glazed and fixed on the second hand of the mirrored clock over the fireplace, chanting to myself, "Don't listen to him. Don't listen to him. He's going to fuck up your head. Don't listen to him." I think he managed to scramble things a bit anyway.

I was removed from his custody twice by Social Services because neighbors or friends' parents turned him in for child abuse. After a month or so, they'd send me back saying he had been too stressed and now he was all better. He wasn't.

When I was sixteen, after a night of drinking and drugs (I assume) he told me he was going to kill me. He told me how he was going to kill me, and how he would get away with it by dismembering me and burning up my body in the fireplace right across from us. From the many nights before of sitting on that couch, forced to listen as his twisted, drunken demons did their best to crush me, I'd learn to go numb to the experiences. Even this one that threatened my life.

It was at the urging of a friend who knew my father, and completely believed his threat, that I climbed out my bedroom window with only the clothes on my back, and ran away for the last time.

The next morning, I went to my probation officer (never said I was angel) and turned myself in as a runaway. I told her she could lock me up 'til I was 21, I wouldn't go back to my Father's house. She asked if I had some place I could stay and I lied and said I did. She told me to go there, stay in school, keep my nose clean and I'd never have to go back to my father's house again.

At first I stayed with my friend who'd convinced me to run away, but her parents weren't up for that additional challenge for long. Then I stayed with my grandparents for a little while, but by then I was practically feral.

I'd grown up in an uber strict household, then suddenly found myself with whole days and nights where I was alone and completely unsupervised, then lived with a father who wouldn't let me leave the house, except to go to school, yet took me to bars with him all the time, and encouraged me to have wild parties at our house, but then beat me up for being drunk. I'd lived in a world that didn't make sense, where rules were overturned like White Russians on a low coffee table, and staying above the chaos required the skills of a San Francisco skateboarder. I'd lived in a house where I never knew who was in the room with me, my father who was supposed to take care of me, or a lecherous, vicious man that I never knew when something might set him off.

I went kind of crazy for a while. When I stayed with adults who didn't threaten me with beatings, I had a hard time following their rules or believing they were real. I also had a hard time with peace and quiet.

I desperately *needed* to be wild. My subconscious couldn't grapple with things that had happened. Anytime life became too calm I started to fall apart inside and I couldn't let that happen. I somehow knew I wouldn't survive it. Not yet. So I raged.

At one point, I ended up staying with my grandparents. I wanted to "be good" for my grandparents, but I just couldn't. I couldn't settle down enough to let my subconscious mull. I also couldn't keep a curfew, and often came home so drunk that one time I parked my car half in the yard and half in the road. Another time I came home with a twelve foot sapling wedged under a dented fender.

One night I came home slightly less inebriated and discovered that my sweet grandmother had been waiting up for me, just to make sure I got home alive. She said not a word, but I heard her tip toeing back to her room. She'd only wanted to see that I was home safe. Again, I tried to be good, but I just couldn't.

I was finally asked to leave when my sweet, Southern Baptist Mamaw found a pack of condoms in my underwear drawer. I tried to tell them I was still a virgin, which I was, and that I had them just in case, but that didn't seem to improve my standing. For them, sex happened only after a union bound by God. There was no reason to even own condoms.

Unbeknownst to me, she was fighting breast cancer, again, at the time. Would it have made any difference if I'd known? I probably would have left on my own.

From then on, I was on the move, sometimes changing locations weekly. My world spun faster and faster into a terrifying and confusing chaos with only one exit, a B line to beautiful corpse. I was too shell shocked, scared and overwhelmed to know how to face my reality or change my fate. So I picked up a mask, a façade character who went wild with her circumstances: The Wild Child. This character was far better equipped to deal with her reality than the shy little creature who'd had such an extremely sheltered existence most of her life. Actually, I'm not sure if it was a façade or a bonafide reaction to my circumstances, but my character was wild, reckless, angry and absolutely fearless. Sometimes. Okay, a lot of the time, it was a façade, because when the lights went out, fighting the fears back could be pretty daunting.

I turned to music for inspiration and fuel, cranking thrash, metal and punk music into my consciousness, letting the frothy, boiling rhythms and lyrics drown out the frightened voice of my subconscious, who, given half a chance, would wonder whatever was to become of her. That just wouldn't do. I couldn't claw the memories out of my heart. I couldn't drink the past away. But I could drown them out, at least temporarily, seeking louder experiences.

The music also gave me a powerful and possibly invaluable outlet for the voice of my own growing rage. It was a music I could dance to with a wild, cathartic fury until anger gave way to beautiful endorphins. In the beginning, my neck would be sore the mornings after from thrashing my head about. It was also great exercise!

Despite what might appear to outsiders as a genre of music and a lifestyle choice that would only further doom me, after studying psychology as an adult, I learned that, given my circumstances, it was a highly therapeutic choice. And the only one whose wardrobe I could afford: baggy, thrift store jeans, torn or too tight t shirts and flannel shirts.

What? Was I going to try out for the cheerleading squad?? Not that there's anything wrong with cheerleading, but I was grappling with a lot more in life than what to wear to prom and I couldn't have cared less how popular I was.

My crowd was pretty wild, but they also tended to have deep souls, big-hearts, loyalty and conspicuous intelligence (shout out to Billy and Shane) and they looked out for me. I had more in common with the adrenaline junkie boys than I did with hair and make-up oriented girls so I hung out primarily with the guys. Usually it was me and two or three guys with wild, metal-head hair, torn up t shirts and acid worn blue jeans. And no, I wasn't a groupie or sleeping with them. Once, when me, and my friends, Billy, Shane and Tommy got pulled over by the cops, the cop had called me a groupie and I shouted back that I wasn't their groupie, that they were mine. Not quite accurate, but fun to shout at that cop.

Though it seems that I was completely out of control, I think I also managed to make some good decisions for myself during that time. I stayed away from the really nasty drugs and once, when I got invited to go backstage at a Metallica concert but they wouldn't let Shane come too, I reluctantly declined.

And I kept fighting. At first, I fought to prove to myself I was worth fighting for. It would take many more years before I fought for myself because I believed I was worth it.

I probably could have gone back to live with my mother, though she'd said, 'no,' when I'd asked once before. But there's a story in the Bible about just this sort of thing in the book of Luke called the Prodigal Son. The prodigal son had left his family but when he returned, no questions were asked and he was welcomed back with a huge, sibling rivalry-inducing party.

But I would have had to beg. And I would have had to promise absolute allegiance and adherence to her rules and the Southern Baptist faith. I would have been loved, kept safe and firmly guided in the direction of a good, Southern Baptist life. But I would have HAD to be EXACTLY what my mother's idea of a good Christian and a good person were. Any ideas that weren't already firmly entrenched in our family culture were angrily trampled out, like dangerous brush fires. I knew if I went back it would be to life in a cage. I would hear the door swing shut behind me and have to say goodbye to any ideas of my own, any will of my own. "If you're going to live in my house, you're going to live by my rules," doesn't begin to convey the level of control over my own life and mind I would have to give up. In her defense, at the time there was a popular Southern parenting technique called, "Tough Love," which encouraged parents to maintain absolute authoritarian control, and sometimes that technique may actually have saved lives and families. But I literally decided I'd rather die than give up control of my own mind and life direction.

So, rootless, broke and never staying in one place for long, I barely graduated high school, but I did graduate. And I maintained my virginity. On purpose. For a while anyways. Witnessing the debauchery of my father had jaded me to even the most suave of predators and pretty boys. I had no intention of letting what everyone said would happen to me, happen, if I could help it. While I partied like a rock star, sometimes with rock stars, I held fast to a list of principles I believed in my heart, one of which was, either it's a love "he" was willing to fight dragons for or 'Hands off Buddy!' Mostly.

Paradoxically, at the same time I was just saying no to drugs and promiscuity, I started taking dangerous physical risks. I jumped onto moving trains, climbed buildings in the middle of the night, and broke into dilapidated, condemned buildings on the wrong side of downtown Memphis, exploring them with my crazy cousins (Shout out to Carey and Clay!). I refused to go out by contracting HIV or by drug overdose but I grew to love the rush of brushing right up against potential immediate death and barely escaping.

Something about these brushes gave me the courage to continue to exist. Maybe because it showed me that I had some power over my life, that I had the power to stop all of this if I really felt like I had to, and I could do it with a spectacular bang. I used to reassure myself that if things got too bad, there was always Plan B. Plan B was suicide.

I was still scared sometimes if I let myself feel it, but just having Plan B changed everything. With literally nothing to lose, the world opened up. In those moments when my fingertips brushed against the robe of the Grim Reaper, I felt an aliveness, a sparkling, pulsating awakeness…You can only imagine how exciting it was to come to Colorado a few years after this and find an entire tribe of folks who loved that rush too, who showed me how to chase that edge in the mountains and deserts through climbing, bushwhacking and mountain biking.

My teens were scary, but they were also exhilarating and there was a lot I'd loved about living on the edge. It's where I broke through the derogative limitations set down by my parents, Southern society and…scratch that. For someone in my situation, the limitations and judgments came from everywhere. A broken child from a broken home with no one to guide me? According to the books (Literally. I read about kids like me in Child Development class in High School) the situation was pretty hopeless. I was doomed to live a life of misery and violence. And I very well might have if not for many things I can't explain. Sometimes when I just barely managed to pull away from the Grim Reaper's grasp, it was as if God yanked me back by my collar.

One day, I packed everything I could into an old, beat-up Volkswagen beetle, left my hometown of Memphis Tennessee and headed for the widely acclaimed wild, wild West.

After rolling across wide-open prairies and seas of desert sage brush, my Beetle Bug broke down climbing into the Rockies, in the tiny mountain village of Durango, Colorado. I ended up living in the forests of the nearby mountains with a bunch of other wild, rambling teenagers whose parents had either given up on them or whom they'd barely escaped. The beauty of those forests and meeting others like me—poets, dreamers, rebels, outdoor nuts, scholars, future preachers, monks and athletes—all of us struggling to regain or create a sense of ourselves, was rejuvenating and I spent two years living in a tent in those fairy-forested mountains. These were two of the best years of my life and the hardest to explain to anyone else.

Instead of the experience dooming me, it shattered *everything* I thought I knew and I discovered who I really was and who I wasn't.

Turned out, I was pretty damned cool. And a good person. No one should ever get to think they're holier than thou until they've been hungry and desperate and still chose to do the right thing—even when no one was watching. Don't get me wrong, I wasn't a saint. For example, I once stole three cupcakes from a church cafeteria when I was hungry, but I didn't let the poor little rich boy who fell in love with me buy me a car and pay my rent. You can see the distinction?

Also turns out I was smart. Before I'd left Memphis, I'd secretly thought I was mildly retarded all of my life. Coming out West with that syrupy, twangy, Southern-accent that made everybody giggle every time I opened my mouth didn't improve that self-perception. With the accent, even after I clawed my way into college, my professors treated me like a small child.

Then, one day, I watched the old Audrey Hepburn musical, *My Fair Lady*, at a friend's house and I became fascinated with the idea of changing your life by changing the way you speak.

Slowly and painstakingly, I trained myself to sound more like Audrey and less like Betty Lou. The difference in the way people responded to me was dramatic. People started taking me seriously in ways blatantly obvious. My grades went from solid B's and C's to solid A's. I walked in and picked up jobs on the spot, and people stopped listening to me with looks of amusement and started listening with serious attention. I was the same person, with the same mind, the same ideas. Only the way I conveyed them was different. It was eye opening. I'd spent my entire life afraid someone would find out I was retarded, but when I finally graduated from college, I did so with honors.

Course, there was always the little voice inside telling me I shouldn't have changed myself for the world, but that little voice had absolutely nothing to contribute when I was so short of cash I lived off ramen noodles, so she could just keep her self-righteous comments to herself.

After living the life of a wandering poet-writer-dreamer-schemer out of a tent for those two years, each day unzipping it to find myself surrounded by living, pulsating beauty, I'd had a hard time transitioning when I moved into a house with two other girls, and started college. I didn't buy a bed, but continued sleeping in a sleeping bag on the floor and kept my belongings minimal. But I couldn't sleep. I missed the immediate connection with the wild canopy of stars, the serenade of the coyotes, and I found the air in the house too stale to breathe. But I also knew it was my chance to rejoin the world, so I had to acclimate.

During the first weeks indoors, I'd stood on the balcony and felt like a caged animal. I remember watching a red-breasted robin poking about the manicured lawn ten feet below me and feeling as though I'd somehow betrayed my ideals. Something about the living indoors thing felt wrong. Except indoor plumbing. Now that I liked.

One day, I saw some packets of glow-in-the-dark star stickers in a store and I came up with an idea. My room was mostly underground with only a small window to the far edge of a wall. I spent weeks putting up thousands of stars, carefully following constellation patterns for the Northern Hemisphere of stars in the winter. Since I didn't really have furniture, I started the constellations about a foot and a half from the floor, and placed them all over the walls and ceiling. When you turned off the lights and all you could see were stars, it was as if you were floating in space. I left the window permanently open, filling the small room with the sharp, clean smell of winter, and finally I was able to sleep.

Eventually, I adapted. I went outside and played anytime I had free time: Rock climbing, mountain biking, hiking…you name it, if it's done outside, I probably gave it a whirl. But it takes a week of backpacking to feel close to the same level of connection I'd had living in the tent. Or wild adventures so intense they strip your baggage within hours instead of days. Over the years since I'd moved indoors and 'settled down' I was lucky enough to find myself on a few adventures like that, by sheer luck, accident and the grace of God. I survived them the same way: sheer luck, accident and the grace of God.

Now the will power it had taken to spend five years getting my degree then establishing myself as the research assistant to the CEO of a multimillion dollar company, was stressing the restraints I'd had to put in place for so long to get there. There was a part of me that was still feral and she was growing tired of brooding quietly. She wanted out and began pushing ever so slightly on the confines of responsibility. Her push was getting stronger. I longed to throw everything away and return to the wild, so I knew I'd better pacify her quick or she'd wreck everything I'd worked so hard to achieve.

I needed an adventure. One where you have to just keep putting one foot in front of the other and trust the universe to catch you. Often enough it does. Caution though: Sometimes it doesn't. But that's part of the rush. Being forced to think on your feet faced with fairly intense consequences. I wanted to know just enough that I ruled out the most dangerous mistakes I could make. Checking the rock, so to speak, before I started climbing. But what each hold was actually like or whether it would hold I could only discover by heading up. After several years of living by the book of Western Civilization, I felt like I was losing my perspective. While I no longer openly taunted the Grim Reaper, I still craved leaps of faith into the unknown, lunacy or not.

So that's the girl you see heading to the airport in Michelle's car for this next chapter. Maybe you think I'm completely nuts? Well, let's go on with the story and see if I change or confirm your opinion.

Chapter 3: Flights of Fancy

"A ship in harbor is safe. But that's not what ships are for." U.S. Navy Rear Admiral Grace Hopper

When Michelle reluctantly dropped me off at the LA-X airport, I shivered with excitement, but I admit that I also felt a deep stab of loneliness watching her car pull away from the curb. I saw her hit her brakes a couple of times and wondered if she thought I was changing my mind or maybe she was changing hers. But then she turned right and her car disappeared around the next corner. Oh well.

LA-X was the first real eye-opening experience for this small town gal. When I'd flown in, it had been more crowded compared with the Durango airport. Much more than I'd expected. But what I really hadn't expected was to spend an actual two hours standing in line, and then get frisked before I gained entrance to the monument that is LA-X. I'd thought I would have at least an hour to mill about before we boarded, and had planned to grab some breakfast before my flight. Unfortunately, after all the frisking and shoe examinations, I only had fifteen minutes. Since I was new to all of this I decided I'd best just stay by my gate and grab something on my layover in Mexico City.

After I picked a seat, I discreetly surveyed my fellow passengers at the gate. Other than a rowdy trio of college boys who looked straight out of Iowa, I was the only other non-Latino, an unusual situation for me as my town in Colorado was predominantly white. I stole glances of the faces around me and turned my ears to better hear when I heard

20

conversations in Spanish.

It was happening. I was leaving my country. English wasn't going to be the first language. Across from me, two women chatted casually in Spanish, smiling at each other. A mother scolded children who were clambering over and under the seats. The language was different but the situations seemed universal. I looked the other direction and saw a tall, fierce man coming into our gate's seating area. He had a wild mop of black curly hair, cut in a shoulder-length mullet, and a beard and mustache that barely covered the many scars and pock marks on his cheeks. I hoped he wouldn't choose the seat beside me because he looked like he'd either just come from killing someone or was on his way, and boy did he think they had it coming.

He chose a seat on the next row and unraveled a wrinkled brown paper bag, pulling out a leftover sandwich. He finished it off in two enormous bites, working mandibles that looked like they could chew through bone. I scanned the faces around me to see if anyone else took notice of this vicious looking passenger, but no one did.

I shrugged, and pulled my *Lonely Planet* guide book from my pack and flipped open to the section on Villahermosa, where my plane would land later that afternoon. I'd taken a brief look at hotels I might find, but folks on "The Tree," had been almost unanimous about not pre-booking hotel rooms but exploring options first hand after you arrive, you know, for the most authentic cultural experience. Only "wankers" would stay at a chain you could find online. That was actually kind of a relief considering that I hadn't seen many chain hotels when I'd looked. Just a Best Western and a Holiday Inn. I couldn't wait to walk the sandy streets and bargain for cabanas.

One forum member, who went by the avatar name of 'HayDuke Lives,' seemed to be especially knowledgeable. He had some great suggestions, but cautioned me if I arrived after dark, to not go exploring. Just take a cab to one of his suggested establishments. No problem, I assured him, my plane was scheduled to arrive by 4:15 p.m. and the sun wouldn't set for several hours.

Villahermosa is in the Mexican state of Tabasco, neighboring the state of Chiapas, but it's the closest airport to Palenque. My plan was to stay in Villahermosa a night or two so I could visit a museum where they have enormous, boulder-sized heads carved by the Olmec people more than a thousand years ago. Then I'd take a bus several hours into Chiapas to the Maya Bell, a campground in the jungle near Palenque. There, I'd set up camp to explore the ruins for a day or so, then who knew what was next. My schedule was open for come what may.

Come what may would be after I saw Palenque, of course. Palenque.

An ancient city of the Maya that had long been abandoned to the jaguars and monkeys, yet retained exquisite glyphs, sculptures and bas-reliefs. Lingering mysteries still hid under tourists feet and acres upon acres of unexcavated, but seriously suspected, hidden ruins. It's estimated that only 10% of the city has been explored, leaving thousands of magnificent structures still cloaked in a jungle of cedar, mahogany and ceiba trees, whose roots sank into the damp composting soil like bony fingers, threatening to pull the ruins apart as their colony spread.

Then there was the Maya Bell, the campground where'd I'd be staying. I'd found out about it by happy chance. I wasn't having much luck arranging anything online and when I tried to call listed numbers, if anyone answered at all, they didn't speak English. Fortunately, one day I was walking down the sidewalk in Durango when I happened to run into Wes, the Mountain hippie turned drug dealer I'd mentioned before, and told him about my trip and my lodging dilemma.

Turns out he'd been there. He told me about this little hippie paradise just outside the gates of Palenque National Park. He said just show up and I'd be fine. I don't know what made me take his advice. We weren't extremely close, but over the past few years, when he came strolling into Durango we'd still grab coffee and catch up. Back in the day, he'd looked like Jesus, with wild, wavy brown hair, and a full beard and mustache. I'd actually had the biggest crush on him then. But he had been too free-spirited even for me. We ran with the same wild crowd until I changed the course of my life and fought through red tape razor wire to get into college and he chose the far more lucrative career of drug dealer. I was never sure how that really worked for him. He never seemed mean enough for the profession.

After that years went by without us seeing each other, but we'd met at a special time in each other's lives. A time when we were so authentically unveiled, so rawly ourselves. When you meet someone in that place and you are in that place, it doesn't matter how many years go by or how much you seem to have changed. It doesn't matter, because you have met each other's essence. Your true selves, and that is something that never changes.

So it was with us. Every few years he would come wandering back into Durango, glowing like he'd been drinking from the fountain of youth whether he was clean cut, or back to shaggy beard and mane, and we'd have coffee. He was clean cut but still glowing when I saw him just before this trip and he told me about the Maya Bell campground. It was the last time I'd see him. I heard a few years ago that he disappeared, floating down a river in Nicaragua in a kayak. He is presumed dead. I miss him. I miss knowing he's out there.

Before I started college, I really wanted to study archaeology and chase the Indiana Jones dream. But the dream I dreamed could not be met by a bachelor's degree. For the life I wanted, I would need to have wealthy family and friends to fund the kind of digs I wanted to do. Otherwise, archaeology jobs were scarce, low-paying and usually on developing job sites like malls and grocery stores, not wild jungles. Since I didn't have a Mummy and Daddy backing my plays, I needed a degree that would get me a job right after I graduated in time to start making my student loan payments. Poor people have a whole different set of considerations when they're picking their college majors.

I'd originally planned to go to Law School and become an environmental lawyer so I could do a better job protecting the environment than I had already been doing as an uneducated, but passionate, political activist before I started college. It's actually why I started college, truth be told. But in my junior year, I briefly dated an attorney who helped open my eyes to the fact that I would graduate with a huge pile of debt and be forced to work for the bad guys because the good guys couldn't afford to pay me.

I checked into his prediction, even calling executives at Sierra Club and the Audubon society, whom I'd previously represented as an activist, and asked them how much truth there was to what he said. One of them told me they couldn't predict the future. Okay, fair enough. The other one said they'd hire me in a minute, but first they had a vast stable of lawyers with twenty years of experience who worked pro bono to fulfill their own, long-compromised, idealistic inclinations. When they ran out of those, they'd def give me a call. Hmmm, hedging my bets on running out of lawyers wanting to improve their karma?

There went that goal. I decided to keep my major of Political Science, hoping my work as an activist, which involved writing legal appeals not—or not just—chaining myself to trees, my high GPA, and the fact that I worked my way through college picking up a double major in Writing along the way, would convince employers I was way too cool to pass up. It worked well enough to get a job that allowed me to make this trip.

Back in LA-X airport, two elegant Hispanic women approached the gate desk and began shuffling papers. I took that as an indication we were about to start boarding, so I put my book away. One of the women leaned towards the mic and began speaking in Spanish, then repeated instructions clearly in English. It was my first international experience! My plane was boarding. It was time to go.

Chapter 4: They Do Things Differently

"A smooth sea never made a skilled sailor." Franklin Roosevelt

It was an eye-opening experience when I had to change planes in Mexico City and the overhead announcer spoke primarily, and sometimes only, in Español. Really, really fast Español.

At the terminal in Los Angeles, the announcer had spoken in Spanish first, and then repeated their message clearly in English. In Mexico City, almost all of the messages were spoken only in Spanish and came out garbled over an antiquated PA system that sounded like speaking through a cup of sand.

I tried to ask for help finding my seat but no one I approached spoke English. I'd had a couple of years of Spanish classes in college, and I made straight As, but I hadn't had much practice. Ever. Still, I'd somehow assumed that once I was submerged in the culture all those high-grade-earning learnings would just come flowing out, at least enough to get by. They didn't. I couldn't read the signs and I sure as hell couldn't understand the announcements. It was sort of scary to be in this enormous building full of more people than lived in my town, with whom I couldn't communicate and none of whom could give a hill of beans about me and my lack of street smarts.

Finally, I asked a solemn-faced security man shouldering a rifle to help me find my gate. Once there, I didn't budge for fear of missing my flight if I misunderstood something. So I sat. Then walked circles around the seating area. Then sat again. Our flight was delayed by one hour, then two, then three. When we finally boarded I did my calculations and determined that we would land around 11:30 pm. Well after sunset. Hmmm. Didn't someone say NOT to be on the streets after dark? I was sure that was just over-cautious advice, blowing the danger way out of proportion. Besides, I thought, the hotels were probably located all together as they tended to be in the U.S. and I could just try one after the other until I found something. I lost some bargaining ability with the late hour, but I'd at least get a roof over my head and if I didn't like the place I could look elsewhere tomorrow.

I was still excited, but now that little part of me that had started to care whether I lived through my adventures seemed to curl up and kind of started whimpering. The wild lioness of the Colorado Rockies was starting to feel a bit of a scaredy-cat. A different feline altogether. In a few hours, I would be arriving in a remote Mexican city, at midnight, with nowhere to stay.

As I sat fretting this development, who should come strolling onto the plane but the largest, meanest looking Mexican man I'd ever seen. The fierce one who wore the eau de homicide cologne. The one I'd breathed a sigh of relief when he didn't choose the seat next to mine at the gate seating area in L.A.. Now he was slowly making his way down the aisle of the plane, carefully checking the row numbers as he went. He stopped at my row, threw a heavy bag in the overhead compartment and gave me a curt nod as he poured himself into the seat beside me.

I gave him a frightened, tight-lipped smile, and chirped an, "Hola," which he returned but somehow without moving a single muscle in his face. I did what visual examination I could without actually turning my head to look right at him. He reminded me of Danny Trejo, who played Machete in the Spy Kids movies, but twice his size. Up close like this, he seemed more of everything: Bigger, Fiercer, rougher complexioned, but with a curiously fresh scent. Not a cologne scent, more like a freshly-dried-on-a-clothes line scent.

My poor little subconscious, the one with all my fears, preconceptions and prejudices, squeaked to myself, "I'm going to die. When the plane lands and he sees I don't have any idea what to do or where to go, this is the man who's going to kill me." I buckled my seat belt and tried not to rub arms with him. He could have the armrest.

The plane took off out of Mexico City like we were moon bound. Granted this was only the third time I'd ever ridden in a plane, but I swear it took off at a five degree angle and held that position for I don't know how long. Long enough that I either fainted or fell asleep because it was sometime later when someone ever so gently squeezed my arm, and softly said, "¿Perdón? ¿Que quieres cenar?" I looked up and found myself face to face with the giant who shared my row, who was now gently waking me with a kind expression on his face, while the stewardess stood nearby holding a plate. I'll say that again: the stewardess was patiently waiting, holding a plate of actual hot food, while my bunk mate, the apparent gentle giant, woke me to see if I wanted my dinner. To which I gratefully answered, "Si, Por Favor!"

Because I wouldn't leave my gate in Mexico City, I hadn't eaten since early that morning. I was starved, shocked and gratified to learn that international flights, non-American flights, actually served real food. And not something out of a plastic baggie that screamed apocalypse rations. This was real meat and potatoes. For free! Gratis! When I finally took a moment to pause from my gorging, I turned to my row partner, locked eyes and said earnestly, "Gracias." He returned my thanks with just the teensiest of smiles and a quick nod. His face now transformed to friend.

When we landed, the airport was deserted. Buzzing florescent lights shined on a wide hall with a scuffed-up, white vinyl floor. The baggage carrousel ground to a start, slowly spitting up suitcases onto a tattered conveyer belt. My massive "friend" quickly retrieved a dubious looking duffel bag and disappeared, while I broke out my translation book and tried to figure out where to find a taxi. Near the front entrance a small group of Mexican men stood smoking cigarettes and arguing intensely under a sign that said, "Taxi."

Well that part was easy. I shouldered my backpack and walked up to them, confidently flipping through my little phrase book until I came to the transportation section, "Perdón, necesito. Que. Me. lleven," I stumbled out (Pardon, I need. A ride…more or less).

One of the men turned to me impatiently and said, "¿Tiennes Dinero (you have money?)?" His response was so terse, so not the eager-to-please vender demeanor I had expected, that I was momentarily taken aback. Wait. Aren't the taxi drivers just waiting for a tourist to pander to? These men? Not so much.

Abandoning all pretenses of a worldly traveler not to be trifled with, I reached right down to the hidden money belt I wore under my pants—yes, the one you're never supposed to let anyone see—and pulled out one of my American Express travelers checks. I smiled, holding it up triumphantly. The man leaned forward and squinted at the note, then said, "Baaaa," while simultaneously waving me away and returning to his argument. I looked at the travelers check to make sure it was what I thought it was. It was an American Express Traveler's Check, the check supposedly accepted anywhere you are, according to the commercials.

Well, apparently in Tobasco it was dog poopy. But it was all I had. I said, "Hey!" and looking earnest, held out my hands in my best "what gives?" expression. To my shock, and terror, the men simply ignored me.

I began to panic. I was 100 lbs. of nothing, in a world it was really beginning to dawn on me, I didn't know at all. I entreated in my slow, stuttering Spanish, "Por Favor, ¡Señors! ¡Necesito. que me. lleven a hotel! You can't just leave me here," I pleaded, my eyebrows knit together, my arms out in entreaty. It must have been some conversation I was disturbing, but finally one of the men stepped away and asked, "¿Tienes una Tarjeta?" He had a thick, jet black moustache that completely covered his lips even when he spoke. He wore a green baseball hat with the letters of whatever it represented almost completely peeled away.

"¿Hable Inglès?" I asked, hopefully.

"No. No hablo Inglès," he answered stoically. "¿Tienes Tarjeta?"

I pressed my lips together with a worried expression, and began flipping through my book.

For a moment he just stared at me in disbelief, then leaned over my shoulder as I flipped through the book. "Alto," he said holding up his hand. He pointed to the book. "Tarjeta." Card. He was asking if I had any cards, like debit or credit cards.

Did I have any cards? Well, that was kind of a funny story. Another side effect of living in a tiny little mountain town is that you really don't need things like credit cards and ATM cards. I'd only recently qualified for a credit card and I'd never needed an ATM card because in my town, you just wrote checks for whatever you needed, rent, groceries, beers, shots of tequila. Checks were still considered same as cash in the little town I now called home. I just never bothered to get an ATM card.

Until the day I was leaving for this trip. I was taking care of a few last minute details when it occurred to me that I might want an ATM card. So I went into my bank and filled out the request form and took it to the clerk. She smiled warmly and said, "Great, we should get this out to you in the next 10 days." To which I responded, "Ten *days*? But my plane leaves this morning for L.A. and then I fly to Mexico tomorrow. I was hoping I could get it today?" She looked apologetic, "I'm sorry, they mail them from a main branch."

I'd thought they could make them onsite the way they do driver's license and grocery cards. Ah well, I shrugged. No ATM card. I'd never had one before, and I've always gotten along fine.

But now I was in the deep South of Mexico, in the middle of the night, with no where to stay, no one speaks my language, and I'd just been turned down by a whole group of taxi drivers for reasons I couldn't comprehend (I'd find out later there was a big protest taking place that weekend. They had much more serious matters of concern than one loco gringa, showing up in the middle of the night with useless pieces of paper and no grasp of the language.) I had one taxi driver that seemed somewhat interested in driving me, but he didn't want to waste his time or gas if I didn't have the funds to pay. Later I'd wonder just how many American girls arrive, by plane, in Villahermosa, without money, to have caused this caution.

I reached into my not-so-secret-money belt and held up the only card I had, which was a credit card, and I had no idea how to get a cash advance on one. He led me over to an ancient looking ATM machine and gestured towards it. I shook my head and shrugged that I didn't know how to work it. "No sè," I said. I don' know.

"¿PEEEN?" He said slowly.

I shrugged sadly, "No sè peeeen. (I don't know PIN)"

He sighed and looked away, frustrated. I stared at him, pleading with my eyes for him not to abandon me. The florescent lights buzzed loudly overhead. He shook his head and looked back at me, obviously dumbfounded "¿Adonde vas?" He asked, "¿Donde?"

From somewhere deep in the recesses of my brain, a Spanish class I'd taken years ago recognized this word as 'where'? I knew he was asking me where I was going. I almost told him that I didn't know. That I didn't have any reservations anywhere, but I had a feeling that his interest in driving me away from the airport was fading and he had more important matters to attend. I quickly blurted out, "Best Western. I'm going to the Best Western." A wave of relief seemed to come over him. He knew the Best Western. He gestured me to follow him.

A wave of relief was on me as well. That is, until I remembered all 'The Tree' and Department of State advisories. Though I've learned a little something about 'The Tree'. When I first stumbled across the site, I thought I'd discovered where the experts go to swap secrets with the experts. This statement is not to discount any of the fine folks on 'The Tree,' but I have since learned to take each recommendation with a dash or two of salt. For example, when they recommended not getting a hotel reservation and just showing up looking for the establishment that best exemplified the culture of the area, they didn't know they'd be read and taken literally by a silly little white girl, who'd never been out of the country, and didn't speak Spanish.

But some of their other advice may have saved my life if not my luggage. It wasn't always easy to adhere to third world travel best practices, though. For example, I'd been advised never to let the taxi driver put my backpack in the trunk because thugs, working with or without the knowledge of the taxi drivers, sometimes run right up at stop lights, pop the trunk with a crowbar, and take off with your luggage.

Kidnappers do something similar, but with people. These situations all seemed easy to avoid when I was back home, sitting in front of the computer sipping lattes and taking notes. In the real world, when it seemed I was lucky to score any ride at all, I didn't feel I was in the position to make any special requests as to where my backpack was to be stored. I might offend the only driver who'd finally agreed to bring me to a hotel. In the defense of, well, anyone in this story that warrants it, I was basically dressed in rags. I'd sought out the most worn out clothing I could find at the local thrift store and used a beat up looking backpack so I wouldn't look like I was worth the trouble of robbing or kidnapping. Apparently, I didn't even look like I could afford a taxi.

The driver threw my backpack in the trunk and opened the door for me to get in. I climbed in the backseat. The seats were torn in several places and there were no seat belts. An ashtray on the door panel was packed tight with cigarette butts and shook ashes all over the back seat with every bump. The ashes were then blown all over by the wind that rushed through the, apparently permanently, open windows. This was my first taxi ride ever.

I spent most of the forty-five minute drive through the darkness wondering what would happen if we arrived and found no vacancy at the Best Western. Would the driver drive me around to other hotels, let me crash at his place (I'd heard rumors of such kindnesses), or would he simply boot me out on the curb in the city where I'd been warned not to show my pale face on the street after sunset.

It was miles from the airport before we even began to see signs of civilization. In the darkness I could just barely make out an almost unbroken wall of vegetation on either side of the road, with sometimes the shadowy outlines of small homes but with no lights on. When we made the occasional stop, the sounds of a jungle full of bugs both frightened and excited me. The air smelled of damp, rich earth and overripe fruit. Finally I started to see a few lights tucked away in the trees, then what seemed like miles of cinder block walls just off the road way. Many of these walls had broken glass cemented into the top of the wall. The glass sparkled in our headlights. In my ignorance, I'd pictured straw thatched cabana's surrounded by jungle, but this was starting to appear to be a large city…whose houses needed tall, broken glass topped cinder block walls for protection.

It began to dawn on me that I might have gotten in over my head.

That maybe I shouldn't be here at all. I assumed people who worked directly with the public would know how to speak English, but none of the cab drivers spoke English. The stewardesses on the plane didn't speak English. The security guard at the airport didn't speak English. I began to feel like a foolish little girl pretending to be this grand adventurer, but at that moment, I was quaking in my boots.

We pulled into the gates of the Best Western and at first I thought a mistake had been made. This place looked like a Colonial Palace, with an elaborate metal worked front gate and candle-lit entryway. The lobby had tall ceilings, dripping with crystal chandeliers. Arched doorways lead down half a dozen adobe halls hung with tapestries, patina paint and more candlelight. And there I stood in my $2 khakis, 50-cent faded T-shirt, and dumpy looking backpack. The night clerk, who spoke about six English words, took no notice of my dour appearance as he checked me in.

The taxi driver, Jorge, I'd learned from the tag inside his taxi, asked him if he could cash the traveler's checks so I could pay my fare. The clerk agreed and changed one of my two $100 traveler's checks. I turned to the driver to see how much I owed him.

"Bddsddlelsllelelel," he answered.

I understood not a word that he said and by this time I was so flustered, I simply turned the cash into a fan and offered it to him with a pleading look to take only what he needed. He stood surveying me for a minute, took two bills from the stack without breaking eye contact, then took a business card out of his wallet, wrote a number on the back of it, touched me on the shoulder in a surprising show of fatherly concern, handed me the card and said something earnestly as he pointed at the number. I surprised him by throwing my arms around him and giving him a hug. He gave me a pat on the back, looked quizzically at me, said something else earnestly while pointing to the card in my hand, and then he was gone.

I went to my room, shut the door and dropped onto the bed. The room was more modest than the entranceway or hallways. Inside was basically like any other Best Western I've ever stayed in, except that the furniture was prettier. The bed's headboard, the dresser and the desk were all made from a beautiful wood with a rich stain brushed on just enough to protect the wood and give it a sheen, but not enough to hide the swirls and waves of the beautiful grain. All three pieces were carved on the borders and edges in subtle designs that resembled ancient Mayan drawings. It was elegant and comfortable, but not as luxurious as the other areas of the hotel that I had seen. Which was kind of a relief, because it probably meant that I could afford this place, at least for a night or possibly two while I figured out what to do. Should I head back to the airport in the morning and get right back on a plane to LA-X?

What was I thinking? Had anything bad actually happened to me? Thanks to a crazy adolescence, I have been in scarier situations with people way more dangerous than anyone I had encountered here. I'd spent my teenage years homeless, couch-surfing and conning my way through survival in Memphis, Tennessee, Forbes Magazines' 4th most dangerous city in the United States. I don't know about everywhere else, but when you live below the poverty line in Memphis, just knowing what streets to avoid is not enough. You have to learn quick, high-stakes risk-assessment. Every person and every situation gets scanned for angles or danger. Granted, it'd been a long time since Memphis, but it wasn't as if I'd suspended those skills. They'd become a part of my nature. And so far, no one had tried to hurt me in anyway, despite my resemblance to a shivering Chihuahua with my pale skinned, blue-eyed, blond-haired, non-Spanish-speaking, travel-skills-of-a-toddler, practically broadcasting vulnerability. The taxi driver wasn't in cahoots with luggage stealers or kidnappers. That, or they had the night off. No one tried to hijack our car or snag my pack out of the back. I felt unusually vulnerable because I'd never been in a place where no one spoke my language, where I didn't know any of the rules or how things were done. But nothing had been really dangerous.

One thing was certain, I was going to be a lot more patient when I encountered someone stateside who didn't speak English. At any rate, Day 1: I was still alive and had managed to find shelter. Yay me! What the fuck was I doing here and would I stay was a question that could wait 'til the morning. Just then, I felt in way over my head.

Chapter 5: The Breaking of Bad

"I think fearless is having fears but jumping anyway."
Taylor Swift

One always feels braver in the morning, with hours of danger exposing daylight stretched out before you. I first experienced this 'fearlessness-by-day, knees-quaking-by-night' phenomenon, when I left my hometown of Memphis, Tennessee. I had $200 to my name, wasn't sure where I was going, and was traveling in a car much older than I was. By day, I felt like a courageous explorer. At night, curled up in the back of my car in some interstate truck stop parking lot or alone in my tent, fear crept up like a stalking animal and hounded me all night. The next morning the sun would rise and with it my courage, the terrors of the previous night all but forgotten. The same thing happened the next morning in Villahermosa. Like a child I awoke in the morning, giddy from my little triumphs of the night before, humming to myself as I got ready to head down to the lobby for breakfast.

In an attempt to shave weight from my backpack, I packed extremely light for a three-week trip. My plan was to rinse out the clothes I wore every night and let them hang to dry. Altogether, I'd packed two pairs of pants, one of them made from quick drying material (thank God!), two pairs of shorts, one tank top, three T-shirts, one sweater, one rain jacket, two panties, two bras, a pair of wool socks, a swim suit, a sleeping bag, a hammock with a mosquito net (possibly the heaviest thing I packed and the one thing I never used), a travel towel, a headlamp, a small journal, a copy of Kurt Vonnegut's *Player Piano*, the *Lonely Planet* guidebook, fifteen foil envelopes of tuna fish, a box of saltine crackers, a bottle of iodine tablets, a bottle of iodine neutralizer, 2 one-liter Nalgene bottles, a small first aid kit, hand sanitizer, a travel size of shampoo and conditioner, toothpaste, toothbrush, a small English-Spanish translation book, a disposable camera and a small bit of cord based on J. R. R. Tolkien's recommendation, or rather, his elves of Lórien, "Never travel far without a rope." Yes, I take travel tips from science fiction. Note I also had my towel (Douglas Adams, Hitchhiker's Guide to the Galaxy) and after much traveling, I must say both pieces of advice are spot-on.

I'd brought but one pair of shoes: my trusty Teva sandals that had yet to disappointment in any type of terrain. The tread was made from something the company called spider-rubber that helps feet stick to rock, an important feature for someone who likes to head off trail or straight through rivers. Strong, nylon webbing wraps around the foot and attaches by Velcro which somehow doesn't seem to rub blisters on my feet. They're not sexy sandals, but for the adventurous gal, they do come in pink and, no, I have not been paid to endorse Teva sandals. Yet. (Psst! Teva, you may now send me my endorsement checks ☺).

Unfortunately, as I mentioned before, I packed nothing that actually looked good on me and as I approached the waiter at the host podium, he in his clean, pressed, white shirt and black bow tie, he gave me a less than discreet scan and what I was pretty sure was a look of disapproval. He coldly motioned me to follow him to a table, but instead of pulling my chair out for me to sit down, as I'd seen him do for the woman who had been seated just before me, he merely pointed to it, before walking away. I looked around the restaurant at the other patrons, all far more polished than I, and my cheeks grew hot.

Had I planned to stay in such a place, I would have brought appropriate clothes. Back in Durango, I was actually known as a dapper dresser, despite my economic bracket. I'd worked in an upscale clothing store all through college, which had taught me not only an appreciation for nice clothing, but an understanding of when to wear what. It both pained and infuriated me to be appraised and found wanting by this crowd, but it couldn't be helped and ultimately didn't matter. I shrugged and let it go. Nothing could mar the shine on my day.

I was off to El Parque Museo La Venta to see my first Central American artifacts: the ancient Olmec heads of La Venta. The Olmec are sometimes called 'The Mother Culture' because it was believed the Olmec were the first to establish organized cities, with rich cultural symbols in art and architecture, that then spread across Mesoamerica, greatly influencing the Aztec, Zapotec, and Maya. They had a calendar etched in stone three hundred years before the Mayan's calculated theirs.

Though no one knows for sure, most archaeologists believe the great stone heads are monuments to different Olmec rulers. The heads are estimated to be at least two thousand years old, weigh an average of 8 tons, though some weigh considerably more, and are typically around 9 feet high and 14 feet around. They were carved from basalt boulders that were somehow brought from the Tuxtla Mountains, God and the ghosts only know how, without the wheel.

La Venta, where the heads in this park were found, was thought to have been an important government seat for the Olmec. Unfortunately, the site also happened to be built atop a cache of black gold, otherwise known as oil. Much of the area was almost completely lost when Pemex, Mexico's nation-owned and operated oil company, plowed through the area and planted a refinery right on top of the ancient grounds. Fortunately, some of the artifacts were saved and moved to the museum in Villahermosa, including four Olmec heads.

The heads and several other large artifacts are part of a large outdoor jungle park that is explored by hiking a meandering trail through a protected patch of jungle that smelled of composting leaves and over-ripe mango. There was also an indoor museum with more exhibits and a zoo with jaguars, crocodiles, spider monkeys, boa constrictors and more. My guide book said coatimundi (a central American cousin of the raccoon), iguanas and squirrels ran freely, and might try to steal my lunch if given the opportunity. One could only hope! The hotel desk clerk called for a taxi, and within a few minutes I was dropped on the street in front of the El Parque Museo La Venta gates.

The museum entrance featured a miniaturized Olmec head that stood three feet high, and two feet around. It was a replica of one of the heads actually "housed" in the museum. The indoor museum featured local history as well as historical and cultural information about the actual location where the heads were rescued near La Venta – all in Spanish. Photographs papered the walls and stone sculptures, pots and jewelry could be seen in glass cases. It was well worth a walk through, and I took my leisurely time with each exhibit, scanning the Spanish placards featured beside them for any words I recognized from Spanish class. Not many.

As I walked outside to where the zoo began, I passed a blue-eyed, broad-smiling Aussie who gave me a "G'day," as he passed me. It occurred to me that he was the first white person I'd seen in 24 hours, and the only person that I was certain spoke English. At first I wanted to chase him down and ask him to coffee, just to savor the sweet sound of words I understood. But I was there to experience a different culture, and I didn't want to cloud the experience by attaching myself to another gringo within the first 24 hours of my trip. So I walked on, feeling strangely liberated by my decision.

When I walked out the museum doors into the zoo portion, I had the pretty, well-kept grounds almost all to myself. Enormous trees shaded most of the area while still allowing subtle flows of sunlight and air. The animals were about the happiest animals I've ever seen in a zoo. They lazed about, played or snoozed, some of them pausing briefly to actually look up when I stepped in front of their enclosures. Any other zoo I've been to, the animals usually look like they're trying to forget you're there.

Cheetah cubs climbed all over their dozing mother, occasionally chewing on her ears until she opened her mouth enough to let out a low growl. A couple of little pig-like peccaries played tag. Birds squawked and monkeys chattered. The jaguar walked right up to his bars, his hips and shoulders moving in a counter-swaying swagger. He pushed his black-velvety nose through the bars, sniffing at the air, trying to smell me. I leaned forward, peering into his eyes, talking softly about the pros and cons of cage life, when I heard an eruption of giggles break out from behind me and excited shouts of, "Una Gringa Americana! Una Gringa Americana!!" How they knew that, I have no idea.

I turned around to see three little girls around six or seven years old, giggling at me. I smiled and said, "¡Hola! ¿Cómo Estás?" which was pretty much the extent of my conversational Spanish skills, but they took it as an invitation and ran over to me. Through spurts of giggling they spoke all at once, pushing their notebooks into my hands. They were so funny, they soon had me laughing and giggling, too. I'd read online that I might be approached by poverty-stricken children selling chiclets (yes, the little gum squares) or begging for money, and I was somewhat prepared for that, but I wasn't sure what this was. These girls weren't beggars. They were all neatly dressed in smart little matching school uniforms: white short-sleeve button-down shirts, plaid skirts, and blue knee high socks with brown leather loafers. Their dark hair was neatly combed and pulled back in pony tails or braids. Their little faces broadcast friendliness, but they talked so quickly, I had no idea what they wanted.

They motioned to my camera so I thought they wanted me to take their picture. This was great news to me because I'd also had the childhood dream of seeing my work in *The Smithsonian* or *National Geographic* Magazine and as a wannabe-magazine journalist I definitely wanted locals in my pictures. I just hadn't wanted to offend anyone by asking to take them. I raised my camera to take their picture, but they shook their heads in a *"No, Silly!"* fashion, and chastised me in their brilliant Spanish. I shrugged, confused, and said, "No comprendo." The tallest of the girls came up to me, smiling and showing two missing front teeth and spoke again, but much slower, and a little louder, holding up her own disposable camera. Apparently that's a technique practiced everywhere when trying to be understood by someone who doesn't understand you: Slower pronunciation combined with more volume.

I finally realized that what they were doing was asking if they could take *my* picture. Apparently, I was every bit as novel to these children as the jaguars and peccaries were to me. "Ha!" I laughed and shook my head, "Yes. Si." I wore the biggest smile as one of the teachers took our picture with one of the girl's cameras. I sat on a nearby metal bench and the girls took turns practicing their English skills with me, which were about on par with my own Spanish speaking skills.

After a few minutes of our hello-how-are-you-my-name-is game, they each placed a notebook on my lap and the cutie pie with the two missing front teeth handed me a pencil. I assumed that maybe they thought I was someone famous and they wanted my autograph. I've had people tell me I look like Jennifer Aniston—no, really, I have! Okay, so one person. One near-sighted old man. Anyway. What else could I do? I signed my name on one of the girl's notebooks. She furrowed her eyebrows opening her mouth wide like I'd just scribbled on a work of art. The other girls shook their heads, grabbed their notebooks and ran after the rest of their class, shouting, "Gracias" and "Goodbye" as they went.

Speaking slowly, my number one fan patiently said, "Nooooooo." And she opened the notebook to a page that had a list of questions in English. She pointed to it, still speaking slowly, and handed me her pencil, smiling encouragingly. The page had a list of questions written in English. Apparently they had been looking for Gringos as some sort of educational scavenger hunt and I was a big prize. Ahhhhhh. Now I understood! I was being interviewed by a six-year-old!

I said, "Ohhhhh," smiled and nodded and set to work filling in the blanks about my nationality, age, occupation and marital status. When I finished I handed it back to the girl. She reviewed it thoroughly, slowly trying to sound out the words. She finally nodded approvingly, said, "Muchas Gracias!" as she threw her arms around me, and hugged me before taking off after her class.

Did that just happen?

I continued through the zoo to the jungle trail portion of the museum to see the Olmec heads, stellae and other Olmeckian artifacts. The exhibits were sprinkled over a 20-acre parcel of wild jungle preserve, tucked in their own individual enclaves of tangled vines and vegetation so thick, peering into them was like peering into a cave. There could be anything in there. I walked through foliage so dense all the displays were hidden from each other so that when I stumbled on an exhibit, I got a hint of the sensation of discovery, especially since there were hardly any other people on the trail.

Some of the artifacts were 30 centuries old, and looked it, with most of their features smoothed away by the hands of weather and time, almost unrecognizable as anything more than stone. I stood, staring at a dark, lichen covered rock and suddenly the pattern just emerged. I saw enormous, empty eyes staring boldly back at me. I longed to put my hands on the exhibit, to trace my fingers over the places where two or three thousand years ago, an artist labored for hours, days or maybe even months to create this face. I looked around me. There was no enclosure or guard to stop me. I started to reach out my hand, then stopped. I knew that the oils from our hands can cause treasures like this to break down more quickly, so I sighed, letting my hand drop.

When I left the museum some hours later, I entered a different world. One that buzzed and rumbled with the comings and goings of hundreds of thousands of people in their cars, busses and motorcycles. I saw taxi's but they zoomed quickly past in a surging river of traffic I had no idea how to navigate. Small-town girl that I was, I didn't know how to hail a taxi. Was it really just like in the movies where you hold up your hand and yell, "TAXI!"

How would I communicate if the driver didn't speak English? How do you make sure you pay the right fare and not the fare of the moment? I stood on the sidewalk waiting to see what everybody else did, but no one seemed to be traveling by taxi. I looked for someone who looked like they spoke English, but no one stood out. I started listening to the people around me talking until I heard a few words of English sprinkled into one family's conversation. I shrugged and decided, "Well, what the heck?" I walked right over and asked them if they habla inglès-ed, and they did! More or less.

I shared my predicament. They laughed good-naturedly and the daughter, whose name was Miriam and was probably just a little younger than I, walked to the curb with me to show me how to hail a taxi.

While we waited for the next one to drive by, she politely asked in her soft spoken voice how I came to be in Villahermosa. When I told her my story, she spontaneously asked if I might like to join her family the next morning for a trip to Comalcalco and to see a Cocoa plantation.

"Well, why not?" I said, enthusiastically accepting her invitation.

We quickly decided on a time and as the next taxi appeared up the road, Miriam held her arm high, waving her hand and shouting in a much stronger voice, a voice possibly reserved for taxis and future children, "TAXI!"

When the driver pulled up she stuck her head in and spoke to him in Spanish, with surprising directness, and then turned to me, told me the fare and not to pay any more than that. Then she smiled sweetly and said, "Okay, see you in the morning!"

"¡Hasta Mañana!" I said as I hopped inside.

Back at the hotel, I checked with the clerk to see if the room was available for another evening, as I didn't know how long it would take us on our trip. This time the clerk surveyed me with a curiously suspicious gaze. I think he was starting to wonder if I could actually pay for the services I was receiving, room and board, including breakfast, lunch and dinner. But he checked and yes, the room was again available so I went upstairs and laid around the room flipping through channels, looking for anything remotely familiar on TV.

Despite the fact that I was having the time of my life, a fish being out of water can be exhausting and I craved some hint, any hint, of home. The only shows remotely familiar were *SpongeBob SquarePants*, in Spanish, *Die Hard*, showing in Spanish with English subtitles. I didn't care. It was good old American, Bruce Willis' familiar face, in a classic American film. It may have been the first or only time *Die Hard* has been chosen for its soothing properties. Yippee-ki-yay, MudderFudders!

By the time bad guy Alan Rickman plummeted to his doom and Bruce Willis saved and properly kissed the girl, it was only 2 p.m. What to do, What to do? I wished I could just go to sleep and wake up for my trip to Comalcalco with my new friend, Miriam. But it was far too early to turn in.

I wanted to do more exploring, but I was a bit anxious about leaving the safety of the hotel for the unknown world with my limited travel skills. The city was so much bigger than I had been expecting! How would I know safe streets from bad ones? Back in Memphis, that kind of mistake could be fatal. And I had no idea where else I might go.

This would be the downside of low preparation and leaving life open for the unexpected surprises. There could be a phenomenal attraction a block away and I would have no idea.

There's a lot to be said for unexpected adventures, but this was a lot of no idea of what's coming. One of the biggest surprises was that I thought there would always be at least *someone* who spoke English around. It was beginning to dawn on me that America wasn't the center of the universe I had, apparently, once believed it to be.

In a day or so I was supposed to be getting on a bus to head into the far more remote jungle, where I had always wanted to go, but where the likelihood of others speaking English now seemed more…remote. My subconscious offered me up an out. Maybe I didn't even need to go to Palanque. Villahermosa was quite an adventure in and of itself. I could just stay here in this nice hotel, you know, close to the airport and possibly an American embassy. I could explore this city thoroughly from end to end. There was really no need to go to the trouble of getting on a bus when there was so much adventure to be had right in Villahermosa.

Then some other darned voice said, "You didn't come all this way to hole up in a freaking Best Western." I looked at the clock again. 2:15. Hmmm.

Perhaps a little walk around the block, then?

I felt a ridiculous amount of anxiety when I first started walking. The faces that passed me wore expressions difficult for me to read. They may have been thinking, "Now I wonder what Tia Maria has been up to today?" or "Did I feed the goat this morning?" But in my vulnerable state, they all seemed to be passing by thinking about the evil Americanos and how they were eating the planet like locusts. I had quite a few people in Durango recommend my finding some Canadian leaf patches and sewing them onto my backpack so people would think I was Canadian instead of American. Some of them thought that between the whole snagging of Texas, New Mexico, Arizona and California, the signing of the North American Free Trade Agreement (NAFTA) and eight years of George W. Bush's presidency, some folks down there might not like Americans. Then again, there are an awful lot of Mexicans moving to America, so those people might be mistaken.

These were just people, like people anywhere else. They were thinking about their own lives, their own families, their own grocery lists and errands.

I decided on an experiment. I had a lot of friends who were more experienced Latin American travelers, and they'd recommended that I actually try to speak in Spanish whenever I could, that the people would appreciate the gesture, even if I made a complete fool of myself and used all the wrong words. So I decided to put my best foot forward, and the next person who passed me, I smiled warmly and said, "Hola." And bowed my head slightly in deference, a habit drawn from teaching and practicing yoga and meditation. Oh yea, btw, I study, practice and teach yoga. Possibly the only reason I'm sane. Ish. Anyhoo.

The first person to pass was an old woman with her long, gray hair pulled back in a neat bun. She wore a calf-length, black skirt embroidered with bright flowers and a white embroidered blouse,

40

untucked. Her face was a leathery map of many challenging years. Over her arm was slung a cloth bag that bulged in all directions and looked quite heavy. She wore a stern grimace, one that, had she been from my town back in Durango, would have meant bears had gotten into her garbage and she'd had to spend the morning picking it up. But when I smiled and said, "Hola," she transformed. She returned my smile with one ten times brighter. Her warmth beamed from her entire being as she returned my greeting.

So rewarded, I walked on and the next time a set of eyes met mine, it was a middle-aged man dressed in slacks and a blue, short sleeve, button down shirt. He had a clean shaven face except for a thin, neatly trimmed mustache. I smiled warmly and said, "Hola." He smiled back, scanning me unmercifully from foot to boobs and back again, before meeting my eyes and saying provocatively, "Ho-la." Shocked, I quickly looked away.

I decided it might be best if I saved my "Holas" for women, children and perhaps very old men.

I kept walking, and I smiled, and I Hola-ed, and over and over again, my smiles were met with broader smiles. I walked for hours until my feet were screaming. I was used to hiking for miles on dirt trails, but concrete sidewalks were another matter. Eventually, I decided to start looping back towards my hotel.

I walked a few more blocks, then turned left again, continuing my experiment and continuing to be rewarded with the results. I stopped bracing myself for assault, relaxed and even enjoyed the sheen of sweat on my skin from the thick humidity, a sensation I never felt back in the high mountain deserts around Durango.

In a little while, I found myself walking through a courtyard that had a row of shops on either side of it. I saw signs with words I had learned in my college Spanish classes: ¡Zappatos! ¡Bolsas! ¡Pantalones! (Shoes! Shirts! Pants!)! The sidewalk was lined with neat rows of trees and large, ornamental pots overflowed with flowers. An outdoor patio crowded with espresso drinkers at bistro tables conjured images of Europe. I turned left again, planning to be approximately in the general area of my hotel, but nothing looked familiar. Turns out streets don't run parallel there, but follow ancient foot paths that wound through now non-existent jungle. I thought I could walk in a square. Turns out it was a squiggle and I was nowhere near my hotel.

The buildings had taken on a decidedly more formal, and much older, air. As I came to a street corner I saw a beautifully ornate church. The sides were covered in carved scrolling reliefs and gothic-looking spires shot into the sky from every corner. A set of scaffolding climbed up one side, indicating it was undergoing some repairs, but as I passed, I heard voices from inside and I couldn't help myself. I poked my head in. I stood with my feet just outside the door, and leaned my body awkwardly forward as if my feet were cemented at the entrance. An older woman with a kind smile approached me from the side and motioned for me to come inside. I smiled, shaking my head, and said, "No, gracias," brushing my hand in front of me to indicate I wasn't dressed for church. She shook her head back at me. The soft crow's feet at the corners of her eyes, crinkled with her kind smile, telling me I was silly and waved me inside more earnestly, motioning towards a seat in the back pew, within easy access of the door.

I was drawn in by her kindness as much as by my feet's desire for a break, and I smiled and nodded, accepting her invitation.

As I entered the doors I instinctively reached out my fingers for the holy water font, one of which I knew would be on either side of the doorway. When I was 13, I'd spent a year in a Catholic, ahem, boarding school, where we attended mass twice weekly. I quickly made the sign of the cross from forehead to heart, then shoulder to shoulder. The masses we were encouraged (forced) to attend had become genuine highlights for me during my stay at the school and I'd enjoyed participating in rituals that had been reverently practiced for hundreds of years or more. I enjoyed the messages delivered by the priest who seemed more philosopher than campaigner, appealing more to our sense of rationality rather than preying on our fears. Though I'd long since become disenchanted with organized religion, the church experience at the school had been a good one. It was with a real sense of reverence that I knelt and bowed my head towards the crucifix of Christ at the front of the church, before scooting to my seat.

The sanctuary was as beautiful inside as it was outside. Jeweled stained glass windows portraying stories of biblical miracles filled the windows and velvet draped everything. The priest spoke with the passion of a Baptist, but the attire and formality of a Catholic and, whether because of my personal experience or because of inarguable fact, I felt God in that place with these, my darker skinned brothers and sisters. I was deeply struck that sons and daughters of God are we all. (I said I became disenchanted with organized religion. Never with God.) After the service was concluded, I smiled and nodded to the kind woman who had urged me in. I stopped briefly just off the front steps and snapped a couple of pictures before continuing on my way, now filled to the brim with this awesome growing suspicion of connectedness. It was another breaking point for expecting something bad and the beginning of taking it as it actually came.

A few blocks later, I came upon a city park full of tents and a large crowd of people all listening to a man speaking through a loudspeaker. He wore a straw cowboy hat, long sleeve, plaid shirt and jeans. He stood at the top of a flight of concrete steps that lead to a grand, dome-topped building. I think it was the city's capital building. The people had gathered here hoping to make themselves heard, though at the time I had no idea of what they wanted people to hear. The man was an impassioned speaker, periodically raising his fist to the sky, which was a gesture the crowd returned with equal gusto and sometimes the word "¡Viva!

The crowd was a mix of men, women, and children, all of them from a modest class. Some were dressed in western clothing, some in beautiful, colorful clothes with designs that I've never seen before that might have come from the mountains or jungles. Everyone looked determined, even the children. I reached into my backpack for my camera, then thought better of it when I recalled a friend's story that ended with a cautionary tale for wannabe photographer's like myself. The story was about a tourist who was beaten to death by an angry mob when they took some pictures of a riot without asking permission. The moral of the tale was to ask first, but everyone here looked so on edge it just didn't seem at all prudent.

Many people carried cardboard signs mounted on sticks with duct tape. I was surprised to find that I recognized a few of the words: Ya Basta! (Enough!), Libertad (Liberty), La Gente (The People), Nuestra (Our). I recognized these words from an environmental activist campaign I'd taken part in some years before in the San Luis Valley of Colorado. That campaign had at its heart the financial and cultural survival of a small, isolated town. For the people who lived there, stakes were high and I can still feel the tension. I can still hear the rage in their voices. It had felt like the situation could just explode at any moment.

I could feel a similar energy here. This protest wasn't about some minor labor dispute. I looked over the crowd. There was a look in their eyes, a resoluteness drawn from a broiling deep within…I saw an old— an *ancient*—woman, shoulders hunched but yet standing tall, holding her sign high. It read, "Su dolor es nuestra dolor." Their pain is our pain. My first thought was, '*This is about to get real. I'd better get the hell out of here.*' That was self-preservation talking. My very recently ex-ed ex-boyfriend—the one I was still a little hung up on—had told me before I left that if I came upon such a setting, the best thing to do is to steer clear, or risk becoming caught up in a level of violence I wouldn't understand or, worse yet, become a target of vengeance.

Another part of me wanted to join in what appeared to be a David and Goliath fight. Yet another side of me just wanted to witness the events unfold and capture them through words and film. That may have been where I would have done the most good anyway, especially assuming that the demonstration I was witnessing was a continuation of the Zapatista movement that escalated to war just after, and in direct response to, the signing of NAFTA.

I didn't know anything about this at the time I stood on the outskirts of the throng, listening to the impassioned speakers who took turns climbing up the steps and sharing the loudspeaker. I'd heard of the Zapatistas but that was over ten years ago and with my naïve sense of justice I'd thought all wrongs had been made right. Truth be told, I didn't know this struggle was ongoing until I started doing research for this book. Had I known, I would have had a much harder time walking away, going back to my posh hotel for my evening meal. As it was, after a awhile, I did walk away. I hailed my taxi and headed back to my hotel, lounged about, ate dinner and then flipped through channels on the TV, too excited about my trip to Comalcalco in the morning to fall asleep until very, very late.

Chapter 6: The Tipping Point

"A bank is a place that will lend you money if you can prove you don't need it."

Bob Hope

Comalcalco was the Pre-Columbian Mayas northern most settlement. It's located near the Gulf Coast of Tobasco, in an area classified as swampy. I was there during the dry season, which was nice because there were fewer mosquitoes and I wasn't on quinine tablets. Visually, compared to ruins like Tikal or Palenque, the site is underwhelming. The ruins are small by comparison, and considerably less palatial and ornamented than I would see in Palenque. They're appeal is more esoteric rather than ostentatious, but I was just thrilled to be there.

This. This was the beauty of going map-less. It left the world wide open for me to stumble into and discover, where everything came as a surprise and there were no expectations to fail. To my limbic brain, I think it lent the illusion of true exploration as I followed my nose and left a whole lot out to the universe, including, to an extent, my safety. Don't get me wrong. I felt I was perfectly safe with Miriam and her family. They were kind, gracious hosts.

It was with a giggle, like a child might have on a swing rising into the air, that I got into their car that morning and it was with this same, childish wonder that I viewed everywhere they introduced me. Such is the beauty of having no knowledge, and therefore no expectations, for the sites we visited. Taking off on an unplanned trip with perfect strangers was the adventure. Everywhere we went was just icing on the cake. On the flip side, I might have enjoyed Comalcalco even more had I known some of its history.

Miriam, and I and a friend of hers with a kind face that spoke no English (and I'm afraid I've forgotten her name), climbed to the top of one of the pyramids, though I had to take their word for it. To the uninitiated it was merely a rising grassy knoll that covered what appeared to be the remains of a very old brick house that had somehow been almost completely swallowed by a carpet of prickly grass, but now was being slowly dug out.

The bricks were particularly interesting. There was a shortage of limestone near Comalcalco so whereas Mayan temples in other parts of Central America were built from honed limestone, these structures were constructed with a kiln-fired mixture of clay, crushed rock and oyster shells, peculiarly similar to what was used in construction of ancient Rome.[i] This wasn't the only characteristic similar to worlds 5,000 miles over the ocean. Many of the brick tablets also carried mason marks on their backs that are almost identical to marks used by Roman masons around the same time period. Below, the drawing set on the right is taken from Roman bricks. The ones on the left are on the bricks found at Comalcalco. Hmmm.

While no one knows for sure what these mason marks actually mean, historically mason marks are signatures of the mason who worked and placed them, perhaps for tracking payment or accountability purposes. Sometimes they were directions indicating how and where the brick should be placed. The bricks above carry a lot of information.

Archaeologists have also found engineering and architectural features strikingly similar to those used in ancient Roman construction. That was all curious enough, but then they unearthed carved figurines with heads donning distinctly Romanesque beards and hair-dos, and that's pretty much blown everyone's mind.

But wait, there's more. In most of the Mayan world, when people died, at least if they were someone of standing, they were usually cremated, or had corn and/or beads placed in their mouths and were laid to rest in mausoleums. In Comalcalco, the elite were buried within cone shaped mud urns folded into fetal position, similar to the way the dead were treated in India around the same time. Incidentally, the name, Comalcalco, basically translates to Clay Pots, which most have taken to refer to the brick tablets that were used in city construction, but maybe it had something to do with this unique way the Comalcalcoans cared for their dead?

So how did Comalcalco come by these Roman aspects? Nothing is conclusive but some believe these characteristics prove an ancient link with Rome a thousand years before Columbus waded onto the shores of the Americas. There are a few theories of how this could have happened, given the distance of over 5,000 ocean miles between ports, so huge grain of salt with all of these. Some claim that the Satavahana Dynasty of India (200 B.C. to 200 A.D.) who had extensive trade connections with Rome may have touched down at Comalcalco and left the stamp of not only Brahmi script, but Roman influence as well. Perhaps even leaving Roman passengers that became the models for the figurines with the strong Roman resemblances. Or perhaps some Roman ship captain was overly ambitious in his travels, sailed a bit too far out, got caught in a storm, and washed up on the shores of Tobasco where he immediately set about trying to make one more road lead to Rome.

I learned some of this information on site, but it was really, really, REALLY hot the day we were touring the grounds so we mostly only read information postings that were in the shade. Otherwise it just felt like the sun was smooshing us to the ground with its heat.

Workers had built palm roofed canopies over some of the structures they were working on so these were the areas where we spent the most time. Miriam, her mother or her father were kind enough to translate brochures and information placards. Otherwise, I might not have understood why we might bother to drive two hours from the city to come stand in the heat and view these initially underwhelming ruins. They turned out to be fascinating when you learned some of the story, but I think the main reason we were here was because our plans included a tour of the cocoa plantations just a little farther up the road.

The plantation was called the Hacienda Cacoatera Jesús María and was established in 1917, but the local tradition of cocoa growing can be traced back several thousands of years to the Olmecs. It has been the vitalizing beverage for many a king and warrior, and a treasured treat that, if denied, could lead to actual violence. Seventeenth century British explorer, Thomas Gage, recounted a story of how the Bishop of Chiapas had banned the consumption of cocoa during mass, because the women of the villages insisted on drinking hot chocolate while attending. Incensed the Bishop decreed that anyone found drinking cocoa during mass would be excommunicated, which essentially meant they'd be condemned to hell for a cuppa cocoa.

The gallant men of the villages drew swords against any priest who denied a woman the pleasure of her chocolate (they may have been inspired in part by the belief at the time that chocolate was an aphrodisiac). The unrepentant Bishop stood his ground to his own detriment. He died a gruesome death, after drinking a poisoned cup of cocoa.[iii]

The cocoa plantation we visited had exactly the kind of house I thought I'd see more of in Mexico. There was a long, deep front porch lined with arches and dripping with bougainvillea. Beautiful wood chairs and tables invited visitors to rest from the heat in the shade and enjoy chocolates from the small gift shop. Colorful woven hammocks hung from either end of the long porch, inviting not only the indulgence of chocolate, but to have it while hanging in the soft, coastal breeze.

We took a tour of the grounds and strolled under the shade of the cacao trees with an uber-fit machete-wielding gent with dark, almond eyes and thick, wavy black hair, whom I'll call Handsome. The machete was something I was seeing men carry everywhere I went and they used them for a variety of dexterity-demanding jobs. They hacked away at lawns, pruned branches, cleared paths and opened coconuts. At first it was frightening. These machetes are basically only a little shorter than swords and the metal is thicker. One could easily be used for monstrous purposes. But here, they were multi-tools. They were pocket knives too big to carry in the pocket.

I got to see an example of the grace and dexterity of machete wielding up close when we took a tour of the plantation grounds. The cocoa trees had recently been harvested so most of the trees weren't carrying fruit, but when we did come upon one that still had a few fruits attached, Handsome pulled one down. He held the fruit, which looked like a cross between a melon and an avocado, in one hand, wielded the machete in the other and, WHACK! One swift snap with the machete and the fruit was halved, his hands and fingers still intact, thank God. It was done so matter-of-factly, so suddenly, I recoiled and had a hard time paying attention as he showed us the beans inside. I stood blinking, trying not to show my fluster, as I feigned interest in the seeds covered in a soft, squishy white outer shell.

Next we were shown the pressing room where they pressed the cocoa butter for making cakes and then ground the solids to make cocoa powder. Handsome reached into a bin, placed some chunks of pressed cocoa on a plate and offered us a sample. They were nothing like Hershey bars. There was zero sugar in them, which came as a surprise when I bit into one and my mouth was filled with a bitter, earthy taste. I almost spit it right back out again, but Handsome was still standing in front of me smiling while pushing the plate back towards me, encouraging me to take another peice.

"Mmmmmmmmm." I said, smiling through pursed lips and hoping my face didn't show my revulsion. Then a peculiar thing happened. As the cocoa remained sitting in my mouth while I awaited my chance to nonchalantly spit the chunk into a planter, the chocolate melted onto my tongue and that bitter-earth taste became something that I actually enjoyed. There was a hint of the familiar chocolate but it was far richer, deeper. Without thinking about it, I closed my eyes, as if absorbing some magic elixir that would soon transform me. In a way, it could. Dark, unsugared chocolate has been found to have the same antioxidants as red wine, can improve cognitive function, act as an anti-inflammatory, lower cholesterol, and improve insulin sensitivity, among other bennies. Perhaps most importantly, however, the rumors are true: It stimulates endorphins similar to sex!

I decided I liked it and reached for another piece, which caused Miriam and her friend to burst out laughing. I have no idea why, but I laughed along with them. The next piece I took, instead of popping the whole square in my mouth, I nibbled off tiny pieces and then allowed them to slowly melt onto my tongue, enjoying the autonomic desire to close my eyes and reel in bliss.

For lunch we headed for a restaurant in a small coastal village on the beach of Tobasco. I don't want to give *Sunset* or *Outside Magazine* any ideas about the next pristine location to ruin by declaring it a secret, thereby directing thousands of travelers to its unprepared infrastructure, but WoW! Sand as white as that of Sarasota, Florida, with calm, hypnotic waves. Maybe all inner Gulf Coast beaches waves are like this, but I haven't seen any other than Sarasota. The ocean did its infinite stretch thing, but the waves were oily-gentle, lazily rolling in, then laying down upon the shore as if in reverent bows rather than crashing into it, as it had when I played in the surf in San Diego. I'd never seen the ocean with such a spell-binding undulation. It was clean and clear and empty of people or anything decadent as far as my eyes could see. No row of luxury chain hotels displacing anything and everything in their quest to garner the most money possible. No beer companies hosting keg chugging parties on the sand. No one was even on the beach despite phenomenal weather that day.

I rolled up my pant legs and waded shin deep into the clean, clear water. I wanted to take off all of my clothes and let the soft sea surround me. I wanted to swim and feel the water's warm, salty touch run like soft hands over my naked body. But, I was pretty sure if I did that I would have been shunned by my group and left to my own woefully inadequate devices. So no on the skinny dipping.

The restaurant had a small building for a kitchen, while the seating was arranged with white plastic tables and chairs set out on the sand . They stood within a square enclosure designated by white banner streamers strung between posts that were set in white buckets of cement. Their specialty was tilapia that came from a farm just a few miles down the road. I'd seen a sign for the farm on the drive here.

It was delicious in a way only fresh fish can be. Fried in a skillet with butter and savory herbs 'til golden brown and served within minutes of preparation. I could smell the garlic simmering in butter moments after I placed my order, and I could hardly wait to get my fork in it. On the side were freshly peeled, tart mangos, creamy avocados, fresh pepper salsa and papas fritas (French fries). I ate every bite, even scraping my fork against the plate to get the herby drippings.

Then the check arrived. It was there I think I might have made a faux paux, but I'm still not sure. I think I was supposed to buy lunch for my gracious hosts. For just a moment it seemed all eyes flicked to the check, held their ground, then glanced away as though it hadn't been laid down at all. I could feel it. Or rather, I can feel it now. It seems so obvious. I was expected to pick up the check. I considered picking it up, but I wasn't sure about the cultural customs. Would it be rude of me to pick up the tab? After all I was a woman, and they had invited me. Where I came from, when you invite someone, it is your treat.

This was new ground for me. I'd never had extra money before and so had never been in the position that I could have even thought about picking up the tab. All of my adult life as I scrambled to survive and put myself through college, picking up a check was just never an option.

My grandmother used to say that someone who gives a gift then expects something in return is a sneak who deserves to be disappointed, and I've always felt there's a lot of truth to that. But what about in this situation? From their perspective, they'd picked me up from one of the nicest hotels in Villahermosa. They probably thought I was rich, from a rich country with the color of skin that supposedly makes all dreams come true (it so doesn't!). And they had just treated me all day. So maybe I should have picked up the check as a gesture of gratitude for including me in their day? If I could do it over again, I'd probably have a great pen pal friendship with some fabulous people. As it was, Miriam's father paid for lunch and then the ride back was a quiet one, all the while I was trying to decide if I should have paid for lunch, if I should offer some cash for gas?

They dropped me off at my hotel and I thanked them profusely, which was met by only slight smiles and awkward nods. Maybe everyone was tired? I walked into the hotel unable to shake the awkward feelings. (Miriam, I've decided. If you read this, please contact me. I owe you and your family dinner.)

As I passed the front desk, the clerk who spoke a little English came around the desk and in a very brusque manner, informed me that I would need to settle up in the morning as there were no vacancies for the following evening. I was slightly taken a-back. He didn't even apologize for the lack of rooms. Just formally told me it was time to go. It wasn't that I didn't want to go. I already planned to push on for Palenque in the morning, but, and perhaps I was just having a vulnerable day, I distinctly felt like I was getting the boot. Once again, I sensed I'd run afoul of some social convention but couldn't be sure.

It may have been the tipping. On advice from folks on 'The Tree,' I wasn't tipping much. They'd suggested I not be overly generous with my tipping lest I single-handedly destroy the local economy. I'm not really the cheapskate I'm making myself out to be here. I used to wait tables and ever since then, I'm usually an excellent tipper, always erring on the side of leaving a little too much rather than a little too little. But this was a hotel, a new experience in and of itself, and I wasn't sure where to tip or how. And the folks on *Lonely Planet's* Thorn Tree forum had made what sounded like a good argument for not tipping according to American standards.

I had planned to include gratuity when I settled my bill at checkout, without taking into account that they would have no idea who to give what by that method, nor would the folks I was inadvertently stiffing realize my eventual good intentions. Combine my failure to tip with my brilliant plan to dress so horribly that I looked like I didn't have a dime, and who could blame the hotel for suspecting my ability to pay what was becoming a sizable tab. Or maybe they really didn't have any rooms.

Back in my room, I took a long, hot, soaking bath, not knowing when my next chance to bathe might be. I unpacked my backpack one more time, spreading all the contents on the bed where I could see everything and determine if there was something I could do without. I sighed looking at the clothing and wished I'd brought just one thing I actually looked good in, or at least maybe a tube of lipstick and mascara, but I'd gone really bare bones on the packing. The only thing that might not be considered an absolute necessity was my Kurt Vonnegut book, but I decided it was worth the added weight, so I re-packed my bag, put on my nappy clothes and went back downstairs for my last hotel dinner. I had a chicken alfredo and a glass of Chardonnay. The alfredo arrived cold and the Chardonnay warm. Yep, pretty sure I should have asked someone else on the tipping issue. C'est la vie.

After dinner, I decided to turn in early and get a good night's sleep for my departure into the great unknown. I was pretty wiped out from the excitement of the day, and besides, what else was I going to do? Traveling as a woman is a lot different than as a man, though I'm not sure it would have been wise for a white man to go out exploring Villahermosa at night either. But for a woman it's always twice the danger, twice the risk and 'twice' is just a convenient word choice. It's probably higher.

I took out my money belt and tried to organize it so that I might not have to be that obvious when I reached into it. The money belt I had was designed to be worn under clothes and flush against the skin so as to be harder for pickpockets to get at, but also relatively undetectable so no one would even know it was there. But so far, I'd been so flustered I'd reached right down into it in front of everyone, completely giving away my secret stash. Basically using it like a fanny pack.

I put some of the pesos from the traveler's check the clerk had cashed for me my first night in my pocket and left the rest of them and my other American Express travelers check safely tucked away in the money belt. Then, for some reason, I lay back on the bed and began reading the back of the credit card. I don't know why I did this, I mean, who reads that? But there it was in that tiny little type, a note cautioning cardholders to let the company know when you intended to travel abroad, due to the high incidence of identity theft. "Failure to alert "Credit Card" may cause the account to be frozen."

I sat upright in bed. "Wait. What??" It had never occurred to me I might need to call the credit card company before I left the U.S. I was completely counting on this credit card since I'd learned the traveler's checks weren't reliable. In a panic, I grabbed the phone and tried to call the 800 number on the back of the card, but when I picked up the phone, instead of a dial tone I heard a polite woman's voice say, "Si. ¿Cuál es su número de teléfono?" (Yes, what is your number?)

I froze. Apparently, either the hotel or possibly all of Villahermosa still operated by the old school method of picking up a phone to make a call and having a person actually connect you.

I took some deep breaths and wracked my brain for how to say my numbers from one through ten in Spanish. *Uno. Dos. Tres. Cuatro. Cinco. Seis. Siete. Ocho. Nueve. Diez. Okay,* I thought. *I can do this.* I picked up the phone, "Si. ¿Cuál es su número de teléfono?" I took a deep breath and slowly read the numbers, one by one, in Spanish. After the final number the woman said, "Uno momento, por favor." (One moment, please.) She returned almost immediately. "No funciona. ¿Tienes otra número?" I deduced that 'no funciona' meant the number hadn't worked and guessed that she asked either for me to repeat the numbers or give her a different one. I read them off to her again, agonizingly slowly. Within a moment or two she responded in the same way. I said, "Gracias." And hung up. U.S. 800 numbers don't work from outside the country. Just so you know. I sure didn't.

I racked my brain for what to do. All sorts of paranoid scenarios started parading straight down the center of my frontal cortex directly from the freaking-out limbic center.

I had to settle my account in the morning. What if this card doesn't work? What if I can't pay my bill? What do they do if white people come to Mexico, stay at hotels, run up bills and then can't pay? And no one speaks English. How can I explain the mistake, that I didn't call the credit card company before I left? That I don't have other credit cards, or an ATM card? I'm communicating primarily through miming. How the hell can I mime my situation? And I look like a bag lady. I look like a bum who stumbled upon some American's purse. What if they throw me in jail? What if they throw me in jail and no one from home can find me? I've actually heard of that happening.

I was in trouble. Possibly deeper than I had ever been before…and that's saying something. My heart pounded in my chest. I stood up as if about to embark on some course of action. Then sat back down when no course occurred to me. Stood up again. Sat back down. I had to do something but had no idea what that was.

I needed help. I went to the telephone to try calling my friend, Brian, back in Colorado. Brian and I were what you call adventure buddies. He was my absolute favorite person to go hiking with because we had the same taste for adventure. We usually went off trail and occasionally tried things like jumping off of cliffs into trees. He was also someone I always thought I could count on. Even if he couldn't help, at least he could let someone know what was happening.

I picked up the phone and the feminine voice softly inquired, "¿Cuál es su número, por favor?"

I took a deep breath, bringing a small measure of calm to my voice, "Hola. ¿Habla Inglès?" I asked.

"No," she answered, "No, lo siento, no Inglès. ¿Que es su número? (No, I'm sorry. No English. What is your number?"

Another deep breath from my end. Well, here goes, "¿United States?" I inquired.

"Si, ¿Que es su número? (Yes, what is your number?" she answered, not exactly like a machine, but not exactly not either.

I swallowed. "In Colorado, Nueve. Siete. Cero. Tres. Ocho......Por favor."

To which she answered, "Te estoy conectado. Gracias. (I'm connecting you. Thank you.)"

There was a buzzing pattern for a few seconds and then a man's voice, "Hello?"

Relief washed over me just hearing his voice. I spoke fast, terrified we'd get disconnected. Terrified it was my only chance to contact the outside world. "Brian, it's me, Donna. I need you to write everything I say down. Do you have a pen?"

"Wait, What?" he said chuckling slightly.

"I'm in trouble, I need you to write down where I am right now and then I need possibly many other big favors." I rushed.

His tone turned serious, "I've got a pen, go ahead."

"Okay, I'm in the Villahermosa Best Western in Tobasco, Mexico. Hardly anyone here speaks English. I don't have an ATM card, the American Express travelers checks are basically worthless and I've just discovered that I was supposed to alert my credit card company before I left the country and I didn't do that so there's a good chance it's not going to work. They want me to settle my bill tomorrow. Brian, they might send me to jail, because I might not be able to pay my tab and no one speaks English so I won't be able to tell them why!" My voice that had been so steady, suddenly cracked, but afraid of getting disconnected, I spoke as quickly as I could, "I think they think I can't pay my tab because I'm dressed like a bum, and the Thorn Tree told me not to tip too much or I'd ruin the economy so I look like I don't have any money. I'm really scared..." It was probably right about here that I just started sobbing.

"Donna, it's going to be okay. Let's figure this out." He said, his voice sounded so reassuring, I felt somewhat relieved. "What can I do?" he asked.

"I don't know!" I answered, full panic breaking out in my voice again. "Maybe call the credit card company and try to explain to them what's going on? The 800 number on the back doesn't work from Mexico. Can you call them and then can you call me right back ASAP?"

"What's the number and what's your credit card number?"

I paused, but only for a moment. This was a big trust issue, as you can imagine. I was basically handing over my financial information, but I had no choice. Then I realized something. In that instant I realized I completely trusted Brian. That he was my best friend. I slowly read first the phone number and then the credit card number and expiration date. I told him my mother's maiden name for their security question.

"I'll call you right back."

"Thank you, Brian, Thank you, Thank you, Thank you."

"Donna, it's going to be okay," he said reassuringly. And then he hung up.

I sat in the absolute silence of the room praying, even though I wasn't sure of exactly who was on the receiving end of the prayer anymore. I was raised a Southern Baptist, but I had long since dropped any pretense of being a devout Baptist. There was too much hypocrisy, questions we weren't supposed to ask, and what I saw as downright logical inconsistencies, for me to continue blindly following. For example, I know why some sects of Christianity refuse to accept theories of evolution: If man evolved from monkeys and God created man in his image…well, you know.

I was also still angry over the way I had originally been "saved" when I was eight years old. Here's the cliff notes to that: My parents dropped me off at a church out in the middle of nowhere Tennessee with a bunch of other eight-year-old kids where they showed us movies for three hours about people who hadn't been saved getting their heads cut off. After this three hours of horror the preacher stood up and asked the crowd of trembling children if any of them wanted to accept Christ into their heart and of course, everyone did. Even children who had already been saved asked to get saved again just in case it didn't take the first time. I think anywhere outside of Tennessee, that kind of recruitment is illegal.

After years of witnessing hypocrisy, scandals, and contradictions, the final blow came when a good friend of mine died in a car accident. My friend had been an atheist, but he had also been a social activist who spent all of his waking hours working to help the homeless, the environment, basically any underdog that needed him. He was quirky brilliant (Shout out to Nathan Herzog up in heaven). I was with one of my Christian friends when I found out and her immediate question was, "Was he a Christian?" Still reeling from the news, I'd whispered, "No. He was an atheist."

My Christian friend shrugged dismissively, put her arm around me and gave me a quick squeeze and said, "Well, I'm so sorry, but I'm afraid he's gone to hell. Best just let him go 'cause you won't be seeing him again," she said, smiling brightly, completely oblivious to her brutal insensitivity.

I almost slapped her. I didn't, but I did decide that I wanted nothing to do with a religion that would condemn good people just because they couldn't believe a hard to believe story, yet accept all kinds of bad people who uttered their get-out-of-jail-free words.

So I was turned off of organized religion, but not God. I've felt God all my life. He's the warm glow of love I feel when I reach out in pain with prayer. The warmth when nothing else seems left. I have no idea what the real story of God is, but I have a feeling that all the world's religions have somehow captured a bit of the essence, but also lost much of the truth, possibly distorted by leaders who bent messages to suit their own designs. That's not so hard to imagine after studying Political Science.

If you look at the principles of all of the different religions, they are more or less the same. The names are different. The rituals and ceremonies, but the gist? Truth is truth. Is it not possible that God appeared to people all over the planet in ways that were culturally relevant to them at the time? Using language and ideas that fit their unique needs for their unique corner of the world? If that were the case, then we might end up with different interpretations of God all over the planet, each of them still being valid. How do we know that isn't what happened? Why wouldn't it be? And supposing it is? Wouldn't that allow us to be more tolerant of the subtle variations in beliefs and stop fighting each other? Anyhoo.

While I don't know exactly what God looks like, it's absolute fact for me that there is a being out there who cares about us and who time and time again, has saved my hide, often in ways that had to be labeled miraculous because there was no other explanation. One of my scariest nights, I'll tell you more about later, I met God in a dream on top of a mountain. In the dream, God appeared like an incredibly wild, rugged old man who was a cross between Santa Claus and the wizard Gandalf from J. R. R. Tolkien's Lord of the Rings trilogy. He was a kind, wizened old soul with a sense of humor and a non-directive coaching style. I lovingly call him Gandal-Claus when I'm feeling cheeky. It was to this image that I prayed to that night in the hotel in Villahermosa.

In my desperation, I decided to try an old guidance trick that had been suggested back in the bible thumping days. You say a prayer asking for guidance and then flip through the pages of a bible and read the first verse you see. I looked in the drawer of the bedside table and sure enough, they still put bibles there in Mexico. Gratefully I pulled it out and smoothed my hand reverently over the leather cover. I said my prayer and began flipping. I closed my eyes, stopped flipping and put my finger on a page. When I opened my eyes, my finger had landed on 1 Peter 2:18, "Slaves, be subject to your masters with all reverence, not only to those who are good and equitable but also to those who are perverse." Ugh! That was obviously wedged in there by some ancient, perverted, slave owner and not at all comforting. I put the book back in its drawer in the nightstand, and wrapped my arms around my legs. I rocked back and forth, praying. Would the phone never ring?

Then it did, so loudly I jumped out of my skin. The credit card company needed more information. It took several more phone calls to even come close to sorting things out and even then, I wouldn't be sure until the next morning when I went to settle my account at the front desk, if the credit card company would actually authorize payment, but they had told Brian they would. I was hoping that wasn't just to get him to stop calling. They also gave another number for me to call in the morning to set up a PIN so I could draw cash advances, though it would take days for the PIN to go active. This whole time, 'til 2 am, I was terrified that the English barrier or the operator night shift ending would cause communication to come to a screeching halt. If that happened I'd be unable to reach out or be reached until morning. It was a really long night of channel flipping and nail biting.

When I slept, I slept fitfully, jumping up in bed several times throughout the night for fear that I'd overslept and caused some other great problem. The next morning, I went down to the restaurant and ordered the largest breakfast they had, in the event that it might be the last thing I ate besides the tuna foils I'd brought from home, or worse yet, was reduced to prison rations until that day I was finally found, if ever.

After breakfast I packed up my pack and headed downstairs hoping for the best.

Setting my pack against a wall, I smiled nervously at the clerk, the same clerk who seemed ever present at the front desk, the same clerk who had gone from charmed smiles to cold stares. This morning he seemed nervous. I took out my credit card and handed it over, trying to steady my hands from shaking. When my eyes looked up to the clerks, he smiled with a somewhat concerned expression. On my behalf? I wasn't sure. It didn't seem likely as each day I'd stayed at the hotel, his friendliness reduced by 20 percent. Again, it may have been the tipping. But since I didn't have much cash, I had intended to leave gratuity for the staff when I settled my tab. He turned the card over, looking at the signature. Then he looked back to me with a kind smile on his handsome, caramel face. He was so neatly dressed, his clothes pressed and precisely tailored, his hair coiffed. His face smoothly shaved. I fidgeted self-consciously in my purposely chosen rags.

"¿Passporte, por favor?" he asked softly, still with that puzzling look of concern. I handed it over and glanced around the room nervously, and apparently, not without good reason. At the front door, two policemen stood, one watching traffic pass by on the street, the other looking directly at me, scowling. The clerk handed back my passport and said, "Gracias, Señorita. Uno momento, por favor."

He swiped the card, simultaneously glancing up at me. I think we were both holding our breath. I tried to stand nonchalantly, but I think my eyes were wide, javilina-in-the-headlights, on the verge of bursting into tears. I glanced over to where the policeman stood. Yep, still there. Then, out of self-preservation, I scanned for other exits. There was probably no chance I could have gotten away and even if I did, what would I have done? And anyway, the clerk still had my credit card, which seemed to be taking an eternity to clear or not clear. My heart beat faster and faster. I stole another quick look at the policeman at the door, the one had looked away to the dining room, then turned his gaze back, leveling it directly on me. I managed a feeble smile. If he wasn't there for me, I certainly had his attention.

"¿Señorita? Firma aqui, por favor (sign here, please)." The clerk said cheerfully pushing a receipt and pen across the counter with a broad smile and obvious relief. My relief was probably also obvious. It had all probably looked very suspicious. All the stateside calls to my room last night. The worn out clothes and apparently a complete lack of schedule as each morning for the past three I had come down to see if there was vacancy for another night, rather than scheduling three to begin with. I smiled back at the clerk, "Uno momento, por favor," I said as I flipped through my language book.

Finding what I was looking for I looked from the book to the clerk and said, "¿Como me, ah, pro-pin-o?" (How do I add gratuity?)

For a moment he stood regarding me, then smiled warmly and said, "No te preoccupies (Do not worry about it)," he said, waving his hand.

I looked over my shoulder at the front door. The police were gone. I flipped back through my book. "¿Puedo que hacer una mas llamada Telefonica, por favor?" (May I make one more call?) I had to call Brian and let him know that the credit card worked and I was heading to the bus station to check the schedule.

"Claro (of course)," the clerk smiled motioning me to a business center furnished with a few handsome desks, computers and telephones. I called Brian and let him know that the card had worked and showered him lavishly with thank yous and probably a promise or two I have yet to fulfill, one of which, I think, was to call before I left Villahermosa.

I turned back to the clerk once more, "¿Que es precio por la …. (what is the price of the…)?"

He smiled warmly, "Gratis (Free)." And then turned back to his computer.

I smiled, "Gracias, Señor." then flipped through the book once more until I came to the passage I needed, "¿Donde esta la estación del bús (Where is the bus station)?" I sounded out the words like someone trudging through deep sand, but he listened patiently. He nodded when he understood and came around the corner, motioning me to follow him. We stood out on the front steps and he pointed down the street and then held up two fingers and motioned to the right saying, "De recho." Then made his fingers walk in the air and held up two fingers again then motioned to the left, slowly saying "Izquerida." Then walked his fingers, held up one finger then held up both hands in success and said, "Solamente uno mas blocquer." (Only one more block)

I was pretty sure I got that. I took his hand, shook it and said, "Gracias, Señor. Gracias."

Again, the beaming smile. "De nada." Then tipping his head forward and almost taking a bow while still holding my hand, he said, "Buenas Suerte, Señorita (Good luck, Miss)."

Okay, I said to myself hoisting my backpack onto my shoulders. "Let's do this." I stepped out the front doors with the odd sensation that here is where I was really leaving the safety net, and here where the adventure really began. And that I was probably going to be okay. Probably.

Chapter 7: Gandal-Claus

"To believe in God is impossible. Not to believe in him is absurd."
Voltaire

My first conception of God as Gandal-Claus came about just before college, before I even knew I was going to college, towards the end of my National Forest dwelling days. I'd taken a break from the tent and was living in a walk-in closet sized cabin in the mountains twenty miles outside of Durango, Colorado. There wasn't room for a couch or real bed even if I could have afforded one and so I slept in a low-ceilinged loft, accessed by a bunk bed ladder, in, of course, my sleeping bag. If I wanted to have heat, I had to chop wood and start a fire every day. I came to love the ritual of chopping kindling in the brisk, quiet air, then boiling water for tea on my iron woodstove.

My amenities included the woodstove, a small gas stove, a fridge and tiny bathroom with a shower. Really, it was perfect for someone who'd been in a tent for a while. The location was stellar. I was surrounded by rocky, pine covered ridges and the crystal-clear Florida River babbled over granite boulders a stone throw from my door. At night I slept in the loft with my head right under the window where I could watch the massive sky of stars sparkle. Naturally, I left the window open so I could hear the coyotes yip and feel the pure, cold air blow across my face as I slept.

Unfortunately, the landlord was an absolute scumbag. Due to a disagreement about who owed what to whom, it was the last night I had to stay there and I had no idea where I was going next and hardly any money to get me wherever that might be. College was still an inspiration or two away and a place folks from my economic bracket didn't usually go.

My car was all packed up, but I didn't know where I would be driving it in the morning. I was alone and scared...*again*. In and out of my Dad's custody from 13 to 15, then completely on my own at 16, and couch surfing from house to house until I graduated high school by the skin of my teeth, then coming out to Colorado and living in and out of a tent for two years, you'd think I'd gotten used to uncertainty.

While sometimes it was thrilling being so untethered, there was always a bit of terror stewing deep inside that I kept under a cloak of bravado. Most of the time I even kept myself fooled. But that night, I struggled to fall asleep, then slept fitfully, waking up several times with my knees literally knocking together. I thought "knees-knocking" was just a saying, I didn't know they actually did that until that night, but turns out, if you're scared enough, they do.

Finally, I managed a sleep deep enough to allow me to dream and what a dream I had. I dreamt I was walking on top of a mountain, far above tree line, just before dawn with someone it seemed I knew very well, but at the same time had just met. As the horizon line slowly started changing different hues of dark blue, green, and pale pink, heralding the coming of the sun, it was as if part of me had been there all along because when "I" arrived, I was in full rant to whoever I was walking with. I didn't "see" what the other person looked like, but I sensed this presence. It was in the guise of this huge, strong, wise old man with long, curly gray hair, long gray beard and mustache, and eyes that were a combination of sharp intelligence, compassion, strength and playfulness; always on the verge of either roaring laughter or outright war. Basically a combination of Gandalf and Santa Claus. I sensed "he" had terrible powers.

Suddenly the "I" that arrived realized that the "I" that was ranting was actually ranting to the almighty God! I wanted to throw my hands over "her" mouth and pull us both down on our knees to beg forgiveness, but what happened instead was that I merged with "me" and went right on ranting. I was furious, pointing out different moments in my life that had been horrifying or deeply painful and asking, "Why?? What's the big idea?? Why'd I get such a crappy hand of cards to play this stupid game??!!!"

All the while, Gandal-Claus listened patiently, nodding his head in agreement that yes, all of those events were very hard to endure and he acknowledged and sympathized with my pain and sense of injustice.

Then he politely asked me to pause my rant for a moment and pointed off to a spot on the horizon where two mountains overlapped each other, forming a deep V between their peaks.

"Do you see that place, that place between the mountains?" He asked motioning with a great, hard hand.

"Yes?" I answered, wiping my tears with the back of my arm.

"That spot is you." He answered. And he snapped his fingers.

The next instant I was yanked onto this Ebenezer Scrooge-esque roller coaster ride where I blazed through scenes in my future life. In these scenes I was going through more hard times. I saw series of events to come that were fraught with anguish, fear and pain. I saw my face scrunched or twisted in various stages of worry and agony. After I don't know how long of flashing through these grizzly portents I was back on top of the mountain with Gandal-Claus. The sky was growing lighter as the sun's rays began spraying up from behind the mountains in the distance.

I was furious. I shouted at Gandal-Claus, "YOU MEAN THERE'S GOING TO BE MORE OF THIS?"

"Yes," he said smiling, firmly, without the slightest hint of apology.

I stormed away, then came charging back towards him and shouted, "NO! WHY? WHY ARE YOU DOING THIS ME?" Then I fell on my knees and just started crying, and whispered, "I can't. I can't go through anymore."

He put his hand on my shoulder and softly said, "Yes, you can. Why am I doing this? Well, It's not really like that." He said rubbing his great hand on my back, soothingly. "I can promise you this." He said. "Stand up and look."

I wiped my eyes and did as he asked, my shoulders slumping, already defeated by events that had yet to happen.

He put his great arm around me and pointed back to the horizon. "Look. Look at your place on the horizon."

I looked and the sun was rising directly in the place where the two mountains met. Powerful, energizing rays shot out as if from a prism, setting the sky on fire with pinks, reds, purples and oranges. Clouds pulsed with brilliantly changing light and color. My heart felt as though it glowed and pulsed with this brilliant light, and I felt joyous. It was the most beautiful sight I have ever seen.

Gandal-Claus stared appreciatively at the show, nodding, a proud smile on his face. "See?" he said. "It's going to be okay."

The next moment I opened my eyes and I was in my sleeping bag in the loft in my cabin. It was dawn and the sky was just beginning to pale. One of my first realizations was that I was no longer afraid. Not only was I not afraid, but I retained a bit of the joyous sensation in my heart. It lasted a long time and I still feel a bit of it anytime I recall that dream.

Was it adrenal fatigue from my night of fret or because the dream was...*real*? I don't know the answer to that. I kind of feel like it was somehow real and yes, I know how that must sound, but this was one of those near miraculous moments I spoke of earlier that, fortunately, make it impossible for me not to believe in God.

I awoke with faith in my journey. I knew for certain that yes indeedy, things do, in fact, happen for a reason. I knew that bad things could and would still happen. But I also knew, whatever happened, I wasn't alone and that in the end, it would somehow be worth it.

That doesn't mean I changed my ways and headed on back to the church fold. I didn't feel like that was expected in even the slightest way. I actually felt even more certain that none of the world's religions had it completely right, only aspects of the original truths, like I said before, some of which had been twisted and distorted to suit the needs of those in power. Obey even a perverted master, indeed! Give unto Caesar what is Caesar's? Sounds rather convenient for Caesar and the perverted master, don't you think?

There's just enough Southern Baptist terror left in me to feel a little frightened at the very idea of writing what I just did, but now that you mention it, that's another thing that just doesn't make sense to me. In the full throes of proper God-fearing, you're not even supposed to let these kinds of thoughts cross your mind, and if you do, you're letting the devil have free roam of your brain and you'll be doomed, Doomed, DOOMED TO HELL!

But I don't think God's like that. The very idea that God will condemn you if you question what some supposed representative says he said? Well, again, that's very convenient for the representative and kind of insecure of the almighty creator of the universe.

That's one thing I like about the teachings of Buddha. Buddha said, in the face of multiple spiritual leaders claiming different truths, one should use one's reason, common sense and experience, to find the truth. He said to question everything, including his own teachings. For me, I would also add to listen to your heart. Ever have someone try to convince you of something and you immediately get this uncomfortable feeling deep inside of you? That's your heart telling you to get the hell away from that person and not listen to them. The best part is that the more you listen to your heart, the stronger its voice grows. I've learned to use my heart like a dousing rod.

I haven't converted to Buddhism or Hinduism, though I do love a lot of their teachings. For that matter, I also love a lot of the teachings of Jesus Christ and Christianity. However, like Christianity, not everything I've encountered feels true to me when run past the meter of my heart so I haven't made a full conversion, despite the fact that my Buddhism and Hinduism influenced yoga practice is an important part of my spirituality.

Which brings me to yoga. I stumbled into yoga ten years ago by complete accident. A guy I rock climbed with suggested yoga might help improve my rock climbing skills so I started attending a class at our local rock climbing gym. I was immediately hooked by the blend of mental and physical challenge and by the way it felt like I'd just had all forms of toxins squeezed right out of my cells, out of my being, even though sometimes I silently cursed my instructor during parts of class. "Put my leg where, while doing what??? How 'bout you stick your foot up your #@#!!" Then I'd surprise myself by doing whatever it was she suggested, or at least coming closer than I imagined I could.

I loved learning that just because I couldn't do something one day, didn't mean I could never do it. Over the years, I've executed poses I never thought possible for me. I learned that failure was not permanent, and that lesson began to apply to every area of my life.

And I love the peace it brings, even when trying to execute poses that require more strength or flexibility than I have. I love the encouragement, the absolute necessity, of suspending the ego, even if that was only accomplished for seconds or minutes at a time. It's so refreshing to get a break from myself!

I'd attended this weekly class for many months until one day, after class, my luminous instructor asked me if I would be interested in learning to teach because she would need a lot of subbing over the summer. The idea of getting up in front of people and practicing, let alone *teaching* yoga, scared me to death. I also knew that I wasn't a pure devotee of yoga, so I initially said no, citing my lack of absolute adherence to Yogic principles. At that time, I smoked a pack of cigarettes a day and still partied fairly regularly despite my busy college and work schedule.

So I told my instructor, this woman I had so much respect for and wanted so badly to be liked by in return, that I smoked cigarettes and drank tequila. I expected her to be shocked and say, "Oh my goodness! Never mind!"

But that's not what happened. She smiled mysteriously and said, "Don't worry about it. Let me teach you how to teach and you'll change those habits when you're ready…if you want to. Practice and all is coming." At the time I didn't realize that the phrase 'Practice and all is coming' was a key tenet of the teachings of the Great Ashtanga Yoga Guru, Pattabhi Jois, may he rest in peace.

I decided that the fact that it scared me combined with my teacher's acceptance of who I really was, clearly indicated I should absolutely do this. So I did. I apprenticed with her for several months, subbing for any classes she needed me to. At the end of six months, she told me she was moving and suggested I formally take over her class. It was one of the best opportunities that has come my way. An invaluable gift I can take anywhere and use any time. It's done way more for me than improve my rock climbing skills.

Among many gifts (including introducing me to my heart-throb husband and helping me birth my daughter), yoga and meditation taught me to calm my mind so that when I'm facing a challenge and trying to sort something out, I can still the clamoring fear voices and focus on other aspects to determine the right course of action. I've learned that the right course can almost never be determined when one is consumed by fears. At the end of every session whether I'm teaching or practicing, I pray. I've found my motives to be the most pure after a session of yoga has helped me clear away the self-centered garbage. My prayers tend to contain a lot more 'Thank you for's' and a lot less 'Please give me's.'

Despite years of practicing, teaching and studying yoga, however, I'm still not dogmatic about it. I try to maintain an openness to finding truths from many different sources. I like what Gandhi said about spirituality, "Truth is one. Paths are many. There are many paths to God. I hope that yours is not a difficult one."

CHAPTER 8:The God of Fools and Orphans

"Experience keeps a dear school, but fools will learn in no other."
Benjamin Franklin

The streets and sidewalks of Villahermosa swarmed with cars, buses, motorcycles, mopeds, and bicycles, the latter three of which often carried more than one person (and sometimes pets or livestock). Lots and lots of people hurried in all directions, many of whom took at least a second look at me before they passed. My fair complexion, and poof of curly, dirty blond-hair (most hair stylists complain that I have three times the normal number of hairs on my head) made me a bit of a stand-out, but my vagabond clothes made me easy to dismiss. While the street vendors targeted passers-by on whom to press their wares of blankets, ice creams, tamales, and meats-on-sticks, they scarcely addressed me at all, which was great as I was having a hard enough time keeping my focus on following the clerk's directions. With so much activity, I had to be careful not to miss a turn, which could have been easy if I got caught in the pedestrian flow.

After taking the last turn, I stopped at the corner to look for the bus station. It was pretty easy to spot as it was surrounded by buses…and more people. Coming from my little mountain haven, I'd never seen anything like this. People swarmed like ants, occasionally bumping into each other, but without even pausing to say, "Disculpe" Or "Perdón."

My plan was that I would find out what time the bus left for Palenque, then grab some lunch, possibly find another hotel if need be, then call Brian and let him know when I was heading to the jungle.

But when I walked into the bus station, it was chaos. People rushed everywhere. There was shouting, children crying, children laughing, women carrying baskets on their heads, vendors selling all kinds of goods: stuffed animals, toys, blankets, Tupperware, fruits, vegetables, and the Mexican version of Doritos. Everything that was being shouted was being shouted in rapid Spanish and I didn't understand a word of it. Suddenly, out of the mileu, a dark, mustachioed man with a fearsome face was shouting, "Palenque! Palenque! Palenque!"

That word I knew. That would be my destination. I panicked. What if this was the only bus that ran that day? Or that week? What if that was my only chance to get there on this trip? *What about lunch?* What about phoning back home to let them know I was headed to a place I didn't know what I'd find and this might be the last chance I have to call them until I get back to the city?

"Palenque! Palenque! Palenque!" shouted the fearsome man.

People bumped into me, throwing me off balance with my heavy pack. At first I tried to check that nothing had been stolen every time I was bumped. I'd read about thieves slitting the bottom of backpacks, causing the contents to spill onto the ground where they quickly scanned the plunder, dove in and snatched the good stuff, then disappeared into a crowd who wouldn't be interested in helping rich gringos recover goods they would easily replace back home. But I didn't come down there with any extra stuff.

As I made my way to the counter I gave up on checking my backpack every time I was bumped because everyone bumped me. I was like a pinball trying to maneuver my way to the ticket counter, shoved from side to side, forward and backward, always on the verge of toppling.

I hurried up to the window, while other bus drivers shouted out the names of their destinations. "Oaxaxa! Oaxaxa! Oaxaxa!" "San Cristobol! San Cristobal! San Cristobal!" "Tikal! Tikal! Tikal!" "Mexico City! Mexico City! Mexico City!" "Palenque! Palenque! Palenque!"

The girl behind the counter had pretty, but hard, eyes. She wore a faded flowery T-shirt and jeans, and wore her long black hair in a side braid. She asked me something, probably my destination, then fixed her dark brown eyes on me as she waited for my answer.

I tried to flip through my book, looking for how to ask about buses to Palenque, but the man was still shouting, "Palenque! Palenque! Palenque!" in the background and I felt the girl, and the line behind me, growing impatient as I flipped.

I shouted to her over the cacophony, "¿Hable Inglès?" I implored.

"No, hablo Inglès." she shrugged, waiting. Once again, I tried to flip through the book, but behind me the line grew, the straps to my backpack bit into my arms, and the man continued shouting, "Palenque! Palenque! Palenque!"

I bit my lip, closed the book and put it in my pocket, "Uno por Palenque, por favor (One for Palenque, please)."

She told me an amount. Naturally I had no idea what she'd said. I reached into my money belt and pulled out another American Express traveler's check and handed it to her, nervously. She flipped it over, back and forth then shrugged, rattled off something I didn't understand, and handed it back. Again, American Express traveler's checks: Fail.

I reached into my pocket and pulled from the bills the hotel had given me when I originally checked in and needed to pay the taxi driver. I had no idea how much to give her, so again, I fanned out some bills and, pleading with my eyes, motioned for her to grab what she needed.

She looked from me to the bills, and back again, a confused expression on her face. Then she slowly chose two bills from the fan and handed me a ticket. I turned and hurried towards the bus. The driver stood in the door waving me in.

Suddenly, someone grabbed me from behind by my backpack and pulled me to a stop. Startled, I turned to see the woman from the counter. She opened my hand and pressed some bills into it, then, smiling kindly, turned me to a completely different bus. This one had already shut its doors and was preparing to depart. She hammered on the door, and the doors folded inwards. I smiled at her, trying to convey the depth of my gratitude, not only for chasing me down to bring me my change, change that she could have easily kept and probably fed her family for a week. But also for going to the actual trouble of coming from behind the counter, leaving a long line of impatiently waiting people, to stop me from getting on the wrong bus, and getting me on the right one. At least I hoped it was the right one.

I feel the need to really press upon you the depth of this woman's kindness. The Southern States in Mexico are predominantly indigenous populations who have been marginalized since the Spanish landed 500 years ago. According to a World Health Report, more than half the population in the Southern States of Mexico live in extreme poverty. People die of curable diseases every day. One in five children born, die of diarrhea or pneumonia. In Chiapas, **Seventy-Four** percent of the population live in poverty and of the many single parent households, women head 8 out of every 10.[iv] That woman could have been one of those eight.

When the Zapatistas began their rebellion in 1994 they'd said:

"We have nothing to lose, absolutely nothing, no decent roof over our heads, no land, no work, poor health, no food, no education, no right to freely and democratically choose our leaders, no independence from foreign interests, and no justice for ourselves or our children." Zapatista National Liberation Army (EZLN) Declaration of the Lacandon Jungle, 1993[v]

They weren't being overly dramatic in their declaration. Young people, even children as young as seven or eight, from Central America risk their lives every day trying to get to the United States to escape starvation. They come from places where they and their families have run out of improvisations and their parents are powerless to help them. There are no jobs and they've been evicted and barred from their farmlands. They send their children with their blessings, broken hearts, and best hopes. In 2012 the Department of Homeland Security said 24,481 such children crossed the U.S./Mexico border, and that that figure has continued to double and triple.[vi]

Their journeys are not easy. In an article published by the Borgen Project, a humanitarian organization fighting extreme poverty and hunger worldwide, a Women's Refugee Commission official cited a comment by one of 151 detained children she interviewed at a Texas U.S. Air Force Base. The interview was for a 2012 study on what is being called 'the migration.' She said it exemplified what many Central American minors face.

"I said to him, 'It's so dangerous going through Mexico. Why would you want to go through Mexico by yourself?' He rode on top of the train. People die and are kidnapped, and all these horrible things happen," she said.

"And he was like, 'Look. I lived in Honduras. It's so dangerous there. I mean, I would regularly see dead bodies on the street. If I stayed in my country, I would definitely die. If I tried to get to the United States, maybe I would die, but I'd still have a chance,'"[vii]

This is one story of many children's stories from Central America. It's horrifying. Often what they encounter along the way is worse than what they leave. Children risk their lives, surviving horrors most of us wouldn't want to imagine, to reach a country where people simply throw away perfectly good food every day. Tons of it. One NRDC report said that people in the United States throw away half of their food or roughly $165 million a year,[viii] yet half of our predominantly Christian population demand these children be thrown back where they came from and cry for an impenetrable wall to keep "the likes of them" out.

Meanwhile, when I went to the thrift store for my travel wardrobe I actually had trouble finding clothes that looked frayed enough because everyone has so much they throw out clothes that look like they have never even been worn. Some of them still have the tags attached! I'd looked long and hard to find the worn out khakis I was wearing when I got on the bus to Palenque. That is the world where the woman who chased me down to give me my change and see me to right bus, lives.

The bus started moving before the doors had even folded closed behind me. I made my way down the aisle as it lurched forward and dropped from side to side, hitting deep potholes in the road, and I practically fell into other passenger's laps as I walked down the aisle looking for an open seat. A bus ticket didn't guarantee a seat. If there was no seat, I would be left standing until someone got off the bus, maybe hours later.

Finally, I found an open seat beside an older woman who was working on embroidering some fabric. I touched her arm, smiled politely and motioned to the seat beside her. She smiled back and nodded. Grateful to have a roost to wait out the pitching and tossing of the bus, I sat down, finally having a moment to think about the beauty of what just happened to me. I closed my eyes and said a prayer of thanks for every miracle of the morning, and asked God to bless that wonderful woman and her family.

It was pretty unbelievable. This was the place where some of those children have come from, the place where this woman left a long line of impatient travelers to chase me down, give me my change and help me get on the right bus. I was grateful but at the time, I didn't know how truly grateful I should have been. In my extreme ignorance I had assumed that a country that had as much as we had would have done everything in its power to help neighbors in this situation until the problem was fixed. I didn't know there were places where children had to make those kinds of choices. Where parents were absolutely powerless to support their children. They could scarcely afford to feed their families, but they could still afford to teach enough integrity and kindness to help a stranger like me. I know that's not always what happens. But it's what happened to me.

With my Christian upbringing, I had to wonder, how could God let such suffering exist? I wonder every time I allow myself to watch the news. I often have to fall back on the adage, "The Lord works in mysterious ways." But maybe God doesn't have anything to do with it at all. Maybe it's all up to us and God looks on with a broken heart hoping that we'll evolve enough compassion and wisdom to choose to do something, and when I say we, I mean any of us.

Maybe it's an opportunity to give the people in those situations a chance to shine, to become more than most of us can imagine because they've been forged in the fires of such challenges. Or maybe it's an opportunity for us, to give us a chance to stop turning away, pretending their plight has nothing to do with us, and put our hearts and minds together to help them find solutions without letting multinationals and tyrant bullies tear them apart. Perhaps it's to give us a chance to shine by reaching out to help. How do you think we're doing?

On the outer edge of town, I saw the shells of half-finished palatial homes that hopeful investors had built to house the rich and rising middle class that NAFTA had promised was coming. In some places all that remained were remnants of arches and enormous concrete foundations, stripped bare of anything that could be pried loose and hauled off.

The rich didn't come and the middle class was evaporating instead of rising. So half-built houses and neighborhoods stood empty, their rapid deterioration aided by local residents pilfering any useful parts that could be dismantled and carried away, and why not? Otherwise they were just sitting there biodegrading. At least someone got some use from them. As we headed out of the city, the country side unraveled into small villages poking out of long swathes of verdant jungle tangle. Occasionally I saw small, one room round huts sporting a beautifully engraved, and out of place, front door or window. Perhaps a lovely patio railing going around a chicken coup, some touch of trim that seemed far too expensive for the home where it had landed. I thought of those ruins of pilfered palaces. And I chuckled approvingly.

Our bus shared the rough road with some transportation solutions that were terrifying but admirably innovative at the same time. Families of three and four rode on a single bicycle or motorcycle. The resourcefulness was astounding. Pedestrians and cyclists were everywhere and cars were on the road that would have long since been retired, if not for the inventiveness of some resourceful mechanic, banging a car back together with a roll of duct tape and some bailing wire.

My bus, in contrast, was a luxury mobile. Cold air whooshed from the air conditioner vents and made me want to reach in my pack for that one sweater I packed, if my pack hadn't been tossed under the bus's cargo hatch. Every two or three rows, a six-inch television screen folded down from the ceiling and at the moment was showing some old Chuck Norris film that, coincidentally, seemed to be filmed in the same jungle in which this bus traveled. I didn't pay much attention to it. I was far too absorbed in trying to see everything I could of the strange new world out the window. The difference in worlds was such a contrast that in a way it was like I was watching a *National Geographic* episode on Chiapas, but I was not only witnessing this landscape, I was in it, separated only by a veneer of metal and movement. Soon enough I'd be out of the air conditioning and into an honest-to-God jungle.

It seemed far into the drive before the edge of the city finally gave fully away to rising and falling hills covered in trees. Occasionally a large hacienda loomed out of the jungle on some picturesque ledge, but for the most part the homes looked one-roomed, most with the thatched roof made of dried palm leaves. Almost none of them had driveways, but here there were also fewer cars on the road with us. Most people walked or rode bicycles, motorcycles or, occasionally, horses.

I thought about the town I toured and the protest I'd witnessed yesterday and how I saw so much that was the same in our two worlds: families who love each other, people working, shopping, reading, eating, sharing time together. Looking out my window, I saw a woman in a brightly colored skirt leading a skinny cow behind her by a short rope while a little boy trailed behind, swishing a stick through the two inches of loose dirt on the road. Some women carried huge parcels on their heads, steadying them with one arm while the other hand held the hand of a child. Older children carried buckets of something or other, or attended livestock. While everyone seemed hard at work, none of them struck me as what I'd call downtrodden. I saw no slumped shoulders, no downcast, diminutive eyes.

Near a small village center, we passed a large barn that had an enormous picture over its entire front-facing of a man wearing a sombrero. His eyes blazed, and a thick mustache draped over lips that, from the fiery eyes, I deduced were probably in a snarl. It may have been a tribute to the revolutionary Emiliano Zapata, a famous leader in the Mexican Revolution, an inspiration and the namesake of the Zapatista movement.

Just as I'd seen at the protest, some of the people I saw on the streets working around the small houses wore western influenced clothes like button downs, short sleeves, T-shirts and jeans or shorts. But some people wore beautiful clothing with floral patterns, bands of color, or animal symbols in vivid colors embroidered over otherwise solid color cloths, usually a white cotton, though some were red. I saw a few who wore weaves of geometric shapes in repeating patterns, similar to some that I'd seen in the tourist kiosks and I wondered if the patterns were more significant than a fashion choice.

In *Maya Threads: A Woven History of Chiapas*, I'd read that "The design of the Universe is woven with clarity and purpose, line by line into Maya cloth. The weaver maps the motion of the sun through the heavens and the Underworld, through time and space. With the repetition of the "universe" design, the lordly sun is prompted to continue his journey. A Maya woman weaves the cosmos as it awakens." I wondered if the designs I had seen held any of that kind of magnificent significance.

I briefly exchanged emails with one of the authors of *Maya Threads,* Carol Karasik, asking for permission to use the above quote in this book, and she responded, well, she responded with what I'd like to call elegant fire. I sent her an excerpt I'd intended to use and she quite firmly and forthrightly pointed out some erroneous assumptions I had made about some of the clothing I had seen and I have never been so eloquently slammed, while at the same time, grateful for being corrected. The short answer is that, no, the clothing I had seen probably didn't hold that kind of significance. She also said I was writing a lovely travelogue, which probably softened my reaction to her admirably blunt response. She obviously has discerning taste. Besides, I like people who don't beat around the bush. Just say it already!

This might be a good opportunity to remind you of my credentials and limitations as a self-published writer of a book that shares some possibly contentious ideas. For one, I didn't have a crew of fact-checkers on my team, nor did I spend exhaustive amounts of time cross-referencing. Everything I share I learned from sources on the web, books or magazines, but there are many conflicting stories on some of these topics, especially the political ones. I did some cross-referencing, but there's a lot of data out there. If something upsets you or you want to know more, I encourage you to do some research on your own to best inform your own opinion. My position is just one of many, and I didn't earn a doctorate in any of the subjects I cover. Now back to the bus.

The bus bounced and swayed under a jungle canopy so dense, I couldn't get much of a view of the country side. I looked at what the woman beside me was embroidering. She had a black cotton cloth she was embroidering with vivid red, pink and orange flowers and leaf patterns.

"Muy Bonita," I commented, to which she smiled broadly, her eyes causing her entire face to crinkle in appreciation. She wore her hair in two braids on either side of her head. Her hair was still mostly black with only a little gray winding its way through.

"¿Habla español?" She asked.

I smiled back apologetically and said, "Solamente un poco,"

probably saying more with my horrid pronunciation than I did with my words, which meant, "Only a little." She smiled again, nodded, and went back to her embroidery.

After an hour or so we came to the border between Tabasco and Chiapas and the bus rumbled to a stop. I glanced up at the television screen, where Latinos in camouflage moved through the jungles with AK-47s (I assume. I know nothing about guns. To me, they're all AK47s). When I looked back outside the window I saw a young, angry-looking soldier wearing camouflage and carrying an AK47 walk to the front of the bus. I'm sure you'll find this hard to believe, given all the bravado I've shown up to this point, but I started quaking in my boots.

I looked to the passengers around me to see how they were reacting. No one was really reacting one way or the other. The kindly grandmother sitting beside me with the braids, continued her embroidery. Other passengers read books, snored, or looked bored. Another soldier joined the first and waited for the bus driver to fold open the doors. Then they came on the bus.

Had I done my research I might have wondered if this were a routine border check or whether it was members of a paramilitary group operating autonomously for their own, or a boss's, interests. I might have wondered if they were part of a group responsible for the rapes, murders and kidnappings that were taking place in that area at the time, completely unbeknownst to me. Nor was I aware that human rights workers, foreign and domestic, regularly received death threats for their efforts and were sometimes beaten, raped, killed or just simply disappeared. I didn't know that the home of the head of the Human Rights Commission in Chiapas was recently "raked by bullets by an angry mob."[ix] There were many things I didn't know about where I was going besides the fact that no one was likely to speak English or accept American Express Travelers Checks.

I didn't know that near my destination of Palenque, there was a town called Usipà, actually less of a town and more of a camp of many families who'd lost their homes because of the conflict…the "low-intensity" warfare still being waged by the Mexican government, or paramilitary groups (rumored to be backed by the Mexican government.) The group stopping our bus with AK-47s could have been members of the paramilitary group Paz y Justicia (Peace and Justice), a government sanctioned organization suspected of being responsible for the deaths of 200 people according to a PBS Frontline special. Like I said, had I known all of that I might have been even more afraid than I was. I might have wondered who they really represented. I certainly wonder now.

Slowly they walked down the aisle, looking into every face they passed, rifles held in front of them with both hands. I nervously scanned the other passengers, planning to take my cue from them, and as everyone seemed to react to this as though it were routine, I went with that also and sat looking directly in front of me with what I hoped was a bored expression on my face. The soldiers stopped a few rows in front of me and asked a man for his papers, I assume, as he fumbled into his jacket and pulled out papers he handed to the soldier.

The soldier looked the papers over briefly, handed them back and kept making his way down the aisle. He passed me by without a glance, something I found interesting as you'd think the only white person on the bus would get a second look, but I didn't argue the point. I was glad he didn't decide to pull some kind of shakedown, the kind I'd heard stories about and seen in movies, where the white person is "arrested" until the ticket is paid, which conveniently enough can be done on the spot to the arresting officer, no paper work necessary.

Whoever they were looking for, they weren't white. Or Gandal-Claus had briefly granted me invisibility. I've always suspected there is some deep truth to the adage that there is a different God for fools and orphaned children, because I was kind of both and if God interceded on my behalf on this occasion, well, it wouldn't have been the first time, nor thankfully, the last.

The soldier reached the end of the aisle and turned back for the front door. On the drop down TV's, the Latino guerilla soldiers were fully engaged in a firefight, little bursts of fire erupting from the muzzles of their guns. The soldiers left the bus and in a few moments, with a grinding of gears and a lurch that pitched me forward then slammed me back into my seat, we were once more on our way.

People on the bus began talking to each other in soft voices. Several people chuckled to the man whose papers had been checked and patted him affectionately on the back. He shook his head, placed his hand over his heart and laughed the grateful, relieved laugh of a man who feels he just escaped certain death. An aura of tension I hadn't even realized was there, evaporated, and a bus that had been quietly subdued became lighthearted and jovial the further we moved away from that checkpoint. Something just happened, but I had no idea of what. The feeling was contagious and I smiled and laughed right along with everyone else, but I was also wondering: What just happened? What, exactly, was going on around here?

Chapter 9: El Fuego y La Palabra (The fire and the word)

"Welcome to the mountains of the Mexican Southeast. Allow us to introduce ourselves. WE are the Zapatista National liberation army; The voice that arms itself to be heard; The face that hides itself to be seen; the name that hides itself to be named. The tomorrow that is harvested in the past."

Opening words of the 1994 National Democratic Convention in Chiapas

Over the last 500 years, the native people of Chiapas have been enslaved, oppressed, repressed, ravaged by smallpox and other European diseases for which they had no immunity, and thrown off their land. Every now and then, they got good and damned tired of it and threw a little rebellion. In those moments when they dared to raise their voices on their own behalf, their people were slaughtered and their better-armed oppressors made horrific examples to remind them who was boss. Conquistadors tied Indian rebels to long ropes and dragged them by horseback throughout the town until the skin was ripped from their bones. If they lived through that, they might have had their arms and legs tied to trees that had been bowed over and tied to the ground so that when the ropes were simultaneously cut from their ropes, the tree tops would fling to the sky, each in a different direction, tearing the body into four sections. The pieces of the person would then be hung about the land, terrifying reminders of who held the reins. I know that description was pretty gruesome, but I think when we use terms like drawn and quartered, we get the meaning, but sometimes we forget the actual horror. I'm thinking maybe we shouldn't.

The Indians were treated with such cruelty that in 1511, a Dominican friar named Father Antonio de Montesino rebuked his congregation, asking, "tell me, by what right or justice do you keep these Indians in cruel servitude? On what authority have you waged a detestable war against these people, who dwelt quietly and peacefully on their own land? ...Are these not men? Have they not rational souls?"[x]

Father Montesino was not the only one asking such questions and in 1512, the first laws that codified Spanish conduct towards Indigenous people were signed, the Laws of Burgos. These laws, the precursors to international human rights laws, sought to insure that, among other goals, the Indians were treated fairly, and were, ahem, encouraged to convert to Catholicism. But the rule of Spain was a long way away and the application of the laws spotty. The tone of the laws was paternalistic, requiring rulers to look after the well-being of their charges, both physically and spiritually, while still maximizing profits for Spain. But the effect was sometimes a reinforcement of the existing system. This went on for centuries. Occasionally the people were pushed and squeezed to the point that consequences be damned, enough was enough.

Legend has it that one community of Chiapans threw themselves into the Sumidero Canyon rather than submit and become slaves to the Spanish. There really is only so much a people can take before they see only two choices: Rebellion or death.

On October 12, 1992, on the Christopher Columbus quincentenial, several hundred Chiapan Indigenous farmers, ranchers and weavers marched into the colonial city of San Cristobal de Las Casas and into the ornate courtyard of Santo Domingo, once a monastery built around 1712. Santo Domingo is San Cristobal's most decadent piece of architecture. It is richly ornamented on the outside with spires pointing towards heaven and intricate carvings covering the walls. Inside, everything is lavishly gilded. It still proudly displays the double-headed Hapsburg Eagle which was the symbol of the Spanish monarchy at the time it was built. It is one of San Cristobal's most popular tourist sites. All of these characteristics made it a powerful place to make a statement.

In the center of this courtyard stood a statue of the conquistador who finally subdued the Indians and founded the city, Diego de Mazariegos. The people surrounded the effigy of Mazariego and for a moment, stood regarding the statue, this symbol of conqueror's pride.

Then one of the marchers took a sledgehammer and swung with the rage of 500 years, and knocked the statue from its pedestal, sending it crashing to the ground. They tied the effigy to a long rope and drug it behind a horse all through the town, as the conquistadors had once done to Indian rebels. Afterwards, the rest of the protesters pounded it into fragments. As they walked away, some of the people took up fragments of the statue as souvenirs, reminders that they could indeed fight back; That together they could perhaps take down this system as they had taken down this proud statue.

This demonstration at a Catholic church did not come easy for people who are deeply devout Catholics. But as their children slowly starved and their pleas failed to move authorities, they were running out of options. Thrown off their land, they were unable to support themselves and grievances that had been simmering for centuries were beginning to boil over. Giving unto Caesar was starving them out.

Their list of grievances are issues that anyone living in a democracy should appreciate, especially Americans, as their demands aren't terribly different from the issues that caused some of America's ancestors to make the voyage across the sea, then finally wage war with their mother country to attain; Rights that later had to be fought for again by Blacks and Women: The right to participate in the political process, to choose their own leaders, to own their own land and have the right to decide what happens on that land; the right to enjoy the fruits of one's own labor, to be free from discrimination and repression, to participate in the engines of economics; to be indentured servants and slaves to the rich no more; to have decent healthcare and access to education for their children. Basically the rights to life, liberty and the pursuit of happiness. Sound familiar?

With the signing of the North American Trade Agreement (NAFTA) in January of 1994, it seemed conditions would only get worse, as one of the agreements provisions was the removal of Article 27 to ease the path of multinationals. Long considered one of the greatest social achievements of the Mexican Revolution, it was added to the constitution in 1917. Article 27 set the government the lofty goal of promoting conservation, balanced development throughout the nation, improvement in living conditions in rural as well as urban areas, and equitable distribution of the public wealth. Large landholdings and mini fiefdoms, were to be broken up and redistributed, taking care not to infringe on the holdings of small farmers.

More precisely, Article 27 states that "ownership of the land and waters within the boundaries of the national territory is vested originally in the nation, which has had the right to transfer title to private persons thereby constituting private property." In the United States, United Kingdom and other nations this national right is called eminent domain. It also gave the government the sacred trust of protecting its natural resources and breaking up large landholdings and redistributing them appropriately to the greatest benefit of the public as a whole.

Those reforms, however, never gained the traction originally intended. President Làzaro Càrdena, Mexico's president from 1934 to 1940, probably achieved the most for peasants and indigenous people, instituting extensive social and political reforms, like the eight-hour work day, establishment of agrarian collectives, redistribution of 45 million acres to the peasants, nationalizing the oil industry under Pemex and establishing the Department of Indigenous Affairs, whose aim was to represent the interests of Mexico's Indigenous people.

But the ruling class would not yield their power so easily. In 1946, with the origination of the Institutional Revolutionary Party, manned by President Miguel Aleman, large landholders began breaking up their estates, as reforms directed, but only on paper. By assigning them to members of their family, they were able to masquerade as small farmers and by-pass the requirements of Article 27. Periodically there would be land redistributions, but not to the extent of original intentions.

In 1991, President Carlos Salinas de Gortari proposed the removal of Article 27 for the sake of NAFTA, which both houses of the federal legislature overwhelmingly approved, basically ringing the dinner bell for multinational corporations.

Feeble as the Article had been, the fact that it continued to exist had given people reason to hope. To remove it at the same time the nation opened its doors to multinational corporations was to confirm what evidence had suggested all along: That the powers that be had no interest, present or future, in the social goals set down in Article 27 and the poor and Indigenous people would be left defenseless.

For months, labor, environmental and indigenous rights activist groups protested NAFTA's enactment, on the grounds that its enactment and the removal of certain barriers to trade intended to protect small farmers, equated with the summary execution of four million indigenous Mexican people. No one seemed to hear them or care because on January 1, 1994, the United States, Mexico, and Canada's trilateral agreement went into effect.

The name Zapatista comes from another revolution's hero, Emiliano Zapata. Emiliano Zapata fought with Poncho Villa in the Mexican Revolution from 1910 until his betrayal and assassination in 1919. A popular horseman and bullfighter before the war, his dedication to the rights of the poor and his ferocity on the battlefield made him a legend.

Originally from the Mexican state of Morelos, Emiliano united the peasantry into a mighty army that fought for reforms on behalf of the indigenous farmers. Instrumental in the overthrow of the corrupt presidency of Porfirio Diaz, he was betrayed, ambushed and executed in the dark of night by the Mexican army. It was a devastating blow. The rebellion in the South of Mexico never regained its strength. They weren't completely defeated, however. A year after his death, some of his supporters infiltrated government seats and managed to institute some of his visions, though it was a far cry from the land reforms he had believed in and fought so fiercely. Seventy-five years later a new movement took up his name and his cause.

New Year's Day of 1994, the morning NAFTA went into effect, the Zapatistas declared war on the Mexican government. At the time it was estimated that 1 in 5 children born in Chiapas would die of a curable disease like pneumonia or diarrhea. United by poverty, hunger and desperation, people from Tsotsil, Tseltal, Ch'ol, and Tojolabal communities and others from the ranks of Mexico's poor, forgotten peoples, took over several cities in Chiapas. They ransacked buildings, but carefully avoided civilian bloodshed. While a few carried Ak47s, most were armed with ancient rifles leftover from the 1910 Revolution. Some of them marched barefoot and carried only sticks or cardboard cutouts of rifles.

As they marched, they freed political prisoners, burned military outposts and took over large ranches. As part of their uniform they wore bandanas and black ski masks over their faces, leaving only the eyes showing, a characteristic that was to symbolize that theirs was not a movement about rallying around one personality, but was about every man, every woman, and every child. Faceless, behind the masks they could be anyone, even you or I. Everyone was Everyman.

The "technical" battle begun on January 1, 1994, was short, lasting only 12 days, before President Carlos Salinas de Gortari called for a cease fire to discuss terms for peace. Some say 150 people were killed, while others say 500. Some said there were so many that bulldozers had to move the bodies. Most of the dead were Zapatistas.

In a 1994 interview with Ed Bradley of 60 minutes, Juan Enriquez, an academic and businessman who participated on the Mexican government's team during negotiations with the Zapatistas, said that the reason the government called for a cease-fire so quickly was because they "very quickly realized that we weren't dealing with fanatics, that some of these demands were legitimate." He said, "What people realized is that there is a need for important democratic changes in this country, for economic changes, and these communities are getting left behind." If that was the actual reason, then that is a beautiful thing, but the story seems more complicated.

With the historic signing of NAFTA, the whole world had their eyes on Mexico, particularly the two democracies of the United States and Canada. Though the Zapatistan movement was at first perceived as being a small, insignificant uprising, it simply wouldn't do to have one while Mexico's two new business partners were still looking on.

So the government, with the Catholic church acting as mediators, offered the rebels, the "professionals in violence," the Zapatistas, an official pardon. The Zapatistas responded:

What do we have to ask forgiveness for?
What are they going to "pardon" us for?
For not dying of hunger?
For not accepting our misery in silence?[xi]

The Zapatistas did not surrender and thank the government for their benevolent offer of a pardon. They reiterated their demands. And so the "peace talks" commenced. While a portion of the government may have been dedicated to peaceful resolution, evidence suggests that at least some sections of the Mexican government decided that the best response was a military one and they were already planning to deal with this little uprising as they had dealt with Emiliano Zapata's: By taking out the movement's leadership…as soon as it could be ascertained who exactly that was.

But they found that a little difficult. Somewhere along the line, someone in Chiapas had heard Spanish philosopher, George Santayana's adage "Those who do not learn from the past are doomed to repeat it."

Supposedly, there was no one leader to be singled out and eliminated, though much of the communiqué's were delivered by one Subcommandante Marcos, but he claimed to be only a humble messenger. In fact, the very title of "sub" commandante was a reflection that Marcos was merely a mouth piece representing the will of councils. Besides, given that all Zapatistas, men, women and even some children, wear the black ski masks or bandanas over their faces, it was impossible to know exactly who Marcos was or whether he was even one person or many.

Except that even with the black mask, Marcos became unmistakable. With his deep, dark, expressive eyes, philosopher's pipe, modest demeanor and soft, velvet tone that spoke politics with the voice of an idealistic poet…there could be only one. Marcos issued statements to the government and any media who would listen, that were called a blend of analysis and poetry, a genre all his own, full of passion and idealism, el fuego y la palabra (the fire and the word), in his own words. It ended up having profound international appeal, as did his Zorro-esque donning of the black mask.

Enriquez said that Marcos is such a gifted speaker that people are often moved to tears by his words. He said that it was his idealism that charmed the Mexican people, and Marcos possesses a lot of charm. When Marcos was asked about the significance of wearing the masks, Marcos joked that, "handsome men like myself have to be protected." A moment later, he leveraged the opportunity to educate on the importance of not forming a cult of personality around individuals, but to maintain the focus on the people.

But it was hard for the media to resist focusing on this character that, so people told *60 Minutes* Ed Bradley, brought romanticism back to Mexico. Bradley shared that praise with Marcos in his *60 Minutes* interview and Marcos laughed with such obvious surprise and embarrassment—well, it was extremely endearing. As is the image of Zorro or Robin Hood he invokes riding into events on a beautiful white stallion.

It is believed that Marcos is originally from the privileged class, a former college professor who came to Chiapas to teach, but instead, learned. He learned to love the people, the culture and the hills of Chiapas and to care so much about their plight that he gave up everything to help them. This is more or less what he said to Ed Bradley in his *60 minutes* interview in 1994. He said in his elegant Spanish accent that "If you believe in some kind of right for the people…you think that the people have the right of justice, of liberty of democracy, then you fight for these people." And it is for the people. He will probably not be at all pleased with the amount of time I've spent on him in this book, but, Marcos, like it or not, you are an integral, fascinating part of this history. Perhaps even why there were already a lot of academics educated on the plight of Chiapas before the first shot was fired, with a movement poised to launch.

Meanwhile, even as the Mexican government outwardly portrayed a concerned paternal face on the conflict, they also sent more and more troops into Chiapas. While a portion of the government may have been sincerely dedicated to righting wrongs, there is also evidence that the government also backed paramilitary terrorism in Chiapas and may still do so. There are even rumors that the paramilitaries also have support and arms from the United States, which wouldn't be at all surprising considering that at the same time an agreement for tri-lateral cooperation was being signed through NAFTA, the United States also enacted Operation Gatekeeper, militarizing the Mexican/American border for the first time.

Not exactly a show of optimism about the impacts of NAFTA for Mexico. Obviously, turbulence was expected. The Zapatistas, for their part, expected to have high casualties, but they were willing to make the sacrifices if it finally got Mexico to address their concerns.

But then something happened that they didn't expect, that nobody expected, including the Zapatistas: The impact of the W.W.W.—the world wide web. Hey, did you know that the internet actually began as a military project? Arpanet, launched in 1983, was designed as a communication platform that would be immune to strikes on a central location, say, the Pentagon. A net with multiple connections and with no central server, messages could be rerouted if one or more servers were destroyed. Then someone, former Vice President, Al Gore, says it was him, deduced broader applications and later, the internet was opened up to allow for scientific communication among universities, then private corporations further extended the net. Then it just exploded because all that was needed to expand was to add new servers going online.

In 1994, at the time of the Zapatista's declaration of war, academics had been using the internet for years. The general public were just plugging in, but it was spreading faster than anyone anticipated, with broader applications than ever expected.

Before the first shot was *officially* fired, academics had already been discussing the plight of the Indigenous people of Mexico and the possible ramifications of NAFTA. They'd posted information about the conflict, the background of the Zapatistas and the Indigenous people of Chiapas, on the brand-spanking new internet and had been sharing it all over the world. They turned a spotlight on a corner of the world scarcely anyone knew anything about. This exchange resulted in email lists, bulletin boards, websites and networks never before possible because for the first time ever, information spread at the touch of a button, for free.

For the Zapatistas it was a miracle, a divine intervention, whatever you want to call it. Without a doubt, it saved the lives of countless Zapatistas and spread their story around the globe. The *New York Times* called it the world's first Post-Modern Revolution. President Carlos Salinas de Gortari had the honor of being the first in the world to experience the power of the web as every move he made, every shot that was fired in the far off jungles of Chiapas, every picture snapped of a child wounded in the crossfire, went viral on the internet and outcries began pouring in from all over the globe. Gortari had no choice but to at least give the semblance of compassionate concern and fair play. Whether he actually felt it, only God knows.

When the war started in Mexico, demonstrations broke out all over the world on behalf of the Zapatistas. There were write-ins, fax campaigns, and protests. Phone calls flooded the Mexican consulates and the U.S. government urging a nonmilitary resolution of the conflict. Connections were made between other Central American solidarity groups, indigenous rights activists, anti-NAFTA organizers, and universities, spreading way outside the borders of Mexico and the academic camp. In Mexico City alone, 750,000 supporters held demonstrations.

Stories were reprinted from the Mexican media and shared everywhere, as were statements from Mexican officials, and spokespeople for the Zapatista, including everyone's new favorite masked man, Subcommandante Marcos.

Marcos was as gifted at writing letters as he was at public speaking. At first he probably didn't expect these letters to have quite such large audiences, but he hoped they found their way under just the right eyes. He wrote letters to the editors of newspapers and magazines, to generals and presidents that were part political protest, part manifesto and part celebrations of the Chiapan people. He painted vivid pictures of endearing peasant life at the same time he held presidents and generals accountable for injustice. In one line he might accuse the president of supporting paramilitaries while in the next he might describe children in the little village where he hid, sneaking candies from his pocket as he wrote.

For a moment you could forget you were reading the words of a revolutionary and think you were reading from the pages of a novel. Then he masterfully wove in a political point.

One letter, printed in 1994 in the Mexico national newspaper El Financiero, addressed To Whom it May Concern, described a family making ready for a birthday party. He showed us an innocent child looking for balloons, candy, or presents hidden for his upcoming 5th birthday party, then slipped in a jab to then Mexican President Salinas, who called the Zapatistas Transgressors. His jab was merely a sentence among many sentences that appeared to be mainly about the arrangements for the upcoming child's birthday party and all the people going about preparations. As I read, I recognized that he wrote for many audiences in this communiqué. He wrote to gain the sympathy for the indigenous people, revealing them to be what they were: human beings just like human beings anywhere; neighbors who would be willing to help you build that barn or fix that car. Children excited about their birthday party.

But it was also to Congress, and to the fearful of international ridicule, Presidente. As the child poked among the office contents for booty, he pushed through what seemed an innocuous list of randomness: pipe tobacco, photographs of friends and families, bullet cartridge belts (what office doesn't have those lying around?), stacks of letters, "dried tears and gun parts." Then Marcos went on to say that the "headquarters" were more like a kindergarten, they were so full of children and I wondered if that were an appeal to not bomb them because they might be bombing children?

Because of the web, Marcos' audience numbered in the millions, from all over the world. All of this new attention made the Mexican government feel like a matron who'd just had the curtain drawn back on her in the shower. They found it much more difficult to suppress information about its counter insurgency once they were not just running a country but international public relations, and one of the first such entities to experience this exciting new aspect of the internet. Gortari signed NAFTA at the tip of the tail ending of his presidency so he may have thought he could sign NAFTA and duck quickly out, but not at the dawn of the information age.

Here's evidence of divine intervention as far as I'm concerned: the internet was almost non-existent in Chiapas at the time. In 1994, the only Internet hubs were in the state's capitol, Tuxtla Gutierrez and San Cristobol de las Casas. There weren't even telephone lines or electricity in most of the rural areas of the state. The media had at first depicted Marcos as a cyber genius with a laptop sneaking through the jungle, but in reality, he carried a walkie-talkie and communicated with his army with CB radios and smoke signals.

The Zapatistas weren't driving the cyber-awareness. It was being driven by sympathizers from outside of Chiapas. Attempts by the government to suppress information were futile as every move made somehow found itself broadcasted by webbers, some of whom had gone down to Chiapas themselves to witness events first hand and shared what they learned as soon as they found an internet plug-in. The communiqués prepared by Marcos and other spokespeople were posted to the net within hours of their completion, where previously they would have been lucky to see them in print sometimes even after days or weeks.

The Zapatistas were just as surprised as the Mexican government to suddenly find themselves flush with international supporters not only on this Internet thingy but coming down to actually join them in their villages.

After months of enduring low-intensity warfare while supposedly engaged in peace talks, the Zapatistas rejected the government's first proposal in July 1994. Rightly fearing there could be some ramifications, some intensifying of the low-intensity warfare, they devised a way to keep the world's eyes on them while at the same time, spreading the discussion of equality. They called for a National Democratic Convention, inviting people from all over the world. Held in August 1994, it was attended by thousands of national and international participants from various social movements— inviting dialogue while at the same time keeping the umbrella over their villages of the world's scrutinizing gaze. It only helped a little. Low-intensity warfare tactics continued. I'll talk about low-intensity warfare in a sec, in the meantime, don't let the benign language fool you into thinking it was mild, like I did.

On January 5, 1995, one year after the initial uprising, Presidente Ernesto Zedillo Ponce de Leon initiated a meeting with someone representing themselves as Marcos, calling the meeting "Steps Toward Peace." In this meeting, both parties produced lists of compromises and demands and the meeting seemed to be going so well that Marcos was rumored to have joked, "I am being threatened with unemployment." The meeting concluded with both parties signing a document titled The San Andres Accord, which entailed granting special rights, including autonomy, to indigenous people. However, upon Zedillo's return to the capital he did not begin deploying the concessions made. He sent the Mexican army into the jungle to execute Marcos. Instead of celebrating the beginning of peace, the Zapatistas found themselves under siege. Course, these actions were all over the internet almost immediately, and again, the letters and calls poured in.

In a tit for tat combat, the Mexican army far out-gunned the Zapatistas who were mostly simple farmers and ranchers. The Zapatistas knew they'd lose an all-out war before they ever declared it. They hadn't expected to win that way. Their hope was that the media would bring awareness to the rest of the country of their plight and that the good people of Mexico would rise to their aid.

And boy did they. Chiapas had the world's attention and if they could keep it, then they could lay down their guns and wield the pen which has long been rumored to out-might the sword. It was worth a try. Negotiations continued, mock or not, as did low-intensity warfare, but instead of firing back, the Zapatistas, through the eloquent voice of Marcos, fired off communiqués, press releases and personalized letters, charming the world with his literary talents and references, painting an image of the Zapatistas as romantic, intellectual, and most importantly, rational, non-communist, poets. Passionate about their ideals, but not in a maniacal way. In the words of Canadian author, activist and filmmaker, Naomi Klein, they showed themselves as "revolutionaries who don't want power." In marches and demonstrations, they tied white ribbons to the ends of their rusty old rifles to symbolize the paradox of guns that want to be silenced.

In 1996, Presidente Zedillo and the Zapatista's signed another peace agreement. The agreement promised…well, it doesn't really matter what it promised, nothing ever came of it and the low-intensity warfare continued. It may have been another ploy for the worldly onlookers. The ploy didn't work however and the government realized that every action on both sides was still being broadcast to the world almost as quickly as they were made, as were the letters and responses of Subcommandante Marcos. In a letter to Presidente Ernesto Zedillo, Marcos said what I think so many of us, Americans, Mexicans, humans the world over feel in the face of political rhetoric:

"Your words today are the same ones we have heard at the beginning of other administrations…You should know that the political system which you represent (the one to whom you owe your position of power, although not your legitimacy) has prostituted the language to such a degree, that today "politics" is synonymous to lies, crime, treachery. I only say to you what millions of Mexicans would like to say: we don't believe it."[xii]

Amen.

President Zedillo tried to counter public opinion (both domestic and international) by using the media to criticize, villainize and outright dismiss the concerns of the Zapatistas, claiming that the movement's worst fears would never come to pass. Unfortunately, the years that followed the signing of NAFTA witnessed many of those fears realized as farm after farm went out of business. The meager provisions to protect Mexican labor and environment were toothless, too weak to prevent the onslaught of exploitation unleashed by NAFTA and big business.

A 2008 *Economist* article cited the benefits to Mexico of NAFTA saying that since implementation, Mexico's non-oil exports had grown fourfold, while the stock of foreign direct investment had expanded by 14 times and "even the country's farm exports to its NAFTA partners have risen threefold." Offhandedly, the author does acknowledge that small farmers were greatly disadvantaged and most of the benefits were reaped by large agribusiness. By 2014, Mexico had lost 1.3 million farm jobs.[xiii]

In the years since, U.S. owned companies have moved to border towns and set up shop offering low pay, long hours and not only no benefits, but sometimes hazardous working conditions that would flunk right through even minor American OSHA regulations. That must have been a big incentive for large companies to push this through. They could move their operations where they didn't have to worry so much about worker safety and quality of life for the community.

That could be a major reason why the San Andreas Accords and other attempts to negotiate have repeatedly failed. *La Jornado*, a respected Mexican newspaper, said that, "Instead of establishing a new and inclusive social pact, respectful to the original peoples' right to autonomy, the state decided to maintain the old status quo": forcing autonomous indigenous people to submit to government control and work as cheap labor for capitalism."[xiv]

While many studies have found NAFTA to be a net gain for Mexico and responsible for the rise of a Mexican middle class, the poor and rural people are shouldering a lot of the negative sides of the agreement and of being on the lower end of the labor industry. They were the humble, desperate pool from which to draw cheap labor, with little or no regard given to their well-being.

So yea, a lot of Zapatistan fears are absolutely being realized. It sounds like those that already had the money got to make even more from the good old fashioned blood, sweat and tears of the vulnerable poor. Sounds a bit diabolical, but I'm no political scientist...wait a minute. I did graduate with honors with a Political Science degree. Guess I am a political scientist.

Regardless of the fact that a middle class has risen, is it worth it to grind the bones of the poor so there is a larger middle class that can shop at GAP?

Medea Benjamin, Co-Director at the international human rights organization, Global Exchange, put it well when she said, "We have to start questioning the big picture, we have to start questioning: What are these clothes that we're wearing? What does this tag 'Made in China' or Assembled in Mexico, the Free Trade Zone,' what does that mean? What does it mean that we have allowed our corporations around the world where they get guarantees from governments that workers will not be allowed to organize?"

Now is a good time to talk about "low-intensity warfare." When I first began this research and came across the term, it sounded like something that would be mildly annoying, like poison-ivy, but not horrific, nothing too alarming.

Then I read about what some of these tactics entailed. To the people this happens to, it's anything but mild. Low-intensity warfare takes many different forms and has many different names: counter-insurgency, anti-subversion, and peacekeeping, to name a few. Political philosopher George Caffentzis said in his essay, *The Politics of Massacre*, "One of the open secrets of LIW (Low-intensity Warfare) is the commandment: Avoid Formal Battles."[xv] In the case of the Mexican government versus the peasantry of Chiapas, this manifested as arming, and condoning, as well as refusing acknowledgement of, paramilitary groups who harassed the communities. They raided villages, set up harassing roadblocks, and generally engaged in intimidation tactics designed to prevent the people from working their fields, furthering already precarious food shortages and all kinds of other mean, nasty, sneaky ways to try to wear away the people's resolve, without giving proof of who did what, or giving enough cause for an international scandal.

But that still doesn't really shed light on what this mild terminology really means. I didn't fully appreciate the difference in mental and emotional impact in choices of words until I read the words 'low-intensity warfare' and then a few sentences later I read detailed examples about some of these 'low-intensity' tactics. There was a distinct visceral reaction to the words 'low-intensity warfare' and a completely different visceral reaction to reading about the massacre of Acteal on December 22, 1997, when a few days before Christmas, an entire village was corralled, and 45 men, women and doe-eyed children were shot down or hacked to death with machetes, then how the government-backed paramilitary group threw their bodies over a cliff into a patch of coffee bushes.[xvi]

In an April 2000 interview with Harvard Professor Thomas Benjamin, Pèrez Narvaez, a representative of the Chiapas attorney general, said this about the massacre, "The Zapatista's were advocating socialism and these groups didn't agree with them. They got a little out of hand."[xvii]

A week after the massacre, the government said they wanted to resume peace talks, no doubt in response to world outrage. Then they sent 5000 more troops into Chiapas—for peacekeeping purposes. You know, "peacekeeping." Years later a federal court finally convicted 77 people for this brutality, including one retired general.

Some sources say they targeted women particularly, because women are the glue of the community. They also represent one half of the general command and one-third of the armed forces. Cecilia Rodgriguez, a spokeswoman for the Zapatista's, a social activist, and a citizen of the United States who traveled to Chiapas for humanitarian purposes was gang-raped and sodomized for her participation in the Zapatista movement. In just the first two years of the movement, 50+ women of Chiapas had been raped, and very little investigation resulted. Hardly anything was ever done about it.

The acts are sporadic enough to terrorize the population, but not on a scale large enough to keep the world's attention. In Chiapas this has been ongoing since 1994, right up to the death of a teacher and the wounding of 15 Zapatistas in 2014 by one of those paramilitary groups.

Over this time there have been hundreds of murders and disappearances that have been attributed to paramilitary units sanctioned, if not armed and funded, by the Mexican government. Again, notice the visceral difference between my telling you there have been murders, and telling you that mothers have been slaughtered or snatched from their children's embraces never to be seen again. Or of the four-year-old little boy found crouching, crying, beside the still warm and bleeding body of his father just shot down while walking home from school. That is low-intensity warfare at its worst. Please don't forget it.

Looking out my window on the bus to Palenque, from an American perspective, it didn't appear the Zapatistas had had much success in the years since their initial uprising. The bus occasionally passed a large house of splendor, but for the most part, the homes I saw were of the one-room, dirt floor, palm-thatch-roof variety with perhaps a few chickens scratching around a packed dirt yard. As far as I could tell, hardly any had electricity. To a girl whose best memories included living out of a tent with an amazing star-tapestry ceiling, it also didn't look like they were doing too badly. But even when I lived out of my tent, I had regular access to clean water, showers, light to read by, work when I wanted it, and medical care when I needed it. And I wasn't trying to raise and prepare children for the world under those circumstances.

A report I recently read said that in the nearby town of Ocosingo, half the homes lacked piped water, five out of six lacked septic systems, and three out of four had dirt floors. It said that conditions were even worse in the country side, where I traveled.

However, the report had also said that the people lived in misery, and I didn't necessarily see any misery. I saw some serious faces, but I also saw a lot of smiles and laughter, from both children and adults, though I do realize you can't really gather the full nature of a place by simply reading about it on the internet, nor by staring out the window as your bus speeds passed it. A tourist can breeze right through and wax poetic about the simple agrarian lives being lived out in this place. To be sure, there's an unmistakable beauty and fortune to such a life. But what the tourist on the bus doesn't see are the daily struggles. The tourist breezes right through admiring the charms, completely oblivious to the dangers that embroil, to the hunger, poverty and disease that are also a part of this world.

Chapter 10: The Maya Bell or Bust

"No place is ever as bad as they tell you it's going to be."
Chuck Thompson

I woke up with my head bobbing and jerking around as if it was no longer attached to my body, but held by a string to a stick that a child was wildly batting about. After several sleepless nights, my consciousness was reluctant to come back to the real world, but I had to rally enough to make sure the bus was actually still on the road. It felt like we'd gone commando through the jungle and were driving over boulders and fallen trees.

Then, BAM! The bus crashed to a halt with such force I was flung against the seat in front of me and then thrown back so hard I landed flat on my back in the aisle. I thought for sure we'd just been in an accident, but I was the only one who seemed to take the slightest notice. The woman sitting beside me looked quizzically at me on the floor, while I struggled to get back in my seat. My fellow passengers had shifted their weight around as the bus clunked, thunked and swayed, as skilled as though they were riding horses.

Embarrassed, I made it back to my seat and smiled sheepishly at the woman beside me. I looked in front of us to see what in the world was going on up there, and caught a glimpse of what I assumed was the road, though it looked more like a wide ditch with deep ruts that drug the bus' tires in whatever groove was deepest.

After a few, or thirty, more miles, it was impossible for me to judge the distance, the road once again smoothed, and the grandmother beside

92

me resumed working diligently on her embroidery. I glanced at her progress, impressed at how much she'd finished while I'd been sleeping, and then I looked out the windows.

I saw green. Everything was coated in this subtle hue of a green patina, because all light was being filtered through a woven canopy of dense leaves. The leaves were so dense and of so many sizes, all vying for their splash of sun, that the canopy was virtually a complete woven ceiling. Even my skin appeared a slight pale green.

I wanted to ask the grandmother for the window seat so I could search the jungle for monkeys, tree sloths, or jaguar, but I didn't dare offend her by mispronouncing anything. I'd heard way too many stories about people getting slapped in the face for calling someone a horrible name by mistake.

Though I didn't know it at the time, I was already making that blunder when I tried to tell people to have safe travels. 'Buen viaje' is what I meant to say and it means 'Good Travels.' What I had been saying was, "¡Buen viejei" which, I found out much later, means something like "Good old woman or witch." So I had been parting ways with people who had been friendly towards me, shouting out, with a smile and a wave, "Have a Good old Woman!" Which had caused my new friends to wave back with looks of confusion and, often, no smile.

There were fewer people walking on the roads here and I never saw any other cars, just an occasional microbus or motorcycle. Suddenly the bus came to a stop, and the driver turned and looked directly at me, glaring.

He said something completely incomprehensible to me. I cocked my head to the side and asked, "Palenque?" to which he nodded, opened the door, and motioned for me to get off the bus. I stood up, but then leaned down to see what I could see outside the windows. There was nothing there. No crossroads. No store. Just the road continuing through jungle.

The driver snarled something at me, and I asked again, "Palenque?" He rattled something else off and I looked questioningly to the grandmother beside me. She set her jaw and shook her head no, pulled at my arm and said, "Sentarse! (Sit down)." When I sat down she took my hand in hers and shouted to the driver, "Vamanos!" The driver looked at us for a moment, then shrugged, closed the doors and drove on without another word.

That's how I narrowly escaped God knows what. Maybe nothing, but I couldn't figure out why the bus driver was trying to put me out of the bus in the middle of nowhere. I still have no definitive answer.

Years later I read Chuck Thompson's book, *Smile When You're Lying*, where he relates a similar experience he had in the Philippines, though his was in the dark of night. He was dropped by a bus and left alone in the dark jungle only to be quickly surrounded by a band of machete wielding men up to no good. He also narrowly escaped God only knows what. I liked what he had to say about adventures that carry the potential for this kind of experience. He said that after years of being a travel writer, trekking through the most remote and dangerous places on the planet, that he had "come to understand that a Zen-like acceptance of travel as a highly unpredictable animal is the most effective way of approaching it." I'll add that when you're a foreign woman traveling alone, without a sponsor and no one's going to look very hard for you if you disappear, all sorts of spiritual practices get recruited. Course, Chuck Thompson is more like Indiana Jones and I'm more like, I don't know, Lucille Ball?

The grandmother beside me smiled reassuringly and patted my hand in hers. I smiled back. I guessed I was going wherever she led me.

A few more miles down the road and we came to a cross road where several rusty, 1960 era Volkswagen microbuses awaited the arrival of the big busses. The grandmother asked me where I was going, I think, and I told her I was going to the Maya Bell at Palenque. She threaded her fingers through mine, holding my hand as though I were a child, and began leading me towards a microbus. Her hands were warm, calloused and felt very strong. I was literally in very strong hands. She approached one of the drivers and said a few words to him, then patted me on the back and motioned for me to get in the bus. I turned around, hugged her (I'm big on hugging), and chanted, "Muchas gracias, muchas gracias" over and over again, from the bottom of my heart. She hugged me back and then got back on the other bus. It clanked into gear and swayed on down the road.

I stood beside the microbus for a moment looking at the jungle around me. Out of the air conditioning for the first time since we left the city, I finally felt the "sweltering heat" I'd read about. I giggled. What in the hell was I doing here? In a foreign land—a deeply foreign land—the likes of which I never properly imagined, where no one spoke my language, I had hardly any money, and yet I was stumbling forward with some strange, clueless determination, while over and over again, being scooped up by angels of human kindness and set on my merry, scary way.

This is awesome, I said to myself, climbing into the back of the bus and sliding across the seat to the window. Some part of me that had gotten attached to predictability in the 9 to 5 grind, gave way to the girl who loved not knowing what came next, and at the moment, I was fully embracing it.

Our creamy blue microbus slowly filled with people to near bursting. At one point, I was so smashed against the person beside me that it was impossible to tell if I were covered in their sweat or my own. While there was no air conditioner, after hours of being over-cooled on the luxury bus, I enjoyed the honest breeze from the open windows. Over the roar of the wind, I could just make out American 80s music trying to make its way through the dirt covered speakers.

I couldn't stop smiling. I wanted to reach my head out the open window, let the wind tear through my hair and shout, "Yahoo!!!" But I didn't. I didn't want anyone to think I was, you know, crazy! I was just so damned happy! Something about narrow escapes, even if you only suspect you narrowly escaped something have a tendency to induce this kind of elation.

There was more to it, though. I'd heard horrible things about how many criminals there were in Mexico and how I was sure to be robbed, maybe even kidnapped or murdered. But then I'd also read articles about how it was safer in Mexico than Texas, so there was that. I didn't really want to believe all the bad stories. I believe that people are mostly good. Mostly. And it was invigorating to have first-hand evidence. Course, on the other hand was the possible bad intentions of the bus driver, but several other times on this trip I'd had no choice but to throw myself at the mercy of strangers and they could easily have taken advantage, but they didn't. I threw myself and they caught me. I've been lucky. I'm not so naïve as to not realize that. There are plenty of people who aren't so lucky. When I mentioned this story to Chuck Thompson he said, "Glad you made it off the bus. Here and there, people don't."

But at that moment, I was riding the high of being a beneficiary of human kindness, living proof of its existence and it was invigorating to have the proof while desperately wanting to believe in it.

The ride to the Maya Bell was short and I was relieved when the bus stopped right at the entrance so there was absolutely no question that I was in the right place. I grabbed my backpack from the top of the bus, paid my faire and actually skipped a little up the stone walkway.

To the right of the path, I saw a collection of thatched roof huts. And roofs were all they were. No walls, just four posts holding a palm thatched roof over a packed dirt floor. Under most of them I saw rope hammocks strung, some of them with people in them sleeping or reading. The huts were called palapas, and there were about twelve of them nicely spaced with the jungle just behind them. The hammocks were beautiful, bright reds, oranges and green patterns, woven of soft cotton. I thought of my own army green, nylon hammock with mosquito net and tried to picture it hanging in this pristine setting and made a mental note to stuff it into the bottom of my pack.

The path led to a large, open air café with an enormous thatch roof and walls that were only three feet high, with the rest open air. It was cool in the shade and I was grateful to throw my pack into an empty chair. There were many wooden tables, each with four wooden chairs around them, and a small vase in the center with a single white or red flower. At the moment, the place was empty other than a slim man with dark skin, and darker circles around his sharp blue eyes, drinking coffee and reading a book. His hair was scraggly, black and shoulder length and he had a thin, sharp nose resembling a beak.

I smiled, "Buenas días. ¿Hable Inglès?"

He smiled back, his blue eyes blazing, as I came to learn later, they always did, "Buenas dias, Señorita. Yes, I speak English," he answered with a middle eastern accent.

I let out a sigh of relief. "Wonderful! I'm afraid my Spanish isn't very good yet and it's been a bit of a challenging trip. You're the first person I've spoken English to in days." A little more information than he really needed, but as I said it, it suddenly struck me of how weirdly true that was.

"I'm Hasid. I'm from Jordan," he said, relaxing into his chair and sending those blue eyes over me in unapologetic assessment. It wasn't because I'm a raving beauty, but because this is what most men do every time they see a woman, though some are more discreet about it.

I regretted my revelation of vulnerability almost immediately. "Do you work here?" I asked, hoping the answer would be no.

"No, but what are you looking for? A cabin or a palapa?" He answered.

"I'm camping, so where does that put me?" I answered, trying to strike a balance between being friendly enough for him to want to help me, but not so friendly that he got the wrong idea, another skill a woman traveling alone needed to have.

"Do you have a hammock?" he asked.

I thought about the ridiculous mosquito net hammock I carried that screamed "Paranoid Gringa" that I could no longer imagine hanging, and asked, "Do I absolutely need one?"

"Do you have a tent?" he asked. I shook my head no. He laughed. "You will definitely need a hammock."

He took a sip from his coffee mug, then set it down and went to the back where a few minutes later, he came back with a short, kind faced man who looked slightly Japanese. He had a string hammock in his hand

and he handed it to me saying, "¿Uno noche?"

"I don't know. No sè. ¿dos noches?" He mistakenly assumed I had a better grasp of the language than I did, because he then sputtered out a whole rapid fire sentence to which I took out my little book and began flipping towards the boarding section.

Hasid translated, "He said that all of the palapas are full, but maybe you can find someone who will let you share theirs. I happen to know that the palapa beside mine is being vacated as we speak. You should grab it before someone else does. Go straight up the walkway, it will be the first one on the right. There's a blond Australian guy who looks like he could be your brother packing his pack as we speak."

I smiled at both of them, said thank you, and almost frantically made my way up the walkway. I'm pretty sure that's something most of those folks never saw around there, someone walking frantically. But I was scared I wouldn't find a palapa and might have to ask Hasid if I could share his. Shudder.

I walked up the walkway and saw a palapa and someone with a wild tangle of curly blond hair leaning over a backpack underneath it. He was shirtless and I could see all of the beautiful, well defined muscles in his fair by nature, but now tanned shoulders. He seemed in a hurry and was talking to someone else who was in the palapa as he zipped zippers and tugged on webbing pulls. I came up behind him and said, "Excuse me, but are you leaving?"

He stopped what he was doing and turned towards me. He had on a nice pair of Bolle sunglasses, which he slowly removed as he turned to face me. He quickly scanned me with his bright, blue eyes, and actually said the word, "Dammit." In an Australian accent. "Yes, dammit, I am," he said, smiling with obvious regret. I smiled back. I was sorry he was leaving, too, because from what I could tell, he was definitely my type. He had a touch of pure wildness, with an air of intelligence. But I'd sworn to myself: no Latin lovers. Even non-Latinos. PPF.

"Do you mind if I go ahead and hang up my hammock? I don't mean to rush you, but there aren't any other palapas so I don't really have the luxury of politely waiting for you to leave."

He stood regarding me for an almost uncomfortably long time. "American?" he asked, in a thick Australian accent.

"Yes," I answered, sighing and shaking my head, "And on behalf of my country: I'm sorry."

Thanks to the controversial reign that was the George W. Bush presidency, we'd lost a lot of respect internationally and part of me really wanted to say, 'Canadian' instead. It had actually been suggested by friends that I get a Canadian patch and put it on my backpack, for fear that being an American might open me up to a whole other set of dangers than other white travelers might experience. But, despite the Bush administration, there was still a lot about America I was proud of, a lot still worth standing up for.

He laughed, nodding, as he threw his humongous backpack onto his shoulders. "Alas, I have a bus to catch. Palapa's yours, Miss." He said, bouncing down the walk as though the pack weighed nothing, blond curls bouncing with his gait. I sighed, watching him go, he turned around once, and smiling, shook his head once more, as he turned to go. Hubba hubba!

"Wait!" I said. He stopped dead in his tracks and turned his head towards me, curious as to what I might have in mind.

"Do they have a pay phone here?" I asked.

I was slightly amused to see his shoulders actually slump and I thought to myself, *Yea, I think you're cute, too, but you're leaving.* He nodded, "Yes indeed, Miss. It's up to the café. You'll need a phone card."

"Muchas Gracias, Señor," I said.

He shrugged, "Doesn't warrant a muchas, Miss. A simple 'gracias' would suffice." He grinned. Accents. What is it about accents? "Adios, chica bonita." He waved and trotted on down to the road just in time to catch a microbus.

Well that was a close call 'cause he was resoundingly my type and his presence might have made the whole, no-Mexico-romance rule harder to keep.

I hung my hammock and went back to the café to get a phone card and call Brian to let him know where I was and that I was okay.

Hasid was sitting at his table reading a book.

I smiled as innocuously as I could, "Excuse me, Hasid, but do you know where I might purchase a phone card and find an ATM?"

He looked up, "Absolutely," he answered authoritatively. "Villahermosa is your best chance, but I'm afraid you just missed the last bus."

"Seriously?" I asked, surprised. "Damnit I just came from there! Does it take coins?"

"Nope. Got to call Mom?" he asked

"No, just a friend," I said. "You wouldn't happen to have a cell phone I could borrow, would you?" I'd thought a cell phone would have made me a target and it was too expensive to risk getting stolen, so I'd left mine with Michelle.

"There's no service. Not for miles. I'm sorry." Hasid answered, then went back to his reading.

"Thanks." Geesh. Sorry, Brian. The morning had been such a chaotic blur, I couldn't remember exactly, but I was pretty sure I needed to call and let him know I was okay. I sighed and thought, "He's going to be worried sick and then he's going to kill me. Well, nothing to be done today. Sorry Bri."

I went back to my palapa and had a foil tuna and cracker dinner, the first meal since breakfast and the last one today. There was the café, but they didn't accept credit cards or, needless to say, American Express Traveler's Checks, so I wanted to save my pesos until I could make sure I could access an ATM with my credit card. So tuna for dinner and tuna for breakfast.

Chapter 11: Roomies

"Never floss with a stranger."
Joan Rivers

All checked in and swinging in my hammock it was still several hours until sunset. What to do, what to do? The campground had a pool, but the water looked pretty murky and I hadn't seen anyone else in it. Though if it had gotten much hotter, I might have decided to risk a little skin infection to cool off. Being born and raised in Memphis, Tennessee, I was probably better suited than most to endure the heat, but even I had my limits.

I decided to take a tour of the grounds and see if I could find a trail or something else interesting. I saw two men hacking away at invading plants with their machetes, fighting the jungle back where it tried to send its tendrils into the sunny spots opened in the canopy by the campground. I wondered if I would ever get used to seeing so many people carrying these swords that were fully capable of hacking off limbs from people as well as trees. Given the political turmoil that had saturated this area over the last decade, some of those blades may have actually shed blood. Shudder.

The grounds were beautiful and very well kept. While it was not quite a resort, it had a lot more to offer than just a hotel. The restaurant was quite elegant for a place that grew straight off the jungle floor. Though it didn't have walls, it did have crystal clear Christmas lights strung across the ceiling that were lit up at night. Though I hadn't tasted the food, I had a suspicion, from the level of care I saw around there (murky pool notwithstanding), that the food would be quite good. The campground was a collection of maybe a dozen of the thatched roof palapas poised against a jungle background with a few tents scattered on open ground.

Another trail led to a collection of cabanas, slightly more upscale than the palapas. They were small one rooms with a bed, small dresser and possibly a desk. Each cabana was surrounded by just enough jungle to give it a private feel. Some of them had their own bathrooms, some of them had none and boarders shared open air showers with the lowly campers. When I say open air, I don't mean there were no privacy walls. There were walls, just no ceiling. Pretty cool actually, showering right out in the jungle surrounded by lush greenery.

Then there was the Temazcal, the spa where people could get massages or indulge in other therapeutic treatments, some labeled as traditional, though I have no idea what that entailed.

A sign said that a few nights of the week there was live music in the café. All this and the grounds were in almost immediate proximity to the ruined city of Palenque. Unfortunately, there were no trails from the campground through the jungle and no other activities to pass the time.

Other than Palenque and the Maya Bell I had no idea what else was around to see, nor whether it was prudent, or spectacularly stupid for a gringa to go walking down the street by herself to find out. This was the downside of being one of those people completely lacking in the planning gene.

It wasn't as though I was new to traveling. I'd traveled all over the Western United States. But my method was to hear about a destination, then head there with the intention to learn what else was in the area when I arrived. Often I was on such a tight budget, my main destination was about all I could afford and once I'd seen whatever that was, I tended to stick to woods, which was just fine by me. While this might have made me miss some big attractions out of sheer ignorance, I learned to appreciate things that most people might pass right on by, like watching wildlife in the woods, or really seeing the graceful, shimmying dance of a tree in the wind. Or, like at that moment, learning to appreciate just sitting and soaking in the sounds of a place, like a heartbeat.

When I got back to my palapa, I noticed a flat patch of green grass just beside it and suddenly my entire being cried out for yoga. I usually practiced for at least a few minutes every day, but I hadn't practiced at all since I got to Mexico. I hadn't realized how bound up I felt until that very moment. I didn't have a yoga mat, but the grass was short and I had on long pants so I decided to have a quick session. The short session ended up lasting at least an hour as I completely surrendered the rest of my afternoon to my body's pleas, that once in yogic motion, seemed to have a pretty long itinerary. It wanted the hamstrings lengthened, the shoulders drawn away from the ears, the waist lengthened and the tension wrung out of everywhere…including my mind.

The form of yoga I practice most is called Astanga. One of the more athletic forms, it calls for a lot of sun salutations. To me, the sun salutation is like being a wave on the ocean, though none of the names of the individual poses reflect this, so maybe it's just me. Starting in Mountain Pose, feet planted firmly on the ground, you sweep your arms out to the side and then rise up high with your fingertips and heart, finding a slight arch of your spine as the wave comes to a crest. Then you, drop, dive forward and fold. Your feet float back into a low pushup position for Chaturanga, as the wave rolls out. Then you swoop your heart to the sky with a graceful arch into Upward-facing Dog and the crest of another wave. Then your hips lift to another crest moving into Downward Dog, you hop forward, reverse diving back up to mountain. It's a flow that moves with the rhythm of your breath, in and out, slow and even. Even the sound of my breath reminds me of the ocean.

I did several sun salutations to clear my mind and get my body warmed from within before adding more poses: Warrior One, Warrior Two, King Pigeon—any pose my body called out for and, after the mental and physical stress of the last few days and the bumpy bus ride, it called for a lot. Finally I ended my session sitting in a cross-legged seated position, my eyes closed, breathing in everything around me, with complete contentment.

I heard bird songs so complicated and melodic they seemed orchestrated. I heard quiet conversations and soft laughter from all over the campground, in many different languages. I heard a machete chopping open coconuts and children giggling in a nearby palapa. It was a symphony. A soft breeze stroked my face and I lifted my chin into it.

"Perdón?" A man's voice inquired softly. I opened my eyes to see a *really* hot man standing a few feet away from me. He had just the slightest bit of a five o'clock shadow beard going, raven-black, wavy hair cut short, a dark complexion, and gorgeous golden brown eyes. The rest of him was just as jaw dropping. I know this because he wasn't wearing a shirt; just a pair of loose fitting brown and white surf shorts and a pair of flip flops. He was in really good shape without looking like his body was his all-consuming hobby. He had a climber's toned physique with just the right amount of chest hair fanning elegantly out from his heart and over his well-defined pecs and abs.

"Yes?" I asked, still riding the serene yoga high.

"You speak English?" he asked.

I smiled and nodded.

He returned my smile. "I am wondering if you would consider sharing your palapa for the night? All of the others are full with three people and more, but here there is only you. Would you mind?" Another accent. His was a thick Spanish accent, the kind always depicted in movies as causing a great deal of swooning among the women-folk.

"Uhhhhh...." I said, pausing as I assessed him and the situation. In a flash, my mind conducted a risk assessment. The palapas were just close enough that if he were the wrong sort he dared not attempt anything. And if he did, he wasn't so much taller than me that I might have been able to kick his ass if I had to. I'm small, but I'm strong. From growing up on a farm and doing chores like hay bucking, splitting wood, carrying five-gallon buckets of water to the horse trough, etc., I'd grown up stronger than most other kids. I'd been told several times in my life that I was freakishly strong and that was before I took up rock climbing five days a week. I always thought if I were ever attacked, my attacker would be in for one helluva surprise. I may be tiny, but I'm not completely defenseless.

Then I considered whether there might be a risk of being charmed out of my panties and my commitment to my PPF and a celibate adventure, but I was quickly able to dismiss any danger there. He was too pretty and suave.

Right after I'd been handed the reins to determine my own destiny at 16, getting swayed by suave men and having my life ruined because of it had been one of my chief fears. I'd worked very hard to become impervious to sweet-talkers. But given that the campground would probably have more people, and therefore he would not be the last one to ask to share my palapa I was bound to end up with a roommate and he seemed pretty benign. And he spoke English. Maybe he could help me with my Spanish. Besides, he hadn't appeared in the least bit attracted to me. He looked like he would prefer dainty women, with perfect hair and makeup, whereas I wore no make-up and at that moment, with the humidity and my Irish heritage, my hair probably made me look like a wild banshee.

"Alright," I said finally, "Permission to come aboard."

He flashed a smile of perfect, white teeth, "Gracias, Capitan!" He said, stepping under the roof and beginning to unroll his hammock.

"My name is Francisco," he said, reaching out his hand.

I smiled and took it, "Hi Francisco. My name is Donna."

"Donna? Donna. I've heard a song about you." He said, smiling with a knowing expression, "Perhaps you've heard it."

I nodded, rolling my eyes, "If you mean the song by Richie Valenz, then yes. About a hundred million times."

He laughed softly and began to sing, "*I had a girl, Donna was her name.*"

"Arrrrrrggggghhhh!" I said, "If you're going to do that, I will have to ask you to leave!" I teased.

He laughed. "Where are you from, Donna? Canada?"

I sighed. "Nope. The United States." I paused, waiting for it, his eyes flicked back to me and I could see in his that he'd heard some bad stories. "Want to find another palapa?" I offered, unrepentant.

Again he laughed softly, "No. Besides there are no others." He shrugged, hanging his backpack from a nail and climbing into his hammock. "I would not have guessed you were American. I was guessing Canadian."

I nodded. "Sorry." I said, feigning interest in my book. Then asked, "And you?"

"I'm from Argentina," he said with obvious pride.

We exchanged small talk for a little while and finally he asked me what I planned to do with the rest of the day.

I shrugged, a little embarrassed that I really had no grand plan to do any epic day-seizing; that swinging in my hammock with Vonnegut's Player Piano was probably it. But since I was alone I was still trying to figure out what would be fun and what would be prudent as a solo gringa in a world where that was a bit unusual. I felt cagey, but wasn't sure walking down the dirt road was a good idea for me. But there was still sooooo much time 'til the sun set.

"Not sure," I answered truthfully. "I'm not planning on going into the park until tomorrow morning. Maybe I'll walk down to the entrance to see what I can find out for a full day tomorrow. Maybe find a place to go for a little hike before sunset." Since I'd walked the boundaries of the campground, I knew there was nothing I could really access from here. I'd peered into the jungle in several places, sizing up my ability to move through the thick foliage and then find my way back again. Back home, I could bushwhack just as well as I could hike on a trail, but the growing greens around here seemed a level of tenacious I hadn't experienced before and wasn't sure I could push my way through. Also, while I had been fortunate to not be allergic to poison ivy or poison oak, the itch-cursing plants of my home lands, no telling what was out in that jungle. Francisco was just as cagey and immediately asked if I minded if he come too.

Seriously? Was the universe out to test me? A hot Argentinean was not only sharing my palapa, but now was offering to be the very chaperone I needed to break out of the safe zone? He knew the language and he knew the culture and customs, at least better than I did. Lottery!

"Well okay, then," I said, "Let's go!" Excitedly I closed my book and stood right up, before he had a chance to change his mind.

I know what you're thinking. How long had I known this guy exactly? Right. About twenty minutes. Is that long enough to know someone before traipsing off into a jungle? Suppose he was up to no good?

Ah, but I have a super power. Being on my own since 16, I've developed a fairly good ability to read other people, and besides, like I said, I probably could have taken him if he got out of line. If I was right, and he was as honorable as he seemed, then we would probably just have a great time. If he tried something, he'd be hobbling back to camp a very disappointed man with more than a few injuries.

It wasn't very far of a walk from the campground to the gates of the park, and had we not gone together and I'd been too scared to walk down the street by myself, I'd have been really disgusted the next day when I discovered the gates were a mere two block stroll around the bend.

On the way, Francisco and I talked a little about different hiking trips we'd gone on and it sounded like he was a pretty accomplished hiker himself. I joked that we should try to find an alternate entrance into the park through the jungle, and he laughed, but I could see that the idea appealed. Then we cleared the bend and saw several armed soldiers with grim, no nonsense facial expressions, standing guard. We stopped talking about an alternate entrance.

We stepped into the office and found the schedule, cost. and guide options, then turned back. That was way too short of a trip. It was too late in the day to justify going into the park, but still too early to just sit around a campground. I could see he wasn't much of a sitting around person either.

"Maybe they have a chess board or some cards at the café," I suggested.

"You play chess?" he asked surprised.

I nodded. "Rather well I'm told," I said smiling.

"Really?" he said, obviously impressed. "Knight to Queen's level three."

I rolled my eyes. "Why do men do that?" I asked.

He laughed, "Do what?"

I shook my head, feigning irritation, "I tell them I play chess and they immediately try starting a verbal game with 'Knight to Queen's level three' or some such nonsense. As if they could actually play out a game that way."

He laughed, "Well then, Grandmaster, what would be your counter move?"

Oh crap, I said to myself. *He plays chess*. Aloud I said, "I don't have enough information to counter yet."

"Such as?" he inquired.

"Such as," I answered, "where are my troops? Where are my bishops? My knights? My queen? Or is this a first move? If so, and that's your first move, the board is set up really wrong."

His eyes went wide as he laughed, "Whoa!" then he gave me a sly smile and said, nodding, "I hope they have a board because I have the feeling this is going to be a very good game."

Just then we were passing a stream that ran under the road and I paused to check its course up the mountain. Back in Durango, I loved following creek beds. They were generally less overgrown than other areas, and on a hot day it was wonderful to trek with your feet in icy cold water. Here, it might just make the difference as far as impenetrable jungles went. I moved from side to side trying to follow its path up the mountain with my eyes.

"What is it?" Francisco said, peering through the brush.

"I kind of want to hike up that creek bed," I said, studying the terrain, "What do you think? Maybe we could even find that "alternate" route into the park?" As I said this an army truck pulled up the road with half a dozen more grim-faced soldiers shoulder-slinging rifles and AK-47s.

We looked at each other and laughed, "On second thought, 20 pesos isn't so much." I said, "But I'd still like to trek up this stream bed."

Francisco shrugged and smiled, "Let's go."

"Really? Have you ever done anything like this?" I asked. I didn't want to be responsible for getting him hurt if something happened out there.

"Have you?" he asked, teasingly.

"Enough times that I own a pair of sandals for just this kind of purpose," I said, holding up one of my feet to show him my rubber soled Teva sandals.

"Ah! That explains the clunky footwear!" he said.

"Hey!" I huffed, "I love these things. Bet you'll be wanting a pair before you reach the top of this hill!" I said, then looked around for witnesses before ducking off the road, hoping it didn't look suspicious to anyone. Especially someone who might be carrying an AK-47 or one of its cousins.

We took off like we'd been unleashed. After several stressful days getting there, being in the woods after a yoga session was exactly what I needed. Like a moving meditation I ducked under and climbed over branches, squeezed past bushes and in particularly thick spots, I got on my belly and dragged myself half submerged in the stream. Occasionally I glanced back to see if Francisco was still with me. Not only was he, but he wasn't very far behind. This surprised me. I was used to having to wait for people to catch up to me when I did this.

Bushwhacking is one of those things I'm particularly good at. I've spent A LOT of time doing it, and I'm just the right size to squeeze under and between, while also being light enough to easily hop or climb over obstacles. I was in my element. We charged on, both of us breathing hard and loving it. The soft voices of the streams, the chatter and chirps of the birds, and a forest so pure we breathed it through our pores, fueling the intensity of our pace, our feet leaping over brush and through the cool stream.

Following a stream is a good way to keep from getting lost in unfamiliar woods, but this was still quite the trek. Several more times we crawled on our bellies through the water to get under branches.

Then we reached the top of the hill and my mind was blown. I stood panting as we gazed at an Eden perfect world. There were several more seeps coming from a small, clear lake that had three slender waterfalls flowing into it. It was beautiful. As if held back by some invisible barrier, the foliage ended at smooth mounds of gray boulders that the water had been cutting routes in since the dawn of time. A thick green canopy still hung overhead. We were in a living dome. I looked up to see a family of monkeys swinging away from us through the trees, relinquishing the grounds to us. We turned round and round marveling at this secret paradise we'd found ourselves in.

Catching his breath, Francisco came up behind me.

"How are those flip-flops treating you," I teased.

Ignoring my jab, he stood panting and looking at me in shock, "You're amazing!" he said, breathing hard and covered in dirt, sweat and no small number of red scratches. "I can take you anywhere! An intellectual, an athlete and astoundingly beautiful." My mouth dropped open.

"Astoundingly?" I said, shocked and beaming. I've been called pretty, but never anything so dramatic as "astoundingly beautiful." Especially not when my hair frizzed in a mad poof and I was covered in sweat and grime. Granted, English wasn't his first language and I was the only gringa for miles, which lent me a hint of the exotic…but still, GOLLY!

I rolled my eyes and blushed. "Well, I don't know about astoundingly," I replied, sheepishly pleased.

He continued, "Really, you struggled under all that brush without complaining, you're bleeding from dozens of scratches and yet you're smiling. You're not even worried about all the spiders. Most women would have shrieked within the first meter and turned back, but you pushed through like a warrior!"

I glowed under the praise, my head beginning to swell to unacceptable measures...but then my smile slowly started to fade. *Spiders?* I thought. *What spiders?*

And then I saw them. I scanned the foliage around me. How I didn't see them before was a mystery, as they were about the size of my palm. Now it seemed everywhere I looked there were giant, palm-sized spiders, legs spread out, waiting. And was it my imagination, or were they looking at us? Immediately, I realized that now I would have to duck and belly crawl the entire way back, but this time knowing there were giant spiders all around me. My mind quickly accessed and offered up spider factoids I'd picked up in my research on Central America. Oh sure, I researched spiders but not social issues, currency precautions or bus schedules. Sigh.

I remembered one set of facts pertaining to a cute little jumping spider, about the size of my pinkie nail, that subsisted almost entirely on a vegetarian diet, supplemented with the occasional ant larvae. Many of them lived out their entire lives on acacia trees[xviii] protected by patrolling armies of ants. The ants were protecting the plant, not the spider, but it works out pretty well for the spider. The ants nest in the folds of the leaves and so they chase off would-be acacia snackers, not realizing they are also protecting the clever little spider. If the ants see the spider, however, they'll attack him, too, so these spiders are like little Shaolin monks, evading attacks, rather than attacking. If that's not fascinating enough, the little buggers are also quasisocial, which in this case means the male and female share responsibility for caring for their brooding baby arachnids. And I loved their scientific name, which, to fully reveal the extent of my geeky nature, is Bagheera Kiplingi. They're named in honor of the author, Rudyard Kipling, one of my favorite writers, and one of his most memorable characters from his book, *The Jungle Book*: the black panther, Bagheera. To me, that made them almost cuddly.

But those weren't the spiders I was seeing scattered liberally through the trees and brush that I would have to push passed to get back to camp. Another Central American species I read about was one that hunted for grasshoppers and cicadas and other larger bugs, nightmarishly enough, in packs. Go ahead and picture that and then ruminate on the Ethiopian proverb: "When spiders unite, they can tie down a lion."

But these spiders were far too large for that species, so then my brain suggested that with their large size they might be a spider called The Huntsman, which would be the best cases scenario as these spiders, while huge, are basically harmless for humans.

The worst one I read about was a spider called the Brazilian Wanderer and they are very much not harmless to humans. According to the Guinness Book of World Records it's the most poisonous spider on the planet. Their bite is lethal and if you're a man your suffering may include a painful erection that lasts up to four hours. Naturally, scientists are researching it's potential to treat erectile dysfunction. Fortunately, these spiders prefer banana groves and we weren't in one so probably not the BeeeDubs.

Whatever they were, I'd pushed my way through the brush to get to the top of this mountain and I'd have to go back the same way. But first, I was boiling alive. "Sweltering hot" was apparently exactly the right description for this climate. I had to get into one of these beautiful clear pools immediately. I waded in and found that they were much deeper than they appeared from above and I was soon in water so deep my toes could no longer feel the ground beneath me.

"This feels amazing!" I shouted to Francisco, rolling over to float on my back. "What are you waiting for?? You HAVE to do this!"

He scanned the water and then all around us, weighing the level of risk involved, thank God one of us did, then peeled off his filthy shirt and hung it on a branch before easing his way into the water. He closed his eyes falling deeper into the pleasure of it.

"Am I right?" I said, slowly rolling from a back stroke to a breast stroke and back again. The water felt so pure I felt like I could absorb it through my skin, and whatever I did absorb was like some sensational drug.

Francisco turned towards me treading water, "It is divine, Bella." He answered. "I just wanted to make sure there weren't any crocodiles before I got in the water."

"Oh my God!" I shouted. "Are you serious??" I looked all around for anything that might even hint a croc, but all looked, as Francisco said, divine.

Francisco laughed, "Well yes, you get used to checking water zones for Crocs in Central and South America. But usually they would be in the water or just on the bank."

Frightened my eyes searched the banks.

"I think," continued Francisco, "there is not enough cover for them to hide in here because of all these rocks and boulders. They like better, how you say, cloudy, brack...swampy water. They like swamps and this water is very clear. Maybe they're not even in this part of Mexico." He laughed, "But what's this? She does have fears!"

In answer I splashed my hands in the water, throwing a fin of water straight into his face.

"Demonia!" he shouted, and turned to splash me back, then swam after me. I turned towards the bank and started to swim, but he seized my foot and pulled me back towards him and then pushed me under. I swam back to the surface and tried to shove him under, too, but he had apparently played this game before and easily stayed afloat. I put a hand on either shoulder and launched into the air to bring my full weight down on him, certain that would duck him under, but my hands slid off his shoulders and I basically slid down his chest and belly with my own body, peeling my shirt up, so that my bare skin slid over his. His hands reflexively caught my waist as if to check my fall, sliding his hands up my body.

Naked belly to naked belly, legs occasionally brushing against each other as we slowly waved them to tread water, there was a pause. An accidental brush of our bodies and suddenly it was tantalizingly obvious that he was a boy and I was a girl. Our faces were so close for a moment that when I inhaled, I inhaled his breath. Slowly he started to move his face closer to mine.

Pretending to be oblivious to this new development, I laughed and leaned back to splash water in his face again, trying to maintain the image that we were merely playmates, not potentials for each other. Slowly his fingers slid away from my waist and I giggled as I swam to the bank. Once my back was turned I took a deep breath and exhaled slowly. Whoa. That was real. I was going to have to play this just right or our wonderful situation would be ruined. Fortunately, again, because of the whole being on my own since 16 thing, managing situations like these were kind of a specialty.

I turned back towards the pool and saw Francisco was diving into what seemed to be the deepest part of the pool. He came back up, took another deep breath and went under again. I wondered if he had seen something cool down there. He stayed down an uncomfortably long time before coming back up, gasping.

"What is it?" I shouted.

"It's really deep right here below the waterfall," he said.

"And?" I asked.

His smile broadened, "And there's a cliff."

With that he swam to the bank and began scrambling up boulders to get to the top of the waterfall. Once on the top, he looked down at me, trickles of water running over every tanned, muscle-rippled inch of him, from his chiseled jaw to his bulging…big toes, and then he coordinated all of that beauty and jumped from the edge. His body moved gracefully into a divers position and when he hit the water, barely a drop bounced up, so smoothly he slid into the water. That looked like fun!

I ran to the cliff and started heading up myself. Once at the top I took a few breaths just staring down into the water, working up the courage to jump.

Francisco treaded water in the pool below and shouted, "Salto! Jump!"

I'd learned the hard way not to pretend my way through a dive a few years before when I jumped off a 95-foot cliff at Navajo Lake in New Mexico. In my head I had visualized executing this beautiful, graceful dive, like the one Francisco just did. But I had never been taught to dive so what happened was that when my feet left the cliff, for just a moment my body was 95 feet over the water. Then I went into shock and was absolutely paralyzed. All except for my throat which screamed my way down the fastest 3.2 seconds ever, to crash with my body horizontal onto the water's surface. It felt like I hit concrete. I came out of the water struggling to breathe, my broken nose turning the water around me red. For a moment I couldn't even see. My eyes felt like they had been shoved to the back of my skull. When my friends had jumped in after me and drug me back to the shore, one of them immediately lectured me on how to jump feet first off of such a high cliff. With a broken nose and three broken ribs, it was advice I never forgot.

This cliff was only about twenty feet, but thanks to the above mentioned experience, it still took some working up to. I used some deep breathing techniques I'd learned from yoga to clear away the fear and reassure myself that the water was deep enough and I'd be fine going feet first. My mind said, "You don't have to do this. You're not trying to impress anyone." Except myself.

I inched my feet as close to the edge as I could. The pool below me looked mystically welcoming. My knees bent and my feet pushed down hard and then sprang up and out, away from the cliff. I felt myself swoosh through the air and then down through the water as if sliding into a sheath made just for me. My toes barely grazed the bottom. I paused for a moment, enjoying the peace of the deep water and then slowly let myself rise to the surface like an air bubble. I came out of the water and noticed I wasn't even breathing hard. Thanks, yoga!

I turned towards Francisco, and smiled eagerly, "Let's do that again!"

We climbed and jumped over and over again, Francisco showing off his diving skills, doing front flips, back flips, spins, something different every time.

For my jumps, I focused on trying to slow the world down and experience microsecond by microsecond of moving through the air and then water, taking longer and longer under water each time. We did it until we were exhausted, as though we were trying to burn the chemistry between us.

After a while, I suggested we follow the widest stream further up and see what else we might find. Once again, Francisco was game.

Thanks to limestone that seemed to swell up out of the earth and then spill over it, the jungle was held at bay and after a few minutes, we came into another enormous clearing where the limestone heaped into knobby hills and the water spilled into clear, cool pools and left us open-mouthed and laughing at the surprise of how beautiful was that place. We climbed up those boulders to find another series of waterfalls, tumbling over playdoh mountains. Once again we climbed to the top. This time, like a falling curtain, the jungle closed back in. We turned to gaze at the series of falls behind us.

It was as though we'd walked into a secret world, a paradise of soft, cool water, exotic flowers and bird song. As impossible as this sounds, the water seemed to flow slower than at other waterfalls I'd been privileged to visit, as if the water were more of an oil that rolled, rather than rushed, so that, despite the series of waterfalls, we could hear the jungle, curious and alarmed, discussing our presence all around us, with calls, and flash swoops of feathery investigation.

At this point, I had not yet seen the great ruins of Palenque, but my imagination poured out stories around this place, this unbelievably magical place, where, perhaps, princes and princesses of Palenque, might have once frolicked just as we were. I picked a handful of flowers, lucky for me of the non-poisonous variety, and set them free from my perch at the top of the waterfall and watched them roll and dive and twirl in the thick, graceful waters. We spent a few minutes trying to determine how close we might be to Palenque and whether we might still find an alternate entrance that might help us both stretch our meager dollars for other ventures. But as we poked and prodded, and peered through the dense jungle, it was a wild tangle of vines, thorn bushes and massive spider webs. It did not allure.

One look at Francisco and then down at my own clothes and it was obvious that if we ever managed to find our way through the jungle and into the park, we'd look exactly like two people who hacked through the jungle and snuck into the park. And then we'd have the guards armed with AK-47s to contend with. Besides, the park deserved our money and we would be truly criminal, figuratively as well as literally, to not pay the fees that help support the park. Even though, in my case, I was eating one packet of tuna fish a day, and saving any money at all might mean I could actually treat myself to a restaurant meal to boost my calories.

Finally, the sun was beginning to set and there was nothing for it. Girl that goes up, up, up into the jungle hills, must come down. Not willing to lose the lofty ground I'd achieved as gorgeous-intelligent-adventure-ess I said not a word about the spiders in the brush, though inwardly I cringed.

We made our way back down the mountain, ducking brush and, again, in some places getting on our bellies and dragging ourselves under it through the stream. When we came out of the brush and back onto the gravel road, I couldn't restrain myself anymore. I jumped around brushing all over myself with my fingers and asking Francisco if there were any spiders on me. He laughed, but checked for me and then turning slowly around, asked, "How about me?"

I laughed because it was obvious he wasn't too comfortable about the idea of carrying giant spiders around, either. After I checked him, he turned serious. "You know, between the jungle, the spiders and the soldiers, I think we better just pay the entrance fee. What do you think."

"Oh hell yeah," I said. And we both laughed.

"But that was a lot of fun. Yes?" he queried, lifting one of his dark eyebrows, hopefully.

"Absolutely," I said. "Thanks for going. I might not have gone that far alone." Who was I kidding. No way I would have gone that far alone. In a Colorado stream? Absolutely, but I knew next to nothing about this area.

We got back to the Maya Bell and met with curious stares from the other guests. We were both covered in sweat, dirt, dozens of red crimson scratches, and, I felt, crawling with bugs. My hair was wild, tangled and had bits of leaves and sticks, stuck in it. But we both had big, big smiles.

"I'm going for a dip in the pool," Francisco said. "You'll come?"

I wrinkled my nose, and looked towards the murky pool, "Ummmm, I think I'll take a shower and then grab a cup of café con leche at the café and read for a while." I answered.

"What are you reading?" he asked.

"A book by Kurt Vonnegut," I answered.

"Ahhh. I love Kurt Vonnegut!" he answered. "Didn't he die recently?"

"Yep." I answered. "I think Kurt Vonnegut is up in heaven now."

"He'll be missed." Francisco said. "Well, enjoy. Hasta luego."

Oh no! No! NO! He's a Vonnegut fan! Universe, why dost thou test me so?

I went to the lockers, got my shower supplies and then locked my pack up. I was about to have my first open air shower. I glanced across the street and saw a herd of cattle sifting through a swampy bog and momentarily wondered where the water for the Maya Bell's shower came from. I turned on the shower and the water came out with a slightly brownish hue. But it smelled okay and I didn't have any other choices so I shrugged and stepped in, making a mental note to extend the length of time to drink from my water bottle after I add the iodine tablets. The water stung on all of my scratches and scrapes, and I winced, but scrubbed them good with my soap. Then scrubbed the clothes I'd worn on the hike 'til they were as clean as I could get them. I got out of the shower, feeling so much better.

I toweled off with the tiny square of a travel towel I'd brought with me, then almost walked off without my travel essentials. What a mistake that would have been, right? I'd be living in a land legendary for its sweltering heat with no soap, shampoo or conditioner probably for the rest of my trip since I had no idea where to find any and no cash to spare for it even if I did. Good thing I remembered, huh?

Except that when I turned back for them, they were gone. Someone had snatched them while I was rinsing, a foot away, behind a very thin nylon privacy sheet! What balls! And Dammit! Now I'd be catching a plane and heading home really, really stinky cause I wouldn't have soap and I would be trekking around a place the guidebooks promised would have me sweating buckets daily. Dammit.

Well, nothing to be done, and most of the people here didn't shower, I think, ever, anyway. At least I was sleeping outside, so it really only mattered when I went back to the states. Still. Dammit!

Back at the palapa, I told Francisco what had happened and he laughed sympathetically, "I'm sorry that happened, Donna, but if it makes you feel any better, I accidentally left my soap in a hostel in Peru weeks ago. It will be alright."

Okay, I thought, *now I'm really glad the palapas are open air.*

"Just rinse off in the water every day or so," he smiled. "Now, may I help you a bit with your Spanish?" he asked with one eyebrow raised, afraid he would offend me with the question.

I think I surprised him with my enthusiastic response, "Yes, please!"

Looking relieved he took a deep breath, like a diver preparing to swim the distance. "Okay. First of all, when you say 'Hola', you need to smile more and draw it out more lazy like, "OOOOOOOOLLAAAAAAAAA," and the same for buenas dias."

I wasn't sure whether to believe him or not. It's not the way I'd heard anyone else say it other than him, and he was from Argentina, which I knew had a very strong Italian influence, and for all I knew was culturally almost as foreign to Mexico as Southern Colorado was. I eyed him skeptically.

"It's more friendly," he assured me. "Now, your r's need a lot of work. Speak to me with rolling r's."

I tried to oblige and made a sound that sounded like gargling phlegm deep within my throat. He squeezed his eyes shut and shook his head with lips pressed together. "No. Listen to closely to me:

Erre con erre guitarra,
erre con erre barril.
Mira que rápido ruedan,
las ruedas del ferrocarril.

I learn this when I am a young boy. It will help to learn to roll your r's." he said giving me an encouraging smile.

I obliged him by trying it out. He smiled, once again closing his eyes, lips pressed together. "Practicar. Practicar. Practicar." He said climbing into his hammock. I tried the tongue twister again. "Quietly." He smiled.

I climbed in my own hammock and tried to practice without making much sound several times. I must have been making some kind of wheezing sound as I did because he winced and said kindly, "Quietly."

I know it's a horrific sound I make because years later I still haven't learned how to roll my r's and yet I'll still try periodically, which evokes a most pained expression from my husband…and, now, also my seven-year-old daughter, who has been a pro-level 'r' roller practically since birth. She has surprisingly also been the one most willing to continue trying to teach me.

I practiced as quietly as I could a few more times before giving it up for the day. I pulled my book out of my backpack to read a few chapters before the sunset. I was ecstatic. It was my first night sleeping in a hammock, in a palapa, and in the jungle, at the end of my first day of traveling by bus, into a jungle, far, far away from an American Embassy or even another American, for that matter. I closed my book as sunlight faded, and then closed my eyes.

I have no idea how much later it was when my eyes flew open at the sound of a loud whispered bellow, like someone shouting in the ujjayi yoga breath. It was coming from the tree just above my palapa. A quick scan through my databank of facts produced one answer: Jaguar!

The rest of the jungle around us was absolutely silent. For a moment, I wondered if I'd imagined the sound. I looked towards Francisco's hammock and could just barely make out the shadowy still outline of his face, mouth hanging open, deep, deep in sleep. "Rooooooooooowwwwwwww." Came the sound, this time, literally as if it were coming from right on top of our palapa. I clutched a tiny LED light I had strung around my neck in case I needed a little light in the night. It barely gave out any light, but might scare a jaguar entering a palapa from a world of the darkest darkness. Maybe.

"Francisco!" I whispered. "Francisco!" I whispered a bit louder. He stirred and in a sexy, sleepy accent said, "Hola, Dona. Como?"

I was quickly losing my status as the uber-brave gringa, but I was too scared to care. "I think there's a jaguar in the tree above us!"

His eyes flew open and he reached for something in his backpack that hung on a hook beside his hammock. Reaching in he pulled out a knife. A really, really big knife. He unsheathed it and sat up in his hammock. A small part of me winced to see him so armed, this kind man I'd trusted to set up his hammock in my palapa and hiked off into the jungle with after knowing less than an hour.

We sat in the darkness, trying to stretch our ears to register more sound. From the rest of the camp came sounds of other Maya Bell guests, snoring in their own hammocks. But no more sounds from the jaguar.

"Como Busca?" he whispered (What did you hear?), I think for a moment forgetting our language handicap.

I didn't need to answer. From only a few feet above our heads came a menacing growl, "Rooooooooooowwwwwwwwwwwwwwww!" causing me to jump nearly out of my hammock. Francisco laughed softly as he sheathed his knife. "It's un mono, a howler monkey. Buenas noches, bella."

"That's a monkey?" I asked, incredulous.

"Es un howler monkey, bella. Zip up your backpack and they will not bother you." He rolled back over, chuckling softly.

Well, I suppose I should go pee while I'm up, I said to myself, swinging my feet out of the hammock. When my feet hit the ground there was a distinct crunch and a new noise to terrify me. My feet landed on something, cold, slick, crunchy and now…slimy, followed by the scritching sound of many little legs running every which way, including over my bare feet. This time I shrieked and jumped back into my hammock, kicking bugs off of my feet, barely keeping my balance as the hammock swung wildly.

Francisco jumped straight out of his hammock, knife unsheathed, squinting in the darkness. "Que demonios!"

I pressed the button on my little flash light and held it down towards the ground, in time to see hundreds of humongous cockroaches scattering in all directions, except, of course, the ones I'd smashed. Their guts now glistened in the dim light, making me painfully aware of what that wet, sticky sensation was on the bottom of my feet.

"HOLY SHIT!!!" I shrieked, watching their clumsy scatter as they ran into, ran around, and climbed over each other.

"Donna!" Francisco loud whispered, using my true name, to which I sat indignantly upright, unjustly chastened. "What the hell?" He shouted.

I was aghast, "What do you mean, 'What the hell!'??? The ground is crawling with cockroaches!"

He sighed as though he were preparing to reason with a child, "Yes, cucurachas. You don't have cucurachas in Colorado?"

"Maybe a few, but, nothing like this! This is unbelievable!"

Another deep, bordering exasperated, sigh, "You must have dropped some food for so many. They are very common here. For this reason, you keep your backpack zipped and hanging. And you keep your shoes in the hammock with you or you shake them out before you put them on in the night." Seeing my obvious shock and terror, he softened. "It is alright. They won't hurt you."

I felt confused. Back home, even the burliest of boys would have freaked his shit if he got out of bed and stood up on multiple layers of giant cockroaches that went squirt as he stepped on them.

Francisco softened more, "What are you doing getting up anyway?"

I was fighting to keep tears tucked away in my throat, but I finally answered softly, "I have to pee."

He cocked his head, smiled kindly and said, "Come on, I'll go with you."

"No, I can go myself. I'm sorry I woke you." I said, humiliated, shaking the roaches off of my Teva sandals.

"No, I have to go to. Come on." He said, holding his hand out to me, that huge, sweet smile on his face.

I smiled back, taking his hand. "Thank you," I said, surprised at my own sincerity.

As we walked to the lavatory, we whispered and giggled as I tried to light the way with my tiny LED light. Finally, I gave up on the light and opted to resurrect my night hiking skills I'd honed during a couple of years when I conducted direct action night campaigns for an environmental group I used to work for. In that capacity, I'd get dropped off a mile or two from a site and have to hike into a location, usually without a flashlight so as to not betray the fact that we were there. Before we'd get dropped off, we'd study topo maps. I'm proud to say that I always managed to get us where we were supposed to be, do our job, which I won't be detailing here, and then get back to our pick up point.

Sure, I could do all that, but cockroaches? Ewwwwww!

I shared this story with Francisco and was pleased that it seemed to gain me back some of the respect I felt I'd lost screeching at everything going bump in the night earlier.

"Really? An ecowarrior, eh?" He asked. "And would you wear your shoes?"

"My shoes?" I asked, confused.

"Those shoes, your badass- yoga-mama-Buddha-sandals you tore up the mountain in earlier today."

"Ha!" I laughed, a little too loudly for how late it was. The entire camp was dark. Everyone was asleep. From other palapas I could hear snoring, some so loud I was extremely grateful my hammock wasn't swinging next to theirs. I nodded, "I like that name. My Yoga-Mama-Buddha-Sandals. But actually, yes. I love these shoes. They're pretty rugged for sandals and they're just wide enough that they offer a little protection when I go bushwhacking. I can tromp through unexpected creeks and have my feet dry minutes later."

"Well, I'm going to have to get some of those. Do they make them for men?"

"Absolutely." I answered. (Ahem, Teva…about my sponsorship?)

Once we were back at the palapa, Francisco paused by my hammock, "Donna, I would very much like to give you a hug. Would that be alright?" he asked.

"Ummmmm…sure," I answered, uncertainly. I stood up and we wrapped our arms awkwardly around each other in the dark. I gave him my best, 'buddy-ole-pal' hug, and then started to pull away, but he drew me back into him, and let his lips brush across my forehead. I melted. It was all I could do to nonchalantly pull away and say, "Well, good night!" and get back into my sleeping bag and hammock. He sighed.

I lay looking at the stars you could see just on the outside of our roof line. A fine dark sky for stargazing. But it was late. My eyes started to drift closed. Before they completely closed I gazed out into the jungle and at first I thought it was my imagination, because the jungle seemed to be sparkling like the sky.

It was lightning bugs. The trees and ground were speckled with them and their off and on patterns of light flirting was breathtaking. Lightening bugs, or fireflies as almost everyone else calls them, are one of my favorite memories from my Memphis childhood. There the woods fill up with fireflies in the deep of summer. We'd catch them, put them in pickle jars and watch them for awhile before setting them all free, watching their little butts light up as they flew away. It was one of the few memories I had that was pure, and free of any taints. I hadn't seen them since my parents were divorced. I felt so childlike in this place, not only vulnerable, but in a constant state of wonder and awe.

"Francisco?" I said

"Yes, Dona?" he replied, half asleep.

"Fireflies." I whispered in awe. Then I fell asleep.

Chapter 12: A Good Cup of Joe

"If it wasn't for the coffee, I'd have no identifiable personality whatsoever."

David Letterman

The next morning I woke up and Francisco was gone. My eyes searched the other palapas, to see if one had come available and he had moved. I wasn't sure how I would feel about that, though I could certainly see why he wouldn't want to share one with me, what with all the shrieking and flapping about in the middle of the night.

It wasn't entirely my fault. This was such a new world to me. I was like a toddler here and wasn't sure what would bite me, so I shrieked and swatted at everything.

I walked down to the café to get my one big splurge of the day, a cup of café con leche (coffee with sweet, warm milk), and sat at a wooden table in the open air restaurant. I sipped and smiled at the warm sweetness, the caramel aroma. There was also just the slightest hint of a spicy kick. I'm not sure if it was because they ground the coffee in a container where they also ground pepper or if they purposely and expertly added this just slightest hint of pepper, but I liked it so much I started adding chili pepper or cayenne into my morning coffee when I came back to the States.

The coffee itself was unbelievably good and I don't think that was just because it's the only thing I was currently ingesting besides tuna fish and cloudy water with a heavy scent and taste of iodine. It was fresh. Probably grown in the jungle not far from the campground, dried under the Chiapan sunshine, ground up and brewed all within a block of where I now sat. Maybe. I don't know that that is actually the case, I only know that coffee was one of the things that Chiapas had going for it.

Coffee was first brought to Mexico early in the 18th century but it really took off when German and Italian farmers settled in Chiapas in the 19th century and built large coffee plantations. Eventually, some of the Indigenous people who once labored on these plantations took what they learned and left to form their own grower-owned and operated cooperatives.

Today, coffee from the highlands of Chiapas are considered among the fullest-flavored, smoothest coffees in the world and proceeds from their farms are building stronger, healthier communities in Chiapas, though it's far from reached its potential impact. For all the money made from growing coffee the farmers have gotten the least cut, especially before the origination of Fair Trade. Fair Trade was founded first and foremost as a social movement, one inspired in large part by the Zapatista Movement.

The coffee cooperative, Maya Vinic, emerged three years after the Christmas Massacre in Acteal in 1997, when a paramilitary group massacred 45 men, women and children as they hid in the Acteal Community Church praying for peace. After the massacre, the founders of Maya Vinic were refugees struggling to hold their community together until they founded Maya Vinic.

Working together they learned everything they could about farming and taking care of the land, but especially about coffee farming. They partnered with Fair Trade advocates to find the best price for their beans and these advocates often became directly involved in the cooperative.

For example, the coffee roaster Higher Grounds helped develop potable water wells in the Maya Vinic Communities, while Alternative Grounds and Development & Peace promoted the Maya Vinic brand in Canada. Maya Vinic hosts assemblies, bringing trade partners and other co-ops together to exchange ideas and help each other trouble shoot challenges. Antonio Ruiz, a founding member of Maya Vinic said that "Our cooperative helped serve as a light to follow…that not only kept us alive economically, but also served to keep our community together."[xix] Maya Vinic now has 643 farmers in the cooperative. They also produce honey…which I like in my coffee.

Starbucks, Green Mountain and Nestle are big customers and supporters of the boutique coffee industry coming out of Chiapas. You can find Chiapan Shade-Grown Fair Trade coffee almost anywhere and if you're a coffee drinker, you should buy these coffees and support the population that Mexico forgot. And I don't really care how preachy that sounds.

Unfortunately, some of the big corporations who purchase items under these type of banners are doing so as a marketing ploy. They are also developing an ever-broadening area of labels that represent different versions, sometimes extremely diluted versions of Fair Trade, confusing choices for the average coffee drinker.

Some of the labels appear socially concerned, but in some cases are only diluting the original standards allowing big plantations to masquerade as small farmers, allowing lesser quality coffee to compete on the same level as higher quality (and therefore more labor and resource cost dependent), making it harder for the farmers with higher standards to make the profit they need to survive. Not just to survive as coffee farmers, but to just simply survive. To live. Period.

They also allow for what Chiapan coffee farmers call 'coyotes,' intermediaries who come to buy coffee, offer poor prices, cheat with the scales or outright steal. They're another reason Fair Trade came about. The market value of coffee exports is over US $30 billion, yet most coffee producers live in poverty, often without even clean drinking water.

The government has supposedly been investing heavily in these extremely poor Southern states, but I'm not sure where the money's going cause they're still struggling pretty hard down there. Besides, they don't want crippling handouts, though a few government protections and a bit of subsidies would be welcomed in the short term. They want to earn their livings. They want to participate in the economy while at the same time, protecting their cultures and traditions.

Josè Pèrez Vasquez, a member of the Maya Vinic cooperative and the social activist group, Las Abejas, has ten children. "We are natives of this community." Josè says. "We are Mayas. We don't want to lose this Maya identity. We want to continue the work of our ancestors, our grandfathers. We also want to work with our mother earth and take care of it."

That's what the Fair Trade movement has been all about: supporting people who are striving to support themselves. "Before traveling to the United States," Vasquez said, "we thought there were no friends and there was no one…but when we got there, we found that there are many friends and many brothers who have the heart to help families that are in need in Chiapas." He smiles, then continues, "And we saw that there are many people and many consumers of coffee!"

By buying Shade Grown Fair Trade Coffee, you help support not only the people, but the rainforests, because shade grown coffee requires the jungle in order to thrive. The indigenous people's other options are to clear the land and farm on soil God didn't design with farming in mind.

The red soil is quickly stripped of most of its nutrients within a few crop rotations and any families dependent on farming have to clear more land for new farming areas within a few crop cycles. But they can't afford to do this unless the market will support their efforts that, in the long run, benefit us all.

In *The End of Poverty*, Icon U2 Rocker and longtime social and environmental activist, Bono, nailed it when he said, "The destinies of the 'haves' are intrinsically linked to the fates of the 'have-nothing-at-alls.'" More and more we are coming to realize that the world is not so indestructible. It is a complex weave of balances. A bird species lost because of poor habitat in one part of the world may cause a spike in mosquito swarms, and therefore malaria or, most recently, the vicious Zika virus, in another part of the world. Just for example.

But what, exactly, do all of these coffee designations like Fair Trade, or shade grown, or rainforest alliance, or direct trade coffees, actually mean, you might ask? I did, and then I did a little digging and found out that Fair Trade Coffee is a certification originally designed to reduce poverty by supporting small farmers who meet specific labor, environmental, and production standards. For people seeking to protect the rain forest and are concerned about the quality of life for those who live in and around them, as well as for farmers who want to support their families and communities, the Fair Trade movement was a godsend.

"Before Fair Trade, farmers were on their own, especially in regions like Chiapas where farmers are isolated and lack a network that can help them level the playing field," said Mary Jo Cook, Chief Impact Officer at Fair Trade USA, an Oakland California-based NGO.

By establishing a price floor, contracts with Fair Trade certification help reduce the negative effects of downswings in the notoriously volatile international market for coffee beans. It can also help farmers gain credibility with lenders, helping them gain access to micro loans. Most importantly, Fair Trade coffee helps to connect small-time farmers with international buyers who are willing to pay a fair price.

The long story, or part of the long story (turns out the world of coffee is very complex. Google Coffee and Ethical Consumerism. Just wow.) is that Fair Trade was intended to empower small farmers to get a fair price for their coffees, create safe working environments with livable wages for farmers and any employee(s), help protect the environment and help reduce poverty in places like Chiapas. In order to don the Fair Trade label, farmer's and producers are prohibited from using harmful agrochemicals and GMOs that harm the future sustainability of the land.

Supporting organizations, such as Oakland, California's Fair Trade USA, ensure the product meets specific standards, and is properly handled, labeled and marketed. To date, Fair Trade coffee still only represents only a small fraction of coffee sales, and for developing countries like Chiapas, Guatemala and Honduras, coffee sales from small farmers make up an enormous share of export earnings, sometimes more than 50 percent of foreign exchange earnings. So drink up, y'all. The Fair Trade Labeling Organization International doesn't just cover coffee, it throws a much broader umbrella, covering bananas, cocoa, sugar, honey, rice, flowers, and other small business items.

Incidentally, Shade Grown, Bird Friendly, Rainforest Alliance or Fair Trade Coffee beans, or any other items with these labels, make great Christmas, Birthday and Bar Mitzvah gifts! What's not to love about making the world a better place by drinking and giving wonderful, energizing, aromatic coffee?

Unfortunately, all of the labels out there do make it pretty confusing when you're trying to make the choice between all those lumpy, crinkly packets you're examining for your home brew. And there are many labels: Organic, Fair Trade International, Rainforest Alliance, Starbucks Coffee, Farmer Equity Café, Smithsonian Migratory Bird Center Bird Friendly (or just Bird Friendly), Shade Grown and Direct Trade. So which one of these certifications should the socially concerned coffee drinker be sipping on?

NPR did a great job breaking down the different designations and exploring their impacts in a January 9, 2014 article titled, "Coffee for a Cause: What Do Those Feel-Good Labels Deliver?" Some labels focus on the farmer, some focus on protecting the environment but make it tough for smaller coffee growers to compete, some try to focus on both, and some labels, like Direct Trade or Sun Grown, are marketing gimmicks masquerading as loftier goals.

If your concern is primarily environmental, the Smithsonian Bird Friendly Coffee designation requires the coffee be grown organically, with no manufactured fertilizer or pesticides, in fields that also contain 10 different species of shade trees, which can be fruit trees. Other crops can also be grown in with the coffee, maximizing garden space. While this is the most environmentally friendly version, not a lot of farmer's can pull this off, so it's not available just anywhere. A quick search in my current town of Boulder, Colorado, one of the most environmentally conscious towns in Colorado, which is one of the most environmentally friendly states in the U.S., turned up one coffee shop carrying brands with the Smithsonian Bird Friendly certification: Whole Foods. If you want to see more of it, contact your favorite grocer or coffee shop. And please be willing to pay the extra buck it'll cost because it's worth it, taste wise, world-wise (I'm going to coin this new definition for the term world-wise right now: world-wise: the understanding and practice of recognizing the world as an interdependent system. You read it here first.).

Rainforest Alliance requires adhering to a set of standards that emphasize not just environmental sustainability, but social, economic and ethical standards as well, though not to the extent of the Bird Friendly. Like Shade grown, there aren't specific regulations of what type of shade and therefore may not necessarily achieve the goals of either land or species protection the name implies. But a farmer who can meet the standards of any of these designations can get a higher per pound price for their coffee beans, which in theory, benefits their community, and is better than nothing from an environmental standpoint.

Then there's the organic seal which requires beans were grown without GMO seeds and synthetic substances, but has no other specific requirements for community support or environmental protection. Still, better than nothing if you just have to have a particular flavor and it's not available from a seal that promotes loftier goals.

Coffee icon, Starbucks claims that 100% of their coffee is ethically sourced, and the wording on their website sounds very similar to that of Fair Trade, but I wondered why they didn't come right out and call it Fair Trade rather than encouraging the spin doctoring that has come to surround the coffee industry? So I contacted them. They responded that they get far too many requests from students so they didn't really have time to answer me. They suggested I look at their website. Which says what I just said but doesn't answer the question at all.

Direct trade is basically only a benefit to the coffee sellers and coffee buyers, where the buyer and the farmer cut out the middle men, or certification requirement enforcers, and therefore both make more money. It has absolutely no social or environmental benefits unless the buyers or farmers have concerns themselves. It's primarily about everyone involved making the most profit. That's not necessarily a bad thing, and not that it can't achieve higher goals, but it also leaves room for the downsides of zero accountability.

Like Direct Trade, Sun Grown sounds like it would be a great, wholesome thing, but in reality it usually means industrial growers who clear-cut every tree and shrub to grow as much coffee as possible under the full brunt of the sun. Devious labeling, eh?

It is a rather strange notion that coffee could hold such power in a country, or that what coffee I choose to drink can affect a whole town in some place like Chiapas, but at the end of the day, the impact is so much greater than if I was contributing to a charity. As the saying goes, Give a man a fish, he'll eat for a day, then either come back tomorrow begging for another fish or starve. Teach a man to fish and he'll eat for a lifetime.

They're learning to fish in Chiapas. Now some of the farmers are further leveraging their plantations by expanding into the lucrative field of ecotourism, offering tours and retreats on their farms. For a modest sum, the adventurous coffee aficionado can stay at a remote coffee plantation, some of which may have been in operation for four generations. They will tour the grounds with knowledgeable staff and sometimes have the opportunity to harvest, roast and sip their very own brews. Some plantations even offer mountain biking, canoeing or kayaking tours. I didn't get a chance to partake in any of those offerings but I have gone inner-tubing in nearby Guatemala and, let me tell you, it was exciting!

To make the trip simple, many of them will also be happy to pick you up from the nearest airport and bring you back. Probably in time for your flight. You'll have to do your own research as to which farms fit your needs, and I do recommend you do your research thoroughly, but I think it would totally be worth it. At the time of this writing, they are starting to promote the Chiapas Coffee Route, a route that winds through the Chiapan Highland Coffee district. Sort of like Napa Valley but with more caffeine and less slurring.

Chapter 13: Palenque: A City of Temples

"We do not follow maps to buried treasure, and X never, ever marks the spot."

Indiana Jones

I thought about Francisco as I enjoyed my amazing coffee. It would probably be better if he had moved to another palapa. It would make it easier to keep my 'No Romance' promise. The trouble was, while I was never what you would call a loose woman, I liked men almost as much as they seemed to like me. Knowing before I left the states how romantic travel can be, I'd taken my PPF (Purely Platonic Friendships) oath. There would be absolutely no hookings-up while in C.A. (Central America).

Scandals circulated about American girls coming to Latin America looking for a taste of the passion rumored to rule the Latin temperament. I'd already had a couple of men who offered me free samples based, I gathered, on those rumors.

The rumor was that American girls were easy. I don't think that was true at all. I think that Latin men can be (no offense, white boys) romantic and passionate in a way their more conservative cousins can't and the girls swoon under the fiery attention. On the outside, it probably looks like they are making themselves easy and willing prey to the suave attentions of dark eyed gents in the know. In reality, the poor girls are probably falling madly in-love. It would be easy to do if one weren't fortified with a history of child abuse and the mistrust and defense mechanisms that go with it. Aren't I the lucky one!

Don't get me wrong. I was certainly curious, but I had no intention of falling for soft, Spanish-tinted-English promises, whispered while being adroitly whisked around a dance floor, and I wouldn't be in town long enough for a potential beau to prove greater intentions. As for flings? For women, there's just too much at stake. Too easy to have your life ruined over a moment of passion. That and I also didn't want to get all caught up in an adventurous encounter that became a torturously doomed, long distance relationship. And, not sure I mentioned it, but I kind of already had a big thing for this guy back home. So no, No, NO! on any hooking up!

But it had been nice to have a friend to play with. A sexy as hell, intelligent and adventurous friend, who, had we all lived in the same country, yea, he might have given aforementioned boyfriend a run for his claim. As it was, I thought he might have been equally thrilled to find someone adventurous and active to play with, too. An adventurer who would come up with and help carry out great ideas like hiking through the jungle, even if sex wasn't included in the amenities. We're not a dime a dozen, ya know. But I guess I made it fairly clear when he attempted a pass or two, and there's nothing wrong with him for moving on if that's where his interest lie. Still, I was bummed.

Oh well, shake it off, Chica Bonita, I said to myself. *You've got some ancient ruins to explore!* I was still super excited to go see the ruins alone, maybe even more so. When you're alone you get to really take things in. You notice details and have mental musings you likely wouldn't if you were with someone else. For a writer, alone is sometimes best. So perhaps it was a good thing I had no distractions while I visited the ruins. I gathered my things and went to the locker to stash my pack then headed towards the road.

As I rounded the corner by the café, I came face to face with Francisco. There was a moment or two of awkwardness. I said, "Buenas dias, Francisco." Which he returned. Then another moment of awkwardness passed 'til I felt it was time to go. I started to wish him a good day, when he said, "I was looking for you. I wondered if you might like to go with me to see the ruins today?"

I should have been embarrassed at the size of my smile, but his grew just as wide as I stumbled out, "Absolutely!" Alone may sometimes be best, but I'd been alone a lot over the last week, and while alone may be great for the writer in me, the giddy child inside wanted someone to marvel with. So we were off. We were practically skipping as we made our way down the path, right past an empty and available palapa—that neither of us acknowledged.

We started with the museum, just a half a mile from the ruins, and spent an hour looking at their displays and artifact collections. I'm a museum nut anyway, but this was all the more fascinating because the items came up out of the soil so close by. There were wall carvings and reliefs of mystical creatures. One particularly compelling piece was more like a sculpture. It was of a being that had the body of a man, but the head of a monkey. It was dressed in royal attire, complete with the headdress of a king. Something about its eyes made the character appear shrewd and cunning.

There was a figurine of a human form but with the head of an eagle, sitting cross-legged and erect. Glass cases were filled with smaller, exquisitely carved figurines and jade jewelry. Replicas of Mayan writing chiseled on huge slabs of limestone leaned against the far wall.

Francisco translated the information placards and I followed each of his translations with polite, "How fascinating!" and "Can you imagine?" When we purchased our tickets, Francisco suggested we forgo the guided tour so I could save money and promised to translate each and every information placard. Besides, he reminded me, the tour would be in Spanish, I wouldn't understand a word and we'd be stuck with a group of 30 inquisitive senior citizens.

"We're adventurers, you and I," he said. "We don't want to be stuck on someone else's schedule, to be hurried here, stalled there. This will be more fun!" He needn't have worked so hard to talk me into an option where I could conserve my meager pesos. I readily agreed and we stepped through the gates. And then my jaw dropped.

When explorer Edward Fitzgerald, the translator of the ancient Persian poems that make up the Rubáiyat of Omar Khayyám, wrote a letter to Lord Kingsborough about Palenque on April 17, 1838 he said, "The galleries are so extraordinary, their construction so curious, so strong, so thick, decorated with embossed devices that I defy any language to do justice to their description or Painter to depict them." At the time Fitzgerald saw Palenque, it was just barely peeking from under the jungle tangle, a magnificent white palace, dripping in green finery. No one had yet tried to reclaim it.

Despite the passing of almost two centuries and sharing the view with dozens of other people, the impact was still profound. It was breathtaking. So breathtaking that in 1987, it was inducted into the UNESCO World Heritage List for its "exceptional and well-conserved architectural and sculptural remains...(and) the elegance and craftsmanship of the construction, as well as the lightness of the sculpted reliefs illustrating Mayan mythology."[xx]

Fifteen hundred years ago or so, Palenque was a pinnacle of Mayan achievement, one of the civilizations most beautiful cities. The palatial grounds were constructed on a limestone shelf at the base of the Sierra de Palenque mountain. It is surrounded by a verdant tropical forest, teaming with life and air. Steep mountains climb 2000 feet above the city including the Don Juan Mountain to the West which is 3,313 ft. or 1010 meters (the name Palenque actually translates to "steep cliffs."). The terrace was 600 feet above a great plain where farmers grew corn and other crops that fed the royalty that looked down on them from above.

Archaeologists believe that Palenque's construction was begun in the first millennium A.D. By 250 A.D., they had evolved social organization enough to accomplish impressive public construction projects: plazas, waterworks, markets, temples, ball courts and administrative palaces.

These metropolis's fostered academics in literature, mathematics, medicine, astronomy, and the arts. Part of their success has been attributed to the remarkably precise 'Long Count,' often referred to as the Maya Long Count Calendar that has been found on monuments all over the Mayan world and other parts of Mesoamerica. According to Dr. John Carlson, Director for the Center for Archaeoastronomy, "It is the most complex calendar system ever developed by people anywhere."[xxi] Palenque flourished until the 10th century A.D. when it seems the city was deserted, for reasons unknown.

It remained lost in the jungle, protected under a web of vegetation, until the 18th century. Lost may not be the right word. Engulfed is perhaps a better one. As pointed out by David and George Stuart in their book, 'Palenque: Eternal City of the Maya,' "...'lost cities' are most often labeled as such by outsiders..." Villagers surely knew of the abandoned city from hunting and gathering excursions into the area and simply chose to leave it be.

I saw paintings done by architect Frederick Catherwood during his visit to Palenque in 1840 with American diplomat, John Stephens. Wrapped in vines, obscured by trees, and dripping with greenery, it danced in splendor.

It was easy to visualize the royalty and their attendants milling about the grounds. Perhaps a monkey or two scampering along a roofline. And for some reason, probably a combination of a childhood growing up watching Walt Disney's *Aladdin* combined with an understanding that the jaguar figured heavily in Mayan mythology, I visualized a pet jaguar at a Mayan Princess' hip.

The grandest of the structures was a temple honoring King Pakal, who became king at the age of twelve and was king from A.D. 615 to 683. Most of the structures on the terrace were built during his reign. Great king or brutal tyrant? Only the trees know for sure. For his temple he had three stone tablets engraved with hieroglyphs recording important events in his reign and the history of his family. The hieroglyphics look like a combination of pictures, mostly of animals, and symbols that had been larger but now were smooshed together to form squares. The tablets were covered with rows and rows of these square glyphs. Two of the tablets were enormous, thirteen feet high. The tablets were mounted on the wall in the hall at the top of the temple steps. These tablets contained the longest Mayan record yet discovered and are believed to be about the Mayan accomplishments in astronomy, mathematics, medicine, and the calendar. The records tell us, near as anyone can tell anyway, that this temple was started eight years before Pakal died at the ripe old age of 80, leaving the temple incomplete. His son saw it to completion.

There were scenes engraved on most of the walls of the buildings, as well as sculptures of mythical creatures and gods. I was ecstatic to see that there was still so much left even after archaeologists and treasure hunters looted it for over a hundred years.

What must it have been like at the pinnacle of the civilization? What must it have been like when the first archaeologists laid eyes on it?? I can imagine the excitement of the archaeologists, dressed in their khaki jungle togs and hats, brushing over the floors and walls, clearing vines and trees—children on Christmas morning!

This particular building is known as the Temple of Inscriptions, a name given by Mexican Archaeologist, Alberto Ruz L'Huillier in 1949, because of the glyphs on the 13-foot stone tablets. This was before he made a far more exciting discovery at this site, a discovery many scholars the world over hail as "one of the greatest discoveries in Mesoamerican archaeology."

Before I tell you about that discovery, I have to digress, significantly, to tell you a little more about Alberto Ruz L'Huillier because, frankly, I found his story so damned interesting and I'm in charge here. I think it is an absolute essential part of the Palenque story.

Alberto Ruz L'Huillier was born in 1906 in Paris, France to a French mother and a Cuban Father. His Father's family had been forced to flee Cuba when his grandfather became the first Cuban landowner to free his slaves, evoking the rage of the other slave owners. Alberto's Father and grandfather continued working towards a more just Cuba even as the family lived in Paris, denouncing slavery and other abuses carried out by Spanish colonialism through editorials and communiqués.

In 1925, Alberto traveled to Cuba, in part, to reclaim the family's landholdings in Santiago de Cuba. Then he fell in love…with Cuba, it's music and its heart, and enrolled at the University of Havana. His transition coincided with the presidency of General Gerardo Machado Morales and a time of intense political turmoil in Cuba. The U.S. backed dictatorship of Morales became increasingly oppressive, consistently in favor of whatever most benefited Cuba's sugar empire and the landholders who were at the heart of it.

In 1929, the stock market crashed and as America scrambled to recover any ground they could, the U.S. Congress passed the Hawley-Smoot Act of 1930, increasing tariffs on Cuban sugar to protect American businesses and farmers. This, combined with the fact that hardly anyone in the entire world had money to spend on travel anymore, meant the Pan American seaplanes flew less frequently to Cuba. A country that relied heavily on tourism found itself empty of tourists. Grand Casino's and luxurious hotels that had cost a fortune to build stood empty and the Cuban economy was all but obliterated. People lost their jobs, some of them their homes, and of those who still had jobs, most experienced significant pay cuts. As the economic turmoil increased so did the crushing oppression of General Machado.

Amidst this turmoil, the strongest and most organized outcries came from the Universities. Students demonstrated against Machado, calling him a puppet dictator who was selling their country to the United States, opening Cuba to Yankee neocolonialism.

One of the strongest voices was that of Antonio Guiteras-Holmes, who, according to the May 20, 1935 issue of *Time Magazine,* was "a little 28-year-old pharmacist with cross-eyes and freckles, his hair parted in the middle, with a childish, open smile and a vocabulary of violent radicalism." This "little" guy became one of the main drivers of a Cuban revolution, a Che Guevarra for the era, and the precursor for Fidel Castro who later instituted many of Guiteras ideas.[xxii]

And he had a sister: Calixta. She was just as politically motivated as he was. Like Ruz, their Father was a deeply patriotic Cuban, living abroad. Their mother was American, with a strong Scotch-Irish heritage. She was well-educated and shared her progressive ideas about the world with her children from very early on, including stories about their uncle, who had been a prominent figure in Ireland's fight for independence.

Being from a politically active family himself, it was inevitable when Ruz became involved with Antonio Guiteras and shortly after, met and fell in love with Calixta. Over the next several years the trio continued to fight for their ideal Cuba, all of them finding themselves arrested and held as political prisoners several times, but they remained undaunted.

Their movement seemed to finally come into its own when Antonio became the Secretary of the Pentarquia, the governor of the Oriente (the province where he had been the leader of the revolutionary forces), and the co-leader of the "Grau-Guiteras Coalition" that came to be called the "Government of One-Hundred Days" when it later failed in as many days. Ruz, appointed by Guiteras, briefly served as head of the Department of Municipal Affairs. Ruz son, Alberto Ruz Buenfil, notes that his Father's involvement in the revolution was always in a more cultural capacity, not a military one.[xxiii]

On May 8, 1935, Guiteras and some of his companions were waiting for a boat to take them to asylum in Mexico when they were attacked by the military. Guiteras and two other men were killed in the ambush. At his funeral his mother was quoted by the *New York Times* as saying, "My son was a great revolutionist against the forces of capitalism and Yankee imperialism. He sacrificed his life for the betterment of people, especially the working classes. While Secretary of the Interior he gave them two great laws: The eight-hour day and minimum wage laws. He was persecuted for these by the government which made him an outlaw, but his followers will continue to fight to preserve the force he created."[xxiv]

After the death of Antonio Guiteras, Alberto Ruz and Calixta were given the choice of exile or death. They chose to leave Cuba and seek a new life elsewhere.

At the time, Mexico's President, Làzaro Càrdenas, considered by many to be the most populist President in Mexican history (he instituted the eight-hour work day in Mexico, you might recall from Chapter 9), had just opened the borders, welcoming intellectuals and refugees from all over the world.

It seemed the right place for the care-worn couple to grieve the loss of Antonio Guiteras and consider their options. Knowing no other life, the couple quickly became involved in Mexican political organizations. Ruz became a member of the Mexican Communist Party as well as Liga de Escritores y Artistas Revolutionarios (LEAR), a group of exiled intellectuals and artists whose members included renowned artists such as Diego Rivera, Bretón and Maria Izquierdo.

Ruz found employment teaching French at the school of Anthropology and traveled throughout Mexico, becoming fascinated with its history and the remnants of civilizations long past. He decided he wanted to know more so he enrolled as a student at the school. The Anthropology department at La Escuela Nacional de Ciencias Biologicas del Politicnico itself was only established the year before, dedicated to educating Mexican archaeologists to help uncover the secrets of the massive ruins strewn all over Mexico. At the time, much of this work had been conducted by American or European Archaeologists, but thanks to this University "No longer would a few Europeans and Americans—and they were valuable investigators—dictate to the world what was known of distant Mexico."[xxv] So once again, Ruz found himself at the forefront of another movement, but this one did not entail social upheaval or, for the most part, running afoul of armed soldiers. Renowned archaeologist, Michael Coe said of Ruz that he was "among the brightest of the younger generation of Mexican Archaeologist."[xxvi]Dr. Ana Luisa Izquierdo, a leading researcher in Mayan studies, said that the professionalization of archaeology began with Ruz graduation.

A few years after reaching Mexico, Calixta and Ruz decided to separate, but they remained close friends, even after Ruz re-married and started a family, with Blanca Alicia Buenfil Blengio, the high-spirited daughter of a lawyer who was also a member of the Campeche intelligentsia during the Mexican Revolution.

Calixta went on to make her own mark in the world of Anthropology. Among other accomplishments she wrote *Perils of the Soul*, the most prominent book on the Maya of the period, and conducted deep and highly praised research on the Tzotzil-Tzeltal communities of Highland Chiapas.

Blanca Alicia Buenfil Blengio did not go to the University but she was well-read, and stood out from her peers with her radical, nonconformist ideas. Alberto Buenfil Ruz (Alberto III), the son of Blanca and Alberto, later said "with humor and affection, that when his Father met his mother, his Father was "a communist (or ex-communist), twice divorced, French, tall, handsome, with blue eyes, long hair, a pirate, and a pre-hippie revolutionary, and obviously my mother was just waiting for this kind of guy."[xxvii]Incidentally, Alberto III inherited the 'make-the-world-a-better-place' gene too and has been called The Father of the Latin American Green Movement by Huffington Post.[xxviii] But that's yet another interesting story. Back to Alberto Ruz.

Ruz first came to Palenque in 1947 to investigate complaints that the administrators weren't doing their jobs and the ruins were being neglected and destroyed. His investigation found that there was neither neglect nor destruction, but rather a feud between the caretakers and the on-site archaeologist, which he reported, graciously casting blame directly at neither party. As part of his survey he took 265 photos of the site, but only used 17 for his report. I know exactly how he felt. The place is so completely otherworldly, with so many complex facets, beautiful works of art and impressive architectural and engineering accomplishments, limiting photographs to fit a report template would be almost impossible.

After his report, he returned to his family in the Yucatan. He was ecstatic when the INAH (Instituto Nacional de Anthropologia e Historia) asked him to return to Palenque in 1949, take over operations and intensify the excavations.

After hacking out a camp and organizing his teams, he chose to start work on the Temple of Inscriptions. First, he had to clear away the vegetation. In a report to his superiors he used the word "vigorous" to describe the jungle's claim on Palenque. After my hike through the jungle, that descriptor gives me the chuckles. Once he laid the stonework bare, he set about his examinations. Now the story gets *Raiders of the Lost Ark*-y.

While Ruz was going about his archaeological floor brushing, he noticed something strange about one of the large flagstones. It had round holes that were filled with stone plugs. He pried out the seals and then used the holes to help lift the large stone away. Beneath it was loose dirt, as opposed to packed dirt that would have indicated a foundation. He started pulling out the loose dirt and discovered stairs leading down into the center of the pyramid.

"Hmmmm," I bet he said. Then, in the words of one of my favorite Calvin and Hobbes cartoons when they found a trickle of water running through the dirt, he probably said, "I'd say our afternoon just got booked solid!"

He and his crew actually spent months carefully removing the dirt and sifting through it before hauling it away. Then the rains came and when I say the rains came, I mean the rains CAME! Chiapas receives 45% of its 85 inches of annual rainfall during the months of August, September, October and November. For L'Huiller's team the world became a shoe-sucking, uncooperative muck and they were forced to stop work for the year.

Alberto came back in 1950, eager to find out what lay at the end of the underground hallway they'd partially uncovered. The work was slow going as it was both difficult to see and, perhaps more importantly, breathe, down there, but by the end of the work season the hall had taken a sharp turn at the bottom of 46 stairs. Alas, the weather forced them to conclude for the season—again.

They returned again in the Spring of 1951, and encountered a game changer. They discovered ventilation shafts the Mayans had designed to funnel in light and air and keep the inside of the pyramid breathable; once these were cleared, work proceeded more quickly.

Finally, they hit a stone wall in their excavations. Literally. It appeared that the Mayans had plugged up the hallway behind them as they left. Either there was something on the other side of that wall, or this was all done for the sake of a hallway.

They poked around and decided to remove the wall and, what do you know, there were more stairs. Then it was muck season again so once more, they had to stop work.

The good news is that the excavation was flush with funding. The Rockefellers, yes those Rockefellers, wanted to know what was at the end of those stairs, too. So Spring of 1952, Ruz and his boys returned with their shovels, picks and brushes and hoped for grander discoveries to report. Someone said that Ruz's wife actually said that he had better not come back 'til the mystery of what lie in the bottom of the pyramid was solved.

Beyond that wall they found a small hallway, blocked by yet another wall, but in front of the wall was a stone box. When they opened the box they found a curious handful of treasures: a single, teardrop shaped earring, three shells painted red, and a small collection of jade earplugs, like the ones you see some folks wearing today that enlarge their earlobes, creating quarter-sized holes you can see straight through. Perhaps this is where the trend got its start.

Shivering with excitement, they set about dismantling the next wall...which took an entire week. Turns out it was twelve feet thick. Whatever was on the other side they really, really didn't want disturbed or they really, really didn't want whatever was on the other side to get out! Kidding! I think.

Once they did bring the other wall down, they found a larger box in front of yet another wall. Expecting to find grander riches, they lift the lid only to stare with confusion at what appear to be the bones of six small people. No jewels, nothing that would indicate the little people were royalty, clergy or anyone of significance.

They poked and prodded at the other walls and found the one to the left to have less compacted soil so they decide to explore that wall and discovered an eight-foot high triangle lodged in the wall. A worker poked his crowbar into the dirt to rest it for a moment and then cried out because, instead of the bar becoming wedged, it pushed straight through into nothingness. Hearts pounding, they enlarged the hole and stuck a light through. Ruz's breath was taken away by what he saw. Shiny, slender stalactites and stalagmites drip from the ceiling and grow from the floor, like crystal icicles, gleaming. But that wasn't the only reason Ruz could scarcely breathe.

Ruz described his experience to *The Saturday Evening Post* in a story co-authored with his friend and fellow archaeologist, J. Alden Mason, thusly:

"Out of the dim shadows emerged a vision from a fairy tale, a fantastic ethereal sight from another world. It seemed a huge magic grotto carved out of ice, the walls sparkling and glistening like snow crystals. Delicate festoons of stalactites hung like tassels of a curtain and the stalagmites on the floor looked like the drippings from a great candle. The impression, in fact, was that of an abandoned chapel. Across the walls marched great stucco figures in low relief. Then my eyes sought the floor. This was almost entirely filled with a great carved stone slab, in perfect condition."[xxix]

The figures that "marched" across the walls were life size stucco sculptures of Mayan royalty who seemed to watch over the great carved slab, or whatever took place on it. The slab was painted with red hieroglyphics on the side. The top was covered with carved images.
They could hardly wait to get inside, take in the full room and lift the lid on the mysterious box.

But wait they would. That eight-foot high triangle was a foot thick and weighed somewhere in the neighborhood of three tons. Eventually they managed to pry it enough to the side that a slender person could get through the entrance.

On June 15, 1952, after three years of exhausting work, Alberto Ruz entered the room for the first time, the first human in over a thousand years to do so. He said of the experience, "I entered the mysterious chamber with the strange sensation natural for the first one to tread the entrance steps in a thousand years." A haunting statement from a man whose remains now rest in front of this temple he worked so hard to explore, an honor bestowed upon him for his extensive dedication and works in Palenque.

So what about the box? The surface of the box was covered with elaborate engravings in near pristine condition. In the center, a man seemed to be reclining almost in the yoga pose, Navasana, boat pose, with legs and torso at 45-degree angle, upon an altar shaped like a monster's head. He is clothed like a King, with elaborate headdress and jewelry. Behind the altar there appears to be a cross, but Ruz recognizes it as the Mayan tree of life, four of which were believed to hold up the flat, four cornered world upon which the Maya believed they lived. The Mayans also believed that in order to pass to the next world, they had to do so through the mouth of a monster. Well, why not?

Ruz believed that was what the engraving conveyed. A King preparing for the underworld, hence the monster waiting under the table.

He was just about ready to conclude the box was an altar used by priests, but one thing bothered him. The altar did not sit on the floor, but on a huge stone block, that itself, sits upon six large stones. What if the slab was more than just a pedestal for the engraved top?

Unfortunately, the rainy season was beginning again, making any type of work impossible, so once more he had to pack it up and leave a question hanging in the air thicker than the humidity.

In November 1952, Ruz was back in the tunnels with his crew. This time he brought an auger so he could drill a hole in the side of the slab and see if it was hollow. It took days, but guess what? The slab was hollow. Now they had to carefully lift the five-ton slab up far enough to get a look inside. They used jacks and it was another all day, all night venture to slowly lift the slab, an inch at a time so they could slide boards under the gained ground to prevent the slab from getting too high or low at any given corner that the unequal weight distribution might cause it to crack. When they had lifted it far enough, guess what they discovered? If you guessed another stone box with a heavy lid, you guessed correctly!

This one had plugged holes just like the flagstone at the top of the pyramid that led down the stairs in the first place. Ruz moved under the engraved lid, removed one of the plugs and shined in his flashlight.

The pale light did not shine into yet another stair portal, however. It moved over jade, shells and the grinning, bared teeth of a skull! It was a tomb.

Inside the box lay the remains of Palenque's great King Pakal, dressed in splendor for his journey through the monster's mouth to his netherworld. He lay face up wearing a great chest piece made of jade beads, a precious stone to the Maya, believed to symbolize life and purity[xxx], over his breast. Over his face they placed a mask, with eyes of abalone shells and obsidian irises amidst a mosaic of 200 pieces of jade. Archaeologists believed that the mask was made by shaping it, piece by piece, to the face of the dead king. Creepy, but beautiful.

The tomb was stocked with other treasures, including necklaces of jade and pearl, elaborate pendants, bracelets, rings, and figurines of animals, people and flowers carved out of jade. Inside the mouth was a perfectly round, deep green jade bead.

This was the first such tomb found by archaeologists in any Mayan ruin, and it changed Mayan archaeology forever. Tombs were found in Chichèn Itzà, Monte Albàn and Campeche. The implications of the findings in Palenque were of a very accomplished social and economic system, one that could feed and maintain the thousands of workers Ruz believed it would have taken to construct a city like Palenque, in addition to the artisans, royalty, priests and warriors.

Francisco and I walked past the Temple of Inscriptions and paused to gaze up the steps of the temple with its dark entrance at the top center of the stairs. That would be the entrance that went down into the pyramid, the one L'Huillier painstakingly excavated over years. The one that was tomb to a king! Oh how it beckoned. I could scarcely resist the long, straight staircase leading to the top of the temple, that led down into the beautifully, musty-smelling vault. It appeared to be closed only by a thin rope that had a sign hanging from it which read "Cerrado Ahora (Closed Now)." Since it wasn't actually gated, I hoped that that meant we could come back another day, but I later learned that the general public hasn't been permitted inside in a very long time. Special tours only.

As we stood gazing longingly up the stairs, there were no guards, and only that flimsy rope barring entrance as far as I could tell. I sorely wamted to sneak a little peak, just a little, teeny, tiny one. Just a whiff of the musty air? If I was in the U.S., under the same circumstances, I very well might have. But the guards here carried more than sticks and the ability to give you a ticket and a stern talking to. They carried AK-47s and national pride.

Don't get me wrong. I had the deepest respect. I wouldn't have tried to chip off a souvenir or anything like that. I just wanted to *see* inside. Francisco translated from the brochure, and then gave my arm a little tug, shaking his head. "Don't even think about it," he cautioned. I looked once more up the stairs, then to the other small groups milling about. Then I thought of the soldiers with their rifles. I sighed and we continued moving through the ruins.

It wasn't that the rest of Palenque wasn't amazing and worth the trip alone. But somehow, now that I knew about the tomb, not getting to see inside of it felt like going to climb a mountain and then turning back before the top. The rest of the climb may have been beautiful, the reasons for turning back sound, but something still vexed. Like needing to see the end of a movie. Something felt unfinished.

We strolled the palace grounds, climbing up and down the other open temple steps for hours. I ran my hands over the smooth limestone columns, feeling their chalky smoothness until Francisco read in the pamphlet that we shouldn't because the oils in our hands would be destructive to the artwork. I was so excited I had momentarily forgotten that. Everywhere I went, my eyes seemed to seek out the dark entryway at the top of Pakal's tomb.

Back out on the terrace, we saw a four story tower, with wide, open windows, possibly for defense or stargazing or both. Columns and walls throughout the palace were covered with life size and larger, engravings of kings, victors, victims and "beautiful" women. I put the beautiful in quotes because their idea of beauty and ours might not be the same thing. Back then mothers tied wooden boards to the top of their children's head, one in the front and one in the back, so that their heads would grow elongated, and the foreheads flat. The professional notion held by archaeologists is that they did this so they would better resemble one of their most important gods, the maize gods, or because it was said that the Maya were created from maize.

According to the Popul Vuh, the creation story of the Maya, the creator of people, Heart of Sky and six other deities, made several attempts to create a people with hearts and minds who could record the days.

First, they made people out of Earth, but those people dissolved in the rain. Then they tried to make people of wood, but they had no hearts or minds and soon forgot the gods. This made the gods angry so they destroyed the wood people with a great flood (wonder if this was the same flood talked about in the Bible?). The wooden people who survived were turned into monkeys.

Finally, they made man from maize, somehow capable of loving and worshipping the gods, and they became the True People of the earth. Again, sure, why not? There are stranger creation stories out there.

Scenes from the Popul Vuh and Maya mythology are depicted all over the interior walls of the palaces and temples and remain in near pristine condition. Traces of paint can still be found on some of them as well as on many of the columns that were once painted brilliant shades of red, blue and yellow.

There was even a courtyard where perhaps children played and a ball court where adults played a game similar to soccer where they kept a ball, or some stories have it, a severed head, in the air using only their heads and upper body. Sometimes the head was encased in rubber gathered from nearby rubber tree forests. Sometimes it was a bloody head that splattered the players as they batted it back and forth. Some of the games were said to be sacred rituals where noble leaders were required to gamble their own lives and power on their ball-playing prowess.

They even had running water. Palenque had an elaborate aqueduct system that channeled water from springs and rivers to the palaces and to the fields below, as well as directing run-off from the heavy rains to prevent damage. One aqueduct runs right under the largest palace, which is 300 feet long and 240 feet wide. Another channel carves around the city. It remains relatively intact. Now that's good designing.

The engineering that went into this place is humbling. We don't even know what other surprises might still be out there because, according to the UNESCO World Heritage Site, only 10% of the site has been explored.

We took a break in the shade under an immense Ceiba tree. Ceiba trees were considered sacred in ancient Maya mythology for connecting the underworld with the terrestrial realm and the skies. And they do look like enormous columns with important charges. They can grow up to 200 feet high with the whole of the trunk completely smooth until the very top, where the limbs spray out like umbrellas. They have huge surface roots that can sometimes be as tall as a person. The roots we sat upon were about two feet high and curved over the ground like a thick ribbon. Once more I wondered what the inside of Pakal's tomb smelled like, or how cool it might be inside. Whether on my deathbed, hopefully many years from then, I would regret not sneaking a peek inside? What would Indiana Jones have done?

Francisco read a few more facts from the brochure as we sipped from our water bottles. Both of us were tired, hot, and dripping with sweat. When Francisco finished reading, neither of us said a word. Our eyes roamed hungrily over mounds of vegetation and soil, wondering what mysterious wonders of a world long gone might still be hiding just beneath the surface.

Chapter 14: Life, the Universe and Everything

"Faith is a passionate intuition."
William Wordsworth

When we returned late that afternoon, I was desperately craving alone time to ruminate over everything I'd seen. Francisco asked if I planned to eat in the café and I told him, no, that I had some food in my backpack. I wasn't super excited about eating another foil of tuna fish, especially since I'd run out of crackers. But it would keep me alive and help me hold onto money I might really need for bus fare back to Villahermosa. If I ate sparingly, I had enough tuna packets to just last me until I could make it to a town with an ATM and see if the credit card company had enabled my ability to draw a cash advance. If not, I had friends who routinely fasted for a week, existing only on honey water or juice. If they could, I could. Either way, I knew I wasn't going to die. You can survive for three weeks without food. It's water you really have to worry about. Depending on circumstances, you can survive only up to 3 days without water. Fortunately, there was plenty of water and I had iodine tablets to purify it.

Francisco shook his head, "Are you eating your tuna fish again?"

I laughed, "Yes, but I'm really not that hungry anyway." And I wasn't lying. I don't know if it was the excitement of this adventure or a

142

survival mechanism that was nice enough to shut off craving what I couldn't have. It may have been a denial talent resurfacing from the years just after my parent's divorce, when food was often scarce, but I really wasn't hungry.

"You must need more than that." he said, confused.

I sighed, not really thrilled about telling him about my other bonehead moves I'd made. But I explained what happened and told him about how my friends fasted back in Durango, how good for them they said it was, and then said cheerfully, "So I'll be fine until I can get to a real town."

"And if your credit card doesn't work?" he asked, with a look of concern.

I took a deep inhale. The thought was really too scary to contemplate, but I didn't want to show it. Yes, what would I do then? Would I have enough for a bus ride and a night at a hotel if I needed it for the return trip? I didn't know the answer to that. I shook my head, "Well, let's hope I don't have to think about that."

"Come, let me buy you dinner." he said, reaching out his hand.

I frowned. I didn't want this to be a date if that was what he was thinking, nor did I want to accept charity, especially from someone I thought came from a third world country and therefore didn't really have much money either. And what about tomorrow? Would he be able to watch me on my tuna fast without feeling obligated to intervene? I knew I'd be fine and so far, it really wasn't a big deal. I had my daily splurge of café con leche and so what if I didn't go, "MmmmMmmm good" for the rest of my meals? At worst I'd lose a few pounds I really didn't mind shedding. Besides, at the moment I just really wanted to be alone with my journal.

I ran my fingers through my sweaty hair. I knew he would keep insisting if I didn't just walk away. I shook my head, "I'm fine. Really. But I sincerely appreciate your offer." I smiled, and then quickly turned away before he could offer a counter argument. I headed for the lockers to grab my other set of clothes and then to the showers for at least a rinse off, even though I no longer had shampoo or soap.

The water was wonderfully cool and it felt good to drop my body temperature and rinse the grit of salt from my skin. That was a lot of salt. Hopefully the sodium from the tuna fish was enough to replenish my stores. While I showered, I also rinsed out the shirt and shorts I'd worn that day. When I got back to the palapa, I took the bit of rope I'd brought based on the advice of J.R. R. Tolkien's Lorien elves and strung it between the poles of the palapa to hang my clothes, hoping they would dry by morning.

I took a short stroll around the camp, trying to be nonchalant as I examined what other people's thatched roof huts looked like. Many of them were empty this time of day and I saw that some folks left all their stuff unguarded in their palapas. I saw backpacks hanging on hooks and open on the ground. Flashlights, cookware and books strewn about on the packed dirt floors.

One palapa looked like it had a family living there full time. A tanned woman with long, brown dreadlocks cooked something in an open fire while a two-year-old baby played in the grass nearby. The woman wore a long, flowing gypsy skirt and a black tank top. She had blue eyes that glowed against her tan skin. Her palapa had a little table, boxes, pots hanging from nails on the poles and a shelf stacked with dishes and cups. It looked like a scene from the Boxcar Children.

What was she and her baby doing here, I wondered. Was she stranded or here by choice? She looked deep in thought as she tended to her pot. Then, for a moment her eyes flicked up and met mine, but there was no real reaction. I was a little embarrassed to be caught staring, but offered a small smile and nodded my head in greeting. She nodded back, without smiling, and turned her attention back to her pot. I walked on.

When I got back to my camp, Hasid was in his palapa next door, sitting on a tree stump and working on a painting. I stepped close enough to see it. It was pretty good. A jungle scene painted with sharp shapes and vivid colors.

"What is it?" I asked him.

Hasid also seemed to be a semi-permanent resident here, having a few extra possessions in his palapa that the typical camper lacked. He had a small round table, several beautifully painted clay pots, a stack of blank canvas, and several completed paintings. He reminded me of someone from the Rainbow Family, a roving band of hippies, artists and (sometimes) intellectuals in the U.S.. They reject traditional social structures and commercialism and rove from national park to national park, primarily living out of tents and campers. I guessed he was somewhere in his forties, though in pretty good shape, as was easy to tell because he never seemed to wear a shirt.

That was a characteristic of many of the male travelers here. Most of them never wore shirts. I found that interesting because none of the local men went about without their shirts on. I wondered what they thought of this habit. Hasid's skin was dark and his crystal blue eyes seemed to cut straight through the fringe of dark hair that hung over his eyes. And he was charming. And mostly harmless. Mostly. I had a feeling he was one of those men that could talk you into just about anything given the chance.

"Do you like it?" he asked, continuing to work without looking at me.

"I do." I said, moving closer to stare over his shoulder. The painting was in the deepest shades of red, blue, yellow, orange and purple. It was a jungle scene painted in deep lines and sharp angles, almost abstract.

He dipped his brush and made a few swipes with it across the canvas, "It is a page from an ancient Mayan story. Here is the story's title in Mayan glyphs across the top and here is a scene from the story.

"The story is called 'The Rabbit and the Coyote.' In this picture, the rabbit has just tricked the coyote into drinking so much water from the pond that he becomes very sick and so the rabbit hops away."

I looked at the picture and saw a coyote with a sharp triangular head, kneeling beside a lake, drinking. A clever looking rabbit with a longer triangular head and long, sharp triangular ears is just turning to leave. It wore a distinctly amused expression.

"How did the bunny trick the coyote?" I asked.

"The rabbit," he corrected me, "told the coyote there was cheese at the bottom of the pond and all he need do is drink all the water from the pond and it would be his. The coyote is stupid and the rabbit is very clever, always playing tricks on everyone."

"Where I come from, it's the coyote who is the clever trickster." I told him. "Though we also have stories about clever bunnies."

He nodded and made a, "Hmmm" sound which seemed a polite way to say 'Yes, now go away. I'm working.' Which I thought was rather polite. After all, just because he was in an open air palapa, it didn't mean I could just invade his space. He didn't actually invite me to view or comment on his painting.

"It's quite beautiful," I said, and then returned to my own palapa.

I pulled my journal out of my backpack and climbed in my hammock. We still had an hour or so of light left before the sunset and my pen flew across the pages while I soaked in the sounds of the jungle at dusk.

I was amazed at how at home I felt right then, how totally comfortable with the way this little village functioned and the place I had settled within it. Amazed at how I'd adapted to climbing into my hammock for everything: sleeping, reading, writing, and even eating.

I pulled out the foil of tuna I had opened at lunch. I'd only eaten half of it. I don't know if you've ever tried dry tuna, but it's not that tasty. It wasn't that hard to only eat half. I pulled out my travel spork and scraped out the rest of the day's sustenance. No longer having soap, I did my best not to drip any of the oil on me. It was surprisingly filling, especially once I washed it down with half a Nalgene of iodine water. Once I was finished I got out of my hammock to take the foil to the trash can. Tuna fish has a pretty strong smell and strong smells in an open air setting surrounded by legions of bugs waiting for the sunset are not things you want to bring together.

Hasid stopped his painting and asked where I was going. I told him, and he said, "Wait, I'll go with you."

"To the trash?" I asked, baffled.

"No, I'm going to have a beer at the café and I'd love to buy you one if you'll let me." he said.

"Oh," I said. "No thank you. I'm just going to wash my hands and call it a day."

Francisco was just coming up the walk and overheard Hasid's invitation, "No, both of you, come back to the café. I'll buy beers for all of us. Please."

In truth, a beer sounded magnificent right then. And I felt a lot more comfortable letting Francisco buy me a beer than Hasid. Francisco and I were adventure buds. It was highly appropriate for us to sip suds after clambering through a jungle. I didn't want to have a beer alone with Hasid, for fear of sending the wrong message. While Hasid had done absolutely nothing inappropriate and had only treated me with courtesy I was still uncomfortable in his presence. I couldn't put my finger on it, but when I had this type of reaction around people, I tended to listen to it.

Perhaps because he reminded me just a teensy bit of my father (that'll send me running every time), or because he was middle eastern and I only had a head full of stereotypes about men from the middle east. I had a headful of stereotypes about a lot of people back then that I never realized. Which means I may still have plenty I'm oblivious to now. I liked him. He was interesting and highly intelligent, but a beer alone? That just did NOT seem like a good idea.

"Oh come on!" Francisco groused. "One beer. We've earned it. We've earned two!" he said.

I reasoned that if he was offering two, it probably wouldn't bankrupt him to buy one, and a beer in that heat sounded so superb, so I shrugged my shoulders, "If you insist, Señor."

"No, no, I buy the second round," Hasid said. "Now that I insist!" The part of my DNA bequeathed by my alcoholic Father's alcoholic family inwardly shouted with glee, "Yay! Two free beers!" Outwardly I wore an expression that suggested I was doing them the favor by letting them buy me beer. And they both acted as though they had won, so win-win. Yeah, I don't get it either, but works for me.

We walked to the café, laughing and joking like children, even Hasid. When we got there, aside from our little party, the café was empty. It was spotlessly clean, each table had it's little vase with its singular flower and a radio played low by the bar.

Another long-term camper came in and asked to join us, offering to buy yet another round. His name was Janez and he was originally from Germany. He was a bit of a paradox. He had the outward appearance of any traveling hippie I've ever encountered. He wore the standard short sleeved tie-dyed t-shirt. A hemp bead necklace was tied around his neck and a hemp bead bracelet was tied around his wrist. He wore a pair of khacki shorts and a pair of flip flops. His face was tanned and his curly brown hair was about three inches long. But he was also so very...German (See? More stereotyping), not that that's a bad thing at all. But his mannerisms seemed so counter to his appearance. Excellent posture, a sharp rigid way of holding and turning his head, a formal way of speaking.

He and Hasid resumed a discussion they had apparently been having earlier that day about religion. It must have gotten quite heated because Hasid stiffened at his approach, then took on a posture that was both non-threatening but also unyielding.

"Janez, religion, per se, isn't bad. I see the mechanics of it." Hasid began. "I see the necessity. It may very well be that the fear of hell is the one thing that stands between some men and murder or other such unsavory acts. If the fear of hell, lack of after-life virgins, or something like that provide much needed buffers between dark natures and the rest of us, well, that's good, right? It's all in who's doing the leveraging. Is religion being leveraged to draw out people's best natures that they otherwise may have lost sense of in their darker moments? Or is it being leveraged by some tyrant or government that has selfish, diabolical intentions without regard for anyone's well-being but their own?"

"Are you suggesting that religion is nothing more than some kind of social control tool?" Janez said, raising his voice slightly. "Have you no respect? No sense of God?"

Hasid leaned back in his chair with an amused expression, then said, "Janez, you've heard of Bertrand Russell—the philosopher? Yes?"

Janez nodded petulantly and rolled his eyes, "Of Course."

"Have you heard how he responded to the question put to him of what he would do on judgement day when God asked why he was not a believer?" Hasid asked.

Janez shook his head, no.

Hasid continued, "He replied, 'not enough evidence, God. Not enough evidence.'" He chuckled, then once more took on a stance that was neither threatening nor yielding. "Actually, there is a difference between believing in God and blindly following a religion. But I'll tell you, my friend, there are some places you can travel to in this world that will make anyone question the existence of God, the existence of some omnipotent that sits idly by while children die from bombs dropped, possibly while the very same children kneeled in prayers for protection just before the bomb hit." As Hasid finished, his eyes seemed no longer in the present but reliving some monstrous memory the rest of us couldn't imagine.

Everyone remained respectfully quiet suspecting this wasn't an illustrative example. This seemed an actual memory for Hasid. I think he'd seen this. I think he'd been there.

In a quiet voice he continued, "I am not a complete unbeliever. I believe there is a God who has some interest in us. Who, like any good parent, wants the best for us. That being said, if that is true, I also think that God must let us find our own way, letting us take the falls we set up for ourselves for our own development. Sometimes children won't learn and evolve any other way. Maybe our bad decisions as a society, as an era in time, will lead to something that we couldn't reach any other way. Hopefully that doesn't mean that we have to bring almost every species on Earth to the brink of extinction to finally understand how precious every creation, how worthy of respect, every life form, IS. I could be wrong, maybe one of these religions on this planet has it absolutely correct and if that's the case, man, I hope I hear about it. I hope I'm swayed, because, my God, what a relief to not have to spend quite so much time sifting through their guidance for errors in logic or morality. What a relief it would be to have a book with the actual directions for life all neatly penned down, 'cause let me tell you: this thinking for yourself crap is exhausting. But so far, in all the religions, almost exhaustively, I see fallible, corruptible men."

Janez, uncertain as to how to continue the argument with Hasid, turned to Francisco and I, "And you, what do you two believe?"

Francisco took Janez' hand, shook it and said, "I'm a devout Catholic, brother." I envied his comfortable position of undoubting believer. Bolstered by Francisco's support, Janez turned to me, "Donna?"

I cleared my throat and prepared for an inevitable bout of proselytizing, something I was plenty used to coming from the Bible belt of the U.S.. "I guess you could say I fall somewhere between Hasid and Francisco in my beliefs. I was raised as a Southern Baptist. I've been "saved" and all that, but then I've had some experiences that make me feel similar to Hasid, that religion, with the exception of Christ himself, perhaps, seems fraught with despicable men. I'm not just talking about the fallen Christian leaders in recent years. In college I studied the Dark Ages, which appear to have been dark primarily because of the church. I studied the horrors of the Spanish Inquisition and the hypocrisy and abuses of religion in that era, not to mention the hypocrisy of today. For the past several months at my job, one of my assignments has been to research the dark side of leadership. To that end, I've spent three months, eight-plus hours a day, reading about child molesting priests and how the Church has protected them. Now I find myself glaring at priests when I see them before I know what I am doing," I paused, taking a couple of gulps from my beer.

Francisco's eyebrows were raised in surprise, while Hasid stared at the condensation on his beer bottle, nodding in sad agreement. I continued as if I were no longer answering Janez question, but saying things aloud I never had before, but had desperately needed to for a long time, "If that's not enough, there's the way Christians seem to view environmentalism—the planet earth. I don't want to offend you or Francisco, and maybe it's just the folks I've personally met—or happen to be related to—but they seem to have this attitude that God made the Earth for man and so we can do anything we want to it. I actually had one Christian, actually a family member, use those exact words. They think that God is coming to take them away from this masterpiece he created," my voice cracked and to my own surprise, I found myself stifling a sob to continue, "so they trash it like some place they think they're never coming back to. This planet is a miracle," I said raising my voice, "We know it to be the only one of its kind in our galaxy, yet it's treated like one can simply go down to Wal-mart and get another one."

I shook my head angrily, "While I believe in God, I'm not so sure He'll be pulling us out of here if we poison the planet. If you were a parent and you bought your kid a beautiful house on a beautiful piece of land and they trashed it, how likely are you to buy another. They also seem to think we have no obligation to see to the well-being of the rest of the life on this planet. They treat other life like it has no value, outside human application." I turned up my bottle and gulped, then accidentally set it back on the table so hard it banged loudly. " Then there's this self-righteous smugness I'm not thrilled about...Am I wrong? Possibly. Like Hasid, if I am, I sure hope I get convinced before it's too late." I finished, slightly embarrassed as I realized how hard I was breathing, *"Why didn't you just decline to discuss religion?"* I thought to myself.

Janez let me finish my tirade without comment. Then, more kindly than he had argued with Hasid, he said, "You have seen the wrong side of Christianity. The media does not focus on the good really being done in this world by Christians, and there are many Christians who are environmentalists. It is one of God's commandments actually."

"Oh?" I questioned. "Where? I'd like to pass that verse along next time I find myself sitting around the family Thanksgiving dinner table."

Janez smiled peacefully, perhaps thinking he had a chance to rescue at least one soul today, "In the beginning of Genesis. There is a verse that says, God "took the man and put him in the Garden of Eden to work it and take care of it.[xxxi] Do not mistake these bad examples as representative of God." he concluded, kindly placing his hand gently on my shoulder.

I hated to disappoint him, but my resurrection as a Christian was going to take a bit more than one Bible verse. I sighed, "Janez, what I would like to hear more about are Christians or Muslims, or representatives of any religion, doing a lot more practicing what they preach, aside from trying to drum up or birth more members, and a lot less killing people who believe differently, yet in the end, the same." I finished, exasperated.

Hasid burst out laughing, "Exactly!"

Janez stiffened visibly. He stood up and very formally turned to Francisco, hands by his side, he took a quick, rigid 'tilt of a bow, "Good night, Francisco." Then he turned to me with such formality he all but clicked his heels together as he tipped forward in only a slight bow, "Fräulein." And then he marched off. Really. He actually called me Fräulein.

"Well, that was interesting." Hasid chuckled.

"These beers are really hitting the spot," I said, trying to shake the tension and change the subject, out of respect for Francisco, though he didn't appear the least bit ruffled by our discussion. He seemed at peace with his beliefs without feeling the need to push them on others, something I found rather noble. Or he had the sense and manners not to discuss religion.

We ordered another round of Pacificos and they went down way too easily. Hasid was happy to drop the religion discussion and asked what we did back in our home countries. I told them I was a research writer for an executive development firm and that I spent most of my time helping the CEO of the company do research, write and edit books on executive development and coaching. Francisco nodded, and took a sip of his beer, then asked, "What is executive development and coaching?"

I took a deep breath for a long explanation.

"The easy way to describe it is that we help executives—typically the highest managers of corporations—remember how to play nice with others after they've been assholes to get to the top. Once they're at the top nobody will tell them what assholes they've become for fear of getting fired so they have to hire people like us to tell them." I laughed at

150

how absurd that must sound. "I mean, they're not all assholes and that's not the only reason we get called in, actually it's usually the exception, but we all could use a friend who will tell us when we're being jerks, sometime. A lot of what we do is help people find and overcome they're individual challenges to peak performance."

"For example?" Hasid asked.

"Well, one of our tools is something we call 360 feedback. For this we interview an executive's peers and the people who work for them. We ask them questions about the executive's management style. Like how they typically motivate people: Is it by maintaining a climate of fear, where people are constantly afraid of losing their jobs? Do they yell and threaten? Are they transparent, honest? Do people trust them? What we've found is that these more mercurial managers typically have teams that are underperforming, or high rates of turnover, which, turns out, cost companies a lot of pretty pennies. If a manager has some of these negative characteristics, we work with them to change their managerial approach. When that happens, profits go up, but more importantly to me, we improve the life of the manager and not only at work. I think it has to effect his personal life as well, so we're improving the lives of his family, the lives of his team, and their families. I like to think we make the world a better place in this way." I finished, taking a swig of my beer. "Ummm...am I talking as much as I think I'm talking?"

Hasid laughed, "You're definitely saying more than I've heard you say all week, but that's the beauty of alcohol. I'm enjoying hearing your voice finally. And good for you. That sounds like great work." he said. "Do you make any money?"

I laughed, "Would I be eating tuna for breakfast, lunch and dinner, if I did?" I rolled my bottle of beer between my hands. "It's not bad, actually. But really, I'm just starting out."

Hasid nodded, "What about you Francisco?"

"My family owns a resort on the coast of Argentina," he said. "Just a few cabanas on the beach." he said modestly.

"Ah, Argentinean Aristocracy!" Hasid proclaimed. For my part, I felt better about allowing Francisco to buy me a beer and suddenly hoped he'd buy me another. Yes, I'd let him buy me beer but not food. It's a family trait.

Francisco smiled showing those fabulously perfect teeth, "We do okay, but that's part of what I'm doing on this trip, seeing how other places operate."

"How about you, Hasid?" I asked.

He sighed, leaning his forearms onto the table as though he were about to share a true tale of woe, "I was a professor at the college in

Jordan, and just got tired of all the bullshit. When my Father died a couple of years ago, I quit my job and took to wandering. I've been here for several months. I'm not sure how long I will stay."

I was surprised. Months? There just wasn't that much to do around here. "What do you do?" I asked, incredulously.

He looked at me plainly and said, "I paint. I walk. I talk to people. It's a fascinating place that attracts fascinating, and sometimes beautiful, people." He said, raising his beer and gesturing towards me. I smiled and looked down, uncomfortably.

Francisco cleared his throat and turned to me, "So, Donna, what have you planned for tomorrow?"

"I'm not sure. I may go back to the ruins. Why?"

"I want to go check out this place near here called Agua Azul and Misol-ha. One is supposed to be a beautiful waterfall and the other is a turquoise blue river with a series of natural slides. Do you want to go?"

That sounded amazing. "Well, yes, I definitely want to go, but until my PIN is activated and I get to an ATM, and make sure I can use it, I have to keep my expenses low so I can make sure I have enough to get back to the airport in Villahermosa."

"How about if it is my treat." he asked, those dark eyes leveling on me. "I just really enjoy your company and it will be more fun than my going alone. You'd be doing me a great favor."

I scanned his face for traces of charity or calculation and saw none. I really wanted to go. I really wanted to see more than Palenque, even though visiting Palenque itself was a trip of a lifetime.

"Really?" I asked. "Because I can probably enjoy spending the rest of the week examining the park."

"Please?" he persisted.

The combination of the beer's relaxing vibes and the new knowledge that he came from a family with at least some wealth and therefore I wouldn't be causing him hardship made the decision easier.

"In that case, I'd love to go! Thank you for inviting me."

He smiled and held his beer up for me to tap in a toast. "Salud." he said. "To Adventures."

Hasid finished his beer and stood. "Thank you, my friends, for the company. I'm going to return to my painting. Buenas noches."

Francisco and I sat sipping our beers in silence for a moment, but I could see that he had something else on his mind. He kept glancing up at me, looking for a moment as though he were about to say something, then he'd once again look down and drum his thumb against his beer bottle, smudging the bubbles of dewy condensation that had formed over the label.

Finally, he looked to me and asked hesitantly, "So, Donna. Tienes un novio? Do you have a boyfriend back home?"

I thought it was interesting the way people would ask about each other's home life, their life outside of the travel life, as though they were asking about a different world. One that didn't necessarily connect to this one. As if we had slipped between dimensions.

I knew this was coming so I wasn't completely taken off guard. "No. I've actually only recently gotten out of a relationship." I said, and found my answer interesting. I didn't sound the least bit mournful. The way I said it sounded like the relationship was something I'd had trouble freeing myself of, when the reality was that I didn't sound mournful because I was pretty sure that relationship wasn't over. I didn't share this with Francisco, though, and I'm not sure why. Perhaps because I enjoyed the level of the friendship so much I didn't want it to change. And I liked the attention. I guess I thought I needed it.

"How long ago?" he asked

I sipped my beer, looked him right in the eyes and said, "A few weeks."

"You broke up with him?" he asked.

I shook my head. "No. He broke up with me. I wanted something different than he did. At least he was honorable enough to be honest about it."

He looked slightly nervous, "And what did you want? Marriage? Children?"

I laughed. "Ha! No. God no! I'm not even sure I ever want to get married. No I want something possibly even scarier."

He raised an eyebrow, "And what is scarier than marriage and children?"

Again I laughed. I looked down at my beer and then raised my eyes to meet his, knowing that what I was about to say would probably scare the hell out of him, but I wasn't apologizing for it. "I want to plumb the depths. I want to see how deeply I can come to know someone else's soul and how completely they can come to know mine. I want to drop all pretenses and show my vulnerabilities and see if I can be loved in spite of them, maybe even because of them. I want to see if something deeper exists out there in the realm of love, something I sense but have not yet felt. I don't know if it exists, but I know I won't find it unless someone is willing to try with me, to be nakedly raw and real." As I finished I looked to him, challenging him to ridicule my revelation.

He sat staring at me with his eyes wide open and both eyebrows lifted. "Holy shit." he said. "You said that to him?"

I nodded, "More or less." I giggled. "I know. It sounds…well, I don't know how it sounds, but I wanted him to know I wasn't interested in anything frivolous. I wanted him to know so that we didn't waste each other's time. Life's too short to waste time, don't you think?"

His eyebrows still slightly raised, he nodded, thoughtfully.

"May I ask, ¿Cuántos años tienes?" he asked me. "How old are you?"

I bristled. This is a question that I have never appreciated, not in my entire life. Not before I turned 21 and certainly not after. In the South, where I was originally from, it is considered extremely rude. In my experience it has also been infuriating, and unjustly limiting.

Try being on your own at 16 and trying to find a job that will pay enough to pay the rent. Try being on your own at 16, experiencing all that can involve, and then try being judged in the same way as a 16 year-old whose had parents and support.

Our system doesn't really know what to think about kids who end up in my position. Too old for foster care, but still required to attend school. No experience or credentials to find a job that will actually support you. If you don't have a family to support you, your options are very, very, VERY limited. So we generally get ignored as much as possible by the system, denied opportunities in the employment sector, then judged by a society that doesn't know a thing about us. Too young to understand, old enough to know better…I'm a little touchy about the age question. When people ask your age they are asking for an easy way to generalize you. Most assumptions about an age haven't defined me for a long time. If you want to know about me, you'll have to take the time to actually find out rather than using something as arbitrary as age.

Francisco naturally could have known nothing about my stance and was probably a bit perplexed when I turned to him somewhat belligerently and asked, "How old are you?"

"Diez y nuevo." he said. To which my mouth dropped open as I repeated his answer to make sure I understood it correctly, with obvious surprise, revealing my own ageist hypocrisy now that I think about it, "Diez y Nuevo???" *Nineteen*?

To which he quickly said, "I'm sorry, I misunderstood you. "Veinte uno." To which he watched me visibly relax. At least some. I thought his first answer was probably the truth, but I think I was also relieved that we were more or less both agreeing to be ageless for the duration of this obviously doomed to be short relationship, so I said, "Veinte cinco." Which was off by a figure I'm not planning to share with you, naturally.

"You have very deep waters." he said, mysteriously, as he raised his beer bottle and tapped mine. He then changed the subject to slightly more benign but far more important matters. We talked about hiking, partying and surfing long after the sun had set.

We walked back to the palapas laughing easily. The beer had loosened everything up nicely. So nicely that when we got back to our palapa, I threw my arms around him reflexively and gave him a warm hug. When I went to disengage, he pulled me closer, laying his cheek against the top of my head.

I pulled away laughing awkwardly like a high school freshman who might have been about to get her first kiss if she hadn't blown it by acting like a goofball.

"Bella..." Francisco said softly.

"Well, good night." I said, still snickering awkwardly. I was confused. Up to this point, the entire relationship had felt so natural. Oddly, as if we'd been friends and known each other always, as if we'd been friends since childhood and were meant to find each other in this place. When I threw my arms around him to hug him, it was on impulse. It wasn't intended as a segue to something more...yummy. Hard to explain. It was like we were kindred-spirit friends, deep and real, but together for only a brush, and not one meant to be romantic.

He shrugged in his own confusion and shook his head, climbing into his hammock.

"Good night, Donna."

Chapter 15: Misol-ha to Agua Azul

"Three things cannot be long hidden: the sun, the moon, and the truth."

Buddha

The next morning, Francisco headed for breakfast while I was still asleep and when I awoke I wondered if he had opted to go without me. The morning was peaceful and cool and at first I was content to hang in my hammock and write in my journal. But then, I decided maybe I should get ready, just in case. I was just finishing up the morning's ration of smelly tuna fish when Francisco came back, hair still dripping from the shower.

"Buenas Dias, Bella!" he said, enthusiastically, obviously a morning person. "Do you have a swim suit?"

"I do!" I said, stretching, lazily.

"Well then, Vamonos!" He said clapping his hands.

"Okay, I'm scrambling, I'm scrambling," I said, getting out of my hammock and digging through my backpack for my bikini.

He shook his head, "How do you sleep so long after the sun comes up?" he asked.

"Practice," I smiled. "I used to wait tables at night and then went out dancing after. Had to learn to sleep through the day sometimes."

He nodded, "Well, the bus will be here in about twenty minutes, so if you want to shower before we go, then..." he hinted.

"I'm off," I said, hurrying down the walk.

I briefly debated the merits of showering without soap, but decided rinsing off would be better than nothing, so I stashed my backpack in a locker, grabbed my weird little towel square and hit the showers. When I got in the shower I saw a travel-sized bottle of Finesse shampoo and conditioner combo on a ledge. "Yes!" I cheered.

It was probably empty, but I figured I could probably pour some water in it, shake it up and get enough soap for a bit of a shampoo, but when I picked it up, I was ecstatic to feel a little bit of weight in the bottom of the slender blue bottle. There was enough for at least one more full shampoo!

Should I or shouldn't I? I wondered. What if someone came back for it and there I was holding the empty bottle with my fresh smelling hair? And I'd be doing almost the same thing someone had done to me. But maybe it was someone who was leaving and they left it there because they wouldn't be needing it anymore. That could be. Then there was the other thing: Someone else's used toiletry item, Ewwwwwwwwww.

But then showering in water that may have come from the cow field across the street...a little soap would be really nice. So I did it. I poured a tiny bit into my hand, careful not to let the water splash even a drop away. I cupped my hands, carefully allowing just enough water in to start a lather and then spread it over my hair. It felt luxurious, the bubblers frothed through my fingers and I lathered and lathered and lathered, massaging my fingers over my scalp. I took my soapy hands, standing back away from the nozzle spray so I could use the soap clinging to my fingers to rub all over my body.

I took the cap off the tiny bottle and held it under the shower stream, filled it halfway with water and shook it vigorously, determined to get use from every clean smelling drop. What luxury!

Just as I was getting ready to shut off the water, a man with a British accent inquired, "Hello, in there. Excuse me?"

"Occupied!" I shouted back.

"Yes, I know," he stuttered. "I'm sorry to bother you, but do you happen to see a bottle of shampoo and conditioner in there?"

"Ummmmmm, let me look." I answered. *Oh drat!* I said to myself. *Busted.* "I don't see any conditioner," I shouted, "but there's an empty bottle of shampoo in here. I'll toss it out."

"Dammit!" He said, then apologized. "I'm sorry. That wasn't directed at you. Sorry to bother you."

"No problem," I said matter-of-factly. I congratulated myself on how cool I played that. So convincing, and with only the slightest hint of guilt. I reasoned that there was really only one serving left, and I probably needed it more than he did. Okay, a little more than a smidge of guilt. But it went away when my clean hair air-dried into the lovely coils of curls it has under just the right, rare, and still mystifying to me, circumstances. The right mixture of moisture in my hair and in the air, the just right place for producing lovely, curls. Mess with that formula even a little and instead the curls go in all directions, coils separate into smaller coils, as if my entire head could only agree on one thing: going POOF! Which is more often than not, sad to say.

I put on my bikini. The fit was quite a bit looser than when I'd tried it on before this trip. A few days of eating nothing but a small handful of tuna three times a day was beginning to take its toll. I wondered if I needed to worry that it might slip off in the water. It also occurred to me that I should be positively ravenously hungry...but I still wasn't. Curious.

I put on my clothes that I'd rinsed the day before, a pink T-shirt with a faded beach scene and my quick dry capris. They had the wonderfully fresh smell of clothing dried outside on a line.

I took out a few peso bills, put them in my money belt, and grabbed my passport, just in case we went through any checkpoints, then hurried to meet Francisco down by the road. He smiled when he saw me, "I was starting to wonder if you'd changed your mind."

I smiled. "I thought about it. I really don't want to be an imposition." I said, slightly uncomfortable to even be in the position where I couldn't go unless he paid. It's a position I knew all too well but hadn't allowed myself to experience for years. Usually I'd just say, "No thank you." And tell myself it probably wasn't that great anyway. But this was adventure land and I had an adventure pal. How could I resist?

Seeing my discomfort he said, "Not at all. Please, allow me in repayment for that most authentic jungle experience you took me on the first day we met."

"Ahhhh, reparations payments for guide services rendered? Now that I can allow you to do. Thank you." It had been an adventure that the pros probably wouldn't have provided, I reasoned.

The bus arrived almost on time to our amazement. A 1970s era Volkswagen Van with duct tape holding the side mirror in place and no glass in two of the rear windows. I looked to Francisco and raised an eyebrow. He laughed, "Come on, gringa. Get in!"

Misol-ha is only about 20 kilometers or 13 miles down the road between Palenque and the much more well-traveled town of San Cristobal De Las Casas. It is a 35 meter/115-foot cascade that falls into a clear, mineral-rich pool of water with such rich shades of blue you'd think it was artificial, but it's not.

Lonely Planet calls Misol-ha spectacular while *TripAdvisor* reviews range from "one of the most amazing places I've ever been" to "I can't believe I wasted xx many hours coming to this rip-off."

To be fair, a lot of the abysmally low reviews were from people who'd been robbed by bandits or swindled by "representatives" of the Zapatista, asking for tourist or road fees. But, also to be fair, there is no infrastructure that sees to the passability of the local roads or the trail down to the falls. They are maintained by the local people who have basically no other way to collect for their labor other than to stop cars and collect the fees on a per car basis.

The area is steeped in poverty, and hunger is a powerful driver. In a true capitalist capacity, the locals had recognized an unfulfilled need, road and trail maintenance, and they assigned themselves the task and set the fee. A fee that, yes, may change from car to car, nationality to nationality, but that's only fair, too, as they know Americans and Europeans can afford to pay more than local citizens. And if locals are going that way, it's probably because they have to, whereas Americans and Europeans? Just out for a stroll.

Keep that in mind if you're ever there or anywhere else where they're still struggling with similar issues. And if you find yourself being pulled over by the police for a shakedown, also keep in mind that your "donation" may be paying the salaries of officers who otherwise might not have been paid in weeks or months. If not for the occasional "speeding ticket" from tourist, there might be no police at all.

The right to survive outranks the needs of the tourist to expect things to function just like back home. If they knew the whole story, those same tourists might admire their solution. The integrity of the poor is far more admirable because they have pressures that can't be comprehended by people who've never been hungry. Not just ready-for-dinner hungry, but so hungry your belly hurts and swells, and you-don't-know-when-or-how-you'll-be-putting-anything-in-it hungry. Worse yet, is when you have hungry children, too.

I've kind of been there a few times. Not quite that bad. And I didn't have children at the time. I think it's why I had yet to feel hunger on this trip. My subconscious kicked me back into survival mode, back to a day when I often had only one meal a day. Trust me, you contemplate all kinds of actions. You wrestle with your principles, of who you want to be, who you hope to be, and then you try to choose the least toxic path for that ideal. Sometimes a thief is not a dishonest man (or woman). It's a man or woman with a hungry family. John Steinbeck's Great Depression era book, *The Grapes of Wrath,* tells the tale of a time in America's history when we had our own droves of displaced, hungry people trying desperately to keep their principles under the pressures of homelessness, cruelty, hunger and indifference. In one passage, one of Steinbeck's characters was trying to explain why the people of California seemed to hate the roving migrants with such ferocity. He said, "They hate you 'cause they're scairt. They know a hungry fella gonna get food, even if he have to take it." Yep. Been there, done that.

Anyhoo.

Is it worth the fees? Well, I'm from the Rocky Mountains. I've stood under the spray of hundreds of pristine waterfalls and jumped from their crests into crystal clear, freezing mountain pools. I've scrambled up them when they're frozen solid in the winter, swinging an ice ax above me and shuffling crampon-capped feet slowly up their crystal cathedrals. In other words, it wasn't my first waterfall. If it had been, I'd probably give it four or five stars, especially given that I wasn't robbed or swindled.

It was pretty spectacular. A hundred and twenty feet of water tumbled over moss-covered cliffs into an aqua-azure pool surrounded by lush jungle. The aqua-azure color is because of a high-mineral content, and it made the pool look like a brilliant watercolor painting

A trail hugs the edge of the pool and leads behind the waterfall where there is a cave about 20 meters or 70 feet deep. For an extra fee, a guide will escort you inside and tell you all about the bats that live there. In Spanish.

Francisco did this but I waited outside. It wasn't the bats. The bats I would have liked to see. It was the gaping hole in the earth. I don't have many phobias, but one of them is being inside a cave at the bottom of millions of tons of rock and dirt whose construction, generally being naturally occurring, has not been built to specs designed by scrutinizing engineers who make sure it won't be caving in anytime soon. When I have gone into caves in the past, I could sense the weight of the mountain above. I found I couldn't breathe, as if the air was crushed out of my lungs by the sheer mass of what was above me. My heart pounded faster and faster, and so hard it was all I could hear and I all I could think was that I had to get out.

So while Francisco took the cave tour, I practiced yoga on a large flat boulder close enough to the falls that a light mist drifted over my body, leaving me feeling dew kissed. I stood on my right leg and brought the sole of my left foot to press against the inner thigh of my right leg and placed my hands together in prayer, focusing on my breath. I became lost in the sound of the waterfall. After a few minutes I switched legs. I closed my eyes and fell into breath and sound. When I opened them again, Francisco was just aiming his camera to snap a photo of me in tree pose. Self-conscious, I lost my balance and practically fell over just as he snapped the picture, immortalizing my fall from grace.

"You know you have to burn that, right?" I said.

Francisco only smiled.

Misol-ha wasn't our primary destination, so soon it was time to get back into the bus and continue on. As the motor started, I suddenly had butterflies in my stomach. Just a slight flutter of nerves, as we moved farther from Palenque and the campground where I'd begun to feel at home and safe.

Now that I was back into the unknown, I became acutely aware that I was traveling with and trusting a man I really knew nothing about. It was one thing to trust him in a campground surrounded by other travelers, many of whom I felt I knew because they reminded me of hippies I had known back home, even if they didn't speak my language. The hippie appearance is apparently one of those universal things. It was a different matter altogether to travel further into the jungle.

We briefly stopped at a small town to purchase permits for Agua Azul. Compared to the peace of Palenque, this town was a hive, buzzing with activity. Francisco followed the bus driver, who moved fast, weaving in and out of a crowd of people all moving in different directions. I tried to stay as close as possible to Francisco so I didn't lose him, but they were moving so fast. Part of me wondered if he was intending to lose me, but that would have made no sense. I'd given him ample opportunity to rescind his invitation. He'd practically had to beg me to go. Still, I almost lost him several times. As we wove in and out of people, I tried to look around for an ATM I could use to check if my credit card PIN was activated yet, but I didn't see one.

I stuck so close to Francisco I kept accidentally stepping on the back of his heels. After the upteenth time, he turned curtly and shouted, "What is wrong, Chica?" I stood speechless, humiliated by my neediness, my reliance, and I hated it.

"Lo lamento." I said, with a mixture of anger and shame.

He softened and smiled, "Perdón is better for this. Perdón or Disculpame."

"Gracias, amigo." I frowned sarcastically, my ego still stinging. "Have you seen any ATM machines where I might try and see if my PIN has been activated yet?

"No, probably no ATMs 'til San Cristobal," he answered.

"Are we going there?" I asked.

Francisco shook his head, "No bella, you'll just have to relax and let me treat you today…including lunch! OH NO!" he teased, biting the back of his hand in mock agony, before turning to pursue our driver.

I pursed my lips, clearly not comfortable with this arrangement. He saw my face when he turned to make sure I was following and his face changed too. His brows furrowed and darkened. He was clearly offended.

Back in the bus, he brooded quietly and answered my questions or comments with as few words as possible. After my third attempt to lighten the mood, he snapped at me, "If you want to learn Spanish, you need to practice. I'm not answering anymore questions unless you ask me in Spanish."

Now, I was irritated. Was it so hard for him to imagine why I might not want him to pay for everything today? Like that I might not want to take advantage of him, or that I, a single female traveling alone in a foreign land, might not want to feel obligated? I folded my arms and gave him my own eyebrow furrowing angry face and raised my voice slightly, "FINE THEN! ¿Que pasa, Amigo? ¿Por que furioso, bub?"

This made him laugh. "¿Bub? ¿Bub? ¿Que es este palabra 'Bub' (What is this word, Bub?)?" he asked, finally looking right at me. "Lo siento, Donna. No estoy enfatado. I'm not mad. Sorry."

"What then?" I asked, still mad myself. "You can't appreciate that I might find it uncomfortable for you to pay for everything?"

He shook his head, "Where I come from it is a great insult to refuse such a gracious offer."

"Where I come from it's a bad position for a woman to put herself in. And it brings up bad memories for me." I answered.

He looked surprised, "Bad memories? Someone wanting to treat you like lady is a bad memory?"

I rolled my eyes, "Look, don't you wonder why I'm not freaking out more about my money situation?"

He nodded, "Now that you mention it, I have thought your reaction to your situation strange."

I sighed, "Well, partly it's because I'm pretty sure that as long as I spend as little as possible I'll have enough to at least get back to Villahermosa even though I might end up having to sleep a night in the airport. But the other reason is because…" I paused, considering whether to go on, "it's not the first time I've been without money and if it comes down to it, I have some skills that helped me get through some hard times in the past and may still help me survive." I finished looking away exasperated.

"Some skills?" He questioned. "Oh," he said quietly, "you mean prostitution."

"Not even once." I said defiantly holding my head high. "Not even ONCE." I repeated with a fierce triumph. Then my chin dropped and my voice lowered as I looked away, "But I was a bit of a con artist."

"A con? With? With what? ¿Que es 'con'?" He asked (con in Spanish means 'with').

"It's a person who gets another person to give them something, usually money, by making them feel like it was their idea, sometimes because there was a promise, or implication of a promise, of something in return." I answered slightly abashed. "I didn't do it much. Only when I had to and I never took anything from anyone who couldn't afford to part with it."

"Ohhhhhh, that kind of con." He said, looking quizzically at me, "Are you planning to con me, Donna?"

"Absolutely not," I declared. Then, "But somehow it feels like it. I keep worrying that my vulnerability in this situation might subconsciously activate a default defense mode that…"

He looked at me shocked, "What?" he coughed.

"I don't know." I stammered. "Do you expect anything in return?"

"You mean like sex?" he exclaimed.

"Sex? A kiss? A green card?" I quizzed.

He laughed out loud, shaking his head, "A *green card*?? Really?" He laughed again, "No Donna, I do not want to leave Argentina for the United States. Not even a little bit. I'll admit, I wouldn't mind a kiss, but it's not expected. You are my friend, and I enjoy your company. I thought today would be so much more fun with you as part of it," he said, kindly. Then asked, "But out of curiosity, what if I did expect something?"

"Well then all bets are off and I owe you no pity." I answered impassively. "I've been on my own since 16. Since then, I've run into many men, and some women, who wanted to take advantage of a girl in my vulnerable position. When I encountered those people I felt completely justified in taking whatever bauble they dangled and then leaving them with an empty net and unfulfilled expectations." That philosophy applies to anyone, man or woman. If someone gives me something with the expectation of covertly getting something, especially compliance, in return, without explicitly establishing their intentions up front, well, anyone who offers a gift expecting something in return isn't offering a gift. It's a trick. It's manipulation. I don't like manipulation.

"Wow." He said, obviously not knowing what to think. "Just wow."

We fell silent letting the wind from the open windows blow through the tension of the bus. I wondered where Francisco's thoughts were taking him. I wondered how much what I had revealed changed his perception of me. I wondered what it had been before?

Why did I say anything? Why not just do as I had to do in the past, take it and if he expected something in return, too bad for him. But he was my friend. Would he now completely lose respect for me now that he knew that I wasn't a first world princess, but a poor, white trash schemer? I mean, I'm not. Not white trash, though there are plenty who might call me that if they knew my history. But I'd like to see them do what I've done with as few moral shadows and as much integrity. I know. I know I could have easily been far more mercenary than I was. I cut people loose if I discovered they couldn't afford the hit or had their heart at stake. But who would recognize what that…that fortitude cost? It would have been easier to take everything that was ever offered and just never looked back.

Still, I winced seeing how shocked Francisco appeared. He didn't get it. I looked directly into his eyes, making sure I had his full attention. "Look, it's just something I had to do to survive. It's not really any different than what a lot of people to do every day in their jobs. They just do it in an office setting. And believe me, my jobs were far more benign than most of those and only born out of necessity. I wouldn't have survived otherwise. I had no choice. No choice I could live with anyway. Since then, I have purposely avoided any situations that might force me to have no other choice."

Francisco looked away, speechless.

I sighed, "That's why allowing you to pay for everything feels so uncomfortable. I hate not having my own money. I hate being dependent or feeling obligated."

I took a deep breath and wiped the sweat away from my eyes, "Once I got into college, and actually added choices, I never wanted to do it again and I haven't. It's not like I was scoring all this money, and pulling off all these big jobs like you see in the movies, or anything. I wasn't a very good con. My heart wasn't in it. I only did it when I had to, only what a person could afford, and only the bare minimum of what I needed. After college, I felt like I finally had a real chance and I hoped I never had to do it again. And I'm not trying to with you, but the fact that I'm in a precarious financial situation right now, and you're footing the bill for today, it brings all of that back. It feels kind of similar, even though once I go home, I'll be fine again. But, letting you pay for everything…well, do you see why it doesn't feel right to let you pay for everything?" I asked.

Francisco didn't say a word, just stared at me with a look I couldn't interpret. How could he understand without living through the same circumstances? A young woman in my position generally had two choices: marriage or prostitution. I found a third way and I'd decided long ago that no one was qualified to judge me for it but God.

As I sat beside Francisco, feeling completely naked and vulnerable, I reminded myself of that fact. I took a deep breath, wiped my face again, straightened up and once more held my head defiantly high. I looked him dead in the eye, challenging him to pass judgment, ready to fight. For a long time, he said not a word.

"Sixteen?" Francisco finally queried, "Where was your family?" he asked.

I shrugged, "Off fighting their own demons." He regarded me with a compassion I both appreciated and resented, then placed his hand on mine, looked out the window and allowed the silence to prevail.

It was another twenty miles down the road to Agua Azul, and by the time we arrived, we'd managed to pick back up where'd we'd been back in Misol-ha—before tempers flared and secrets were revealed.

Agua Azul gets my five-star review. Their full name is Cascadas de Aqua Azul: blue waterfalls. It's a series of cascades ranging from less than a foot to 20-feet high domes of tan limestone. It's a river of waterfalls with the same type of high-mineral content, turquoise blue water as Misol-ha. It flows over a wide river of sugar-coated limestone domes and quirky mineral formations. The mineral content is so high, in fact, that fallen trees or anything else that lies for long in the stream is coated in thick crusts of limestone, making for a menagerie of otherworldly sculptural creations. It also makes for free body slides! Whether from being in just the right path or from repeatedly having boats, inner tubes, or people running over them, the limestone over the falls has smoothed into slick slides.

You can hike up river and then wade in anywhere, put your arms out to the side to keep you afloat while putting your feet out in front of you to push off any submerged trees or rocks, and let the river run away with you. When you come to the falls, you simply let the water, which is running really, really fast, pull you over and you just slide and shoot right through these natural slides.

Just one thing: People drown here *all* the time and there's no fleet of lawyers ready to sue so there's no lifeguard on duty. Swim at your own risk. Actually, there's two important considerations. The second is that burglary is common, so you have to have a trustworthy person to watch your stuff while you take the wild ride. A recent scan of *TripAdvisor* reviews list getting robbed among the possible activities at this attraction.

Sometimes by machete or gunpoint. One reviewer said he was actually shot. He gave the place a one-star rating.

Other reviewers spoke of being stopped by nail strips, or by people holding ropes across the road to stop cars and then asking for money (see previous paragraphs on road maintenance). One reviewer mentioned being stopped three times and being asked to pay fees, only to get to the park and be asked again, this time by the legitimate park authorities...if there really is such a thing. She still gave the place 3 stars.

It's worth mentioning that some of the people who left raving, five-star reviews also left a line or two about the sketchier side of the attraction. Full paragraphs of how beautiful and sublime the place is end with subtle words of caution. Joe Doe, from San Diego, California left this raving review with his five-star recommendation, "...the reward starts from the beginning; the roar of the crystal waters welcomes you as soon as you descend from the small bus. As you get closer to the river, there is a moment when you have to adjust your eyes because the spectacular hue of the waters is something that you have to see for yourself to believe it. If you stay on the beaten path, you will still be able to enjoy the river, but if you feel adventurous and go upstream, you will be rewarded with tranquil waters and beautiful scenery. A word of caution, don't go too far by yourself, it is better to go in a group, for safety reasons..." Jane Doe, from Erie, Pennsylvania left this comment at the end of her five-star review praising the unique beauty of the place, "I would recommend that women hike with others, not solo, in this area."

I was only vaguely aware of any safety issues and we didn't encounter any unofficial toll takers, but that may have been because of the arrangements that were made at our previous stop. Plenty of other reviewers complained about the crowds and the vendors, but I didn't think they were overly intrusive. We grabbed a couple of drinks and lunch, from vendors we were glad were there, and hiked up the river until we came to a place just above some of the 20-feet high cascades.

After lunch Francisco stood up and said, "It's not a good idea to leave our things here unattended, so we will have to take turns. I'll go first and check it out. Then I'll watch your things while you go. Bien?" He asked.

"Sounds good." I said.

With a big smile, Francisco left his belongings with me and trotted up the trail while I watched for his head to come bobbing back down stream, hopefully still attached to his body. There was a strong holiday vibe, and the crowd was predominantly Latino, but I was getting used to that. There were a lot of people and if I were looking for that tranquil, wilderness experience, I would have been deeply disappointed, but I'd had no expectations one way or the other and I thought it was grand. There were so many families, huge multi-generational families, all splashing about, laughing, or just picnicking on blankets. It made me smile to see so many families enjoying each other's company.

There have been some moments while I've been in Mexico that I've been uncomfortable being in this foreign place with these foreign, to me, people. I was brought up in the South and I had no idea how deeply entrenched the culture of white is bright and all other colors are suspect, was, even within me. I didn't think I was a racist. Back in the US of A, I'd often felt more comfortable in the company of minorities, of people who'd had to struggle in some way in their lives as well, than with my white peers, most of whom knew very little about struggle. In fact, whenever something obviously racist happened I was outraged and more than ready to jump in and help correct the wrong. But being raised in a pretty racist culture had left its mark. It was moments like this that I realized it, when I look around me and realized that I was surprised by what I saw.

I saw real joy in the faces of parents as they played with their children. I don't often see parents really getting down in the dirt and playing with their children in the U.S. Pushing their kids on swings, sure, but not really playing. What I do see is a lot of distraction. A lot of kids playing on the playground while Mom or Dad stare at their phones. Seeing these families at play was peeling back and exposing subconscious beliefs I had and at the same time, seeing all that love made me feel safer and more at ease.

I wished I belonged to some of the families I saw around me. They seemed to enjoy each other so much. Nearby I saw three generations, a mother and Father with their four children and even grandmother and grandfather standing out, thigh-deep in a turquoise lagoon, batting a beach ball back and forth to each other. Grandmother's silver and black hair all piled up on top of her head, sparkled from the water that had been splashed onto it.

I looked up the stream searching for Francisco's head. I wondered how far he went because it seemed like it was taking him a long time. Finally, I saw his head, lips spread wide in a big grin, his eyes focused on his direction. He came shooting out over a small cascade, for a moment air-borne, then dropped back into the water, where he sunk below for just a second or two before bobbing back up and struggling to get his feet back in front of him. He still had the big smile but his attention was fully fixed on righting his position. He saw me, turned his body to angle towards me, then glided into the shallows, stopping a few feet from me.

"You are going to LOVE that," he panted.

"Well okay then!" I said, excited to get going. "Anything I should know about?"

"Are you a good swimmer?" he asked still panting. "The current is a lot faster than I thought."

"I'm pretty good. I've done a lot of river swimming." I answered. "I've actually used that same floating form you used in our river back home."

"Well, you should be fine. But just a heads up. She's strong." he replied earnestly motioning to the river. "I wish we could go together, but if we leave our stuff, it *will* disappear."

"I wish, too," I said, "But I have a feeling it's still going to be fun"

He nodded, "Okay, keep going until you see a bench beside the river. That's where I started. You can probably go further if you want, but that was a pretty good workout for me."

"Sounds good," I said.

I'd done something similar to this in the Animas River in Durango, Colorado. Tourists and trustafarian college kids would rent giant rubber inner tubes to float down the Animas, but me and the other poor urchins of the town had learned to float down the river just like the people here, with our feet out in front searching for and bouncing off, around or over submerged rocks and trees. Dangerous, yes. But far more exciting than an inner tube ride!

I left my meager pile of belongings with Francisco and rushed up the trail, eager to jump in. I came to a place just before another set of the 20 foot high cascades with a wooden bench beside the river and strolled out into the water. The current was much quicker than I had thought and I had to fight to keep the water from pulling my feet right out from under me before I was ready.

The water was deliciously frigid for the 100 degree-plus weather we were having that day. I turned to face the direction I'd be rushing down and with a practiced finesse squatted down while simultaneously pulling my feet up, with my knees bent. I dropped one foot a little deeper down into the water to give myself a better chance of feeling a boulder before it slammed into my tuche and precious nethers. It was exhilarating. This river moved faster than the Animas and it was an exciting ride and took my full attention to maneuver around boulders and keep my line going through the rapids.

All at once I came upon a five foot drop I'd noted on the way up as probably being the crux of my route. Like being sucked down a drain I went over the falls with little control and the next thing I knew, I was under water with the weight of the falls pushing me down and behind the waterfall. I panicked as I realized I was stuck. I was pinned against the limestone behind the falls. I fought and kicked to push myself back into the current, but the waterfall kept me pinned. My lungs burned as I twisted, and struggled. Finally, I managed to get my feet on the wall. I pushed my feet against the rock with all my might and finally managed to thrust myself back out into the current, but then I was zooming down the river and my form was all wrong.

Instead of having my feet in front of me I was in a swim position and almost immediately a sharp boulder or tree limb under the water raked across my belly and smacked into my rib cage. It tore across and nearly ripped my bikini top off. I cried out in pain, then flexed and waved my body hoping the current would swing my body back into the right position. Thankfully, it worked. Once I was righted, I made for the shore. I clawed my way to the shallow bank and pulled myself onto the warm rocks, panting and dripping. I looked down at my belly. The rock had pulled my bikini off of one of my breasts and it looked like a little bleeding moon, laid bare for all to see. I quickly pulled my bikini back up and looked around to see if anyone saw it, or the fact that I almost drowned...or that I was bleeding, but no one seemed to have noticed.

Just under my nipple, an angry red welt was swelling that ran in a diagonal line across my ribcage to the other side. It wasn't very deep, but blood was soaking through my bikini top and running down over my belly. No one seemed to notice that either, which made me feel suddenly lonely and frightened.

I splashed water over the scrape to get a better look at it, my heart still pounding, when, out of nowhere, an even more terrifying thought sprang to mind: I'd just left what little money I had, my credit card (that may or may not have worked) and, worst of all, my passport, with someone I'd known for little more than a week. Someone presumably from Argentina, but who really knew the truth. What if he was a passport thief? That was a thing there, people getting passports stolen, right? What if this had been part of his plan all along? To bring me out here, have me hand over everything of value I had, then send me running up a trail while he took off the other direction with all my stuff? Maybe *he* was the con and *I* was the mark! I didn't see any other people floating down this crazy river. Everyone else stayed out of the current.

Every warning I'd been given before I left the states, that the people here would soon as kill me as look at me, that all they cared about was getting my money, that they were all lazy, sneaky thieves just waiting for an opportunity to rob me blind...all of those things that I swore I didn't believe before, now elbowed to the front of my mind, revealing that they'd somehow barnacled onto my subconscious, and were now hitting me with the told-ya-so's.

Furious, I sprang to my feet and tore off down the trail. When I came around the corner to where I had left Francisco with my stuff he was nowhere to be seen. I panicked. I should have suspected something when he called me "astoundingly beautiful." How could I have been so gullible? So stupid?? *"I'm so completely fucked!"* I screamed at myself.

The only thing I could do was run as fast as I could, hope to catch him, and then hope that years of rock climbing had left me strong enough to beat him senseless and get my stuff back. *If* I could find him. I looked around to see if he'd at least had the heart to leave my clothes so I wouldn't be basically a naked, non-Spanish speaking gringa, penniless in the jungle, but I saw nothing. Not even my 'yoga-mama-Buddha sandals.' Now *that* was dirty.

Just before I set off running barefoot through the jungle, I happened to look to my left into the river. Guess what I saw? In the middle of the river, anxiously looking upstream, was Francisco, holding all of our stuff tightly clutched in his arms.

For a moment, I just stood, a look of confusion frozen on my face as several competing voices in my consciousness battled for dominance. Something else was happening deep inside my heart. And then something broke. I stood there, dripping and bleeding and without warning, I just started sobbing. It was at that moment Francisco turned and saw me. His eyes grew wide as he took in the blood soaked bikini, and the blood still running down my belly.

"¡Oh Dios Mio! ¿Que pasa? Are you alright?" he said, splashing out of the river as fast as he could. He lost his footing and fell forward into the water, but he never took his eyes off of me, nor dropped my things in the river, as he clawed his way to shore. I stood there with tears streaming down my face.

He thought I was crying because of pain or fear, but I had had worse than this. Living an outdoor adrenaline junkie life, I'd broken eleven bones, accrued countless scrapes, bruises, and contusions, several of which got stitches, while several others probably should have gotten them. I wasn't crying because I was scared or in pain, as Francisco presumed. I was crying for reasons I didn't completely understand myself. Coming around the corner, suspecting the worst from Francisco, as a Hispanic, as a human being, only to find him standing in the river, anxious for my safety while keeping my meager belongings safe in his arms…He threw everything on the ground and guided me into the shallow water where he used his water bottle to begin rinsing away the blood so he could assess the damage.

Something ugly deep inside that I didn't even know was there shattered. Some blackened gunk of spiritual crud that silently weighed me down, quietly overshadowing my feelings and perceptions about the world...about Mexico, about Francisco, they'd broken through it and it came bleeding out of my pores and now was being rinsed away on the wild current of the Cascadas de Aqua Azul and I knew it would never come back. Not like that. Not Ever again. Gandal-Claus works in mysterious ways. Five Stars.

Chapter 16: The Story of the Little Snail

"We are born of the night. We live in it. We will die in it. But tomorrow there will be light. For those now crying in the night, for those to whom day is denied, to whom death is a gift, to whom life is forbidden."
Subcomandante Marcos, aka Delegate Zero, aka Galleano

Marcos: I know you don't want attention. That you don't want monuments or plaques in your honor. That you don't want books written about you. Rest at ease. This book isn't about you. It's about me. But you are an integral part of this story and...and you're just so damned quotable. Please forgive that you'll be mentioned on two or three more pages. Then again, I'm starting to wonder if this book is really about either one of us.

The Indigenous people of Mexico make up more than one tenth of the population of Mexico. According to the World Health Organization, these Indigenous people live on or own one fifth of the national territory and make the greatest contribution to the nation's wealth.

Here's a shocker: Chiapas is incredibly rich in natural resources. The rocky mountains to the east block the westward flow of moist, Caribbean air, bathing the area in rain and clouds, making the Lacandon jungle possible. And the Lacandon jungle? That rich, earthy smell is because the area is home to the greatest variety of plant and animal species of any other region in Mexico. The vast array of plant life absorbs the water and releases it at a steady rate down the mountain sides where it flows into creeks and rivers that flow into reservoirs, that flow through four hydroelectric dams, that provide forty-five percent of all electricity in Mexico. The homes that surround them are medieval. Now there is a fifth, highly contentious hydroelectric dam construction underway, with five affected communities protesting its completion.

Exploratory drillings have produced gushers of oil, the liquefied residue of millennia of lush jungles, that a United States Geological Survey estimated might imply 19 billion barrels of oil and 83 trillion cubic feet of undiscovered natural gas resources in 10 geologic provinces of Mexico, Guatemala, and Belize. This, despite periodic claims from Mexican government geologists over the years who, at least during the 90s and early 2000s, claimed there wasn't enough oil in the area to bother with the hassle it would take to get it, especially given the political unrest of the area.

In 1999, Subcomandante Marcos said, "The war that the Mexican government is waging against us [Zapatistas/Indigenous/Maya/Peasants] has as its objective this oil-bearing stratum, along with the oil deposits that lie in the Corralchen mountain range, in the Montes Azules preserve and in the Santa Cruz mountain range." There are many who believe the government's real interests are in driving the indigenous people off of the land so they may completely exploit the resources without worry of compensating any population it might effect.

Is it true? Well, I could see where they might feel that way, especially seeing as how here we are in 2016 and there are now, according to one report,[xxxii]twenty oil fields operating in Chiapas with 278 million barrels in oil reserves and probably more fields will open because, after seven decades of operating as a monopoly, Petrolios Mexicanos (PEMEX) is opening up four-fifths of its prospective resources to foreign investors.

In a Wall Street Journal article in 2015, Pemex CEO Emilio Lazoya said that now that Pemex was no longer burdened with "unprofitable projects" previously deemed as necessary to fulfill national development policy, Pemex's "objective was to make money." Investors and oil developers are lining up to bid, mostly undeterred by Mexico's standing as one of the "most dangerous countries to operate within Latin America."[xxxiii]

Mexico has compelling reasons to support the best efforts of PEMEX, as it supplies a huge hunk of government revenue and in recent years it seems both the revenue and the oil production has been declining, a major factor influencing this change in policy. The decline is owed to a combination of questionable policy decisions, internal graft, and lack of necessary expertise. They also lose millions of dollars every year because criminal groups are tapping right into their pipelines. Wonder what they're going to do about that? Advise bidders to bring their own security detail? I suppose they just might.

It's not just the oil industry that's been opened to outside bidders, either. Natural gas production is failing to meet the current needs of the country, even with significant imports from the United States, and analyst believe the shortages are blockading economic progress. To address these issues, on December 20, 2013, President Enrique Peña Nieto signed constitutional reforms regarding Mexico's energy sector. On August 11, 2014, those changes went into effect, opening Mexico's oil, natural gas and power industries to outside investors. In theory, this allows Mexico's industry leaders to partner with outside companies that have more experience, equipment, and capital, all of which is necessary to address Mexico's current energy issues. The law also reduced the tax on oil from a whopping 79% to a slightly more modest 65%.

The language of the law implies a desire to respect the people in the communities that might be affected by any new developments. Companies must conduct social impact assessments and obtain approval from informed, non-coerced community members, who deserve to be treated with respect, fair play and compensation.

That sounds like a good thing, right? Development only by the consent of the community. What a just, enlightened government to include such a clause! Bravo Mexico! Unfortunately, the communities, and social and environmental activists say these requisites are not always enforced in Chiapas, and the people there have little faith in any promises made.[xxxiv]

For one, when the first dam was built in Chicoasèn in 1976, the company promised to pay for the land, bring in clean piped water, and build a school and a health clinic. Forty years later and the people are still waiting for these promises to be fulfilled.

It probably also doesn't help that the community is actively voicing that they do NOT want the new Chicoasèn 2 dam, meanwhile the company claims they have signatures of approval from the community. Community members, however, claim that many of the people who supposedly signed their approval apparently signed posthumously, because many of them are dead.[xxxv] According to a Service for International Peace (SIPAZ) blog, elders from the surrounding communities declared a hunger strike in November of 2015 after the lawyer representing their interests was falsely arrested under charges of mutiny by the Federal Electricity Commission.[xxxvi] My research didn't turn up how this wrapped up before the completion of this book, but these were not great first steps forward.

Oil and gas development sucks if you live nearby it (unless you own the mineral rights) and the sooner we push the industries involved to turn to more sustainable resources the better for every living creature on the planet. And the technology is out there. The Toyota Prius is an amazing piece of work. I recently had to drive one eight-hours over several mountain passes, out and back. I filled the tank once on the way down: $13. On the way back, I filled it again: $15. I'm also a bit of a speed freak and the Prius did not disappoint. I went the speed I hoped to. As soon as they come out with a four wheel drive model (other than the Toyota Highlander which starts at $40K and I can't afford it), I am so getting one!

Most of us can't run right out and trade our cars in for a hybrid. So until alternative options are more affordable, we're kind of stuck on the system. We can't drive cars all over the place and then say 'no oil drilling,' right? We just have to demand that it's done as responsibly, conscionably and transparently as possible. *Somehow.* At the same time, we have to take responsibility for our own contribution to the problems, while working diligently to minimize our oil reliance (i.e. walk, bike, car pool, take a bus, drive a Prius) and keep pushing the industries involved to release more sustainable alternatives. Until then, if we rely on oil, we have to expect to shoulder some of the responsibility...and burden.

But what about places like Chiapas where far more people walk, or ride horses, bikes or motorcycles? Most houses I saw didn't even have driveways. Hardly anyone even has a car...or electricity and running water. So what, then, do they owe the system? What is their responsibility? I'm inclined to say that if they reaped the benefits of being a *part* of the system, you know, defended, protected, benefitted from the infrastructure, equipped with clean drinking water, good schools and decent healthcare, well then I would say they have some responsibility. But what if, as some sources suggest, they derive few benefits, but shoulder a significant percentage of the burden?

And then there's the question for those who are reaping the benefits. Do they (and *they* may very well include *us*) owe anything to the impoverished people who happen to reside in the places that provide our natural resources? What about to impoverished people in general?

Here's a thought: Jeffrey Sachs, an American economist and director of the Earth Institute at Columbia University, said that "When we fight poverty and disease in any impoverished part of the world, and thereby bolster the world's shared commitments to human dignity and survival, the lives we save may truly include our own and our children's in some future turn of fortune."[xxxvii] Course, one of the criticisms that have been leveled at Sachs was his enthusiasm for areas such as Chiapas to join the capitalist train as quickly as possible to solve all their problems, and, at least the Zapatistas of Chiapas, are reluctant to jump completely on that train. It's not that they're communist. They're not. But frankly, it seems the only way they could jump on that train would be by leaving their homes for the cities or join in on the plunder of their lands. That's the last thing they want to do.

You might have picked up that I'm a bit of an environmentalist and my default setting is to rally for the underdog. Of course I want to see these people living in their quaint farming villages, healthy, happy and protected from the downsides of the heartless engines of economics. But just now, as I glanced up from my computer to the window across from me here in Colorado, I see a window that used to frame a view of grassy hills rolling straight out to snowy mountains rising up from the plains.

But the grasslands have been plowed under and packed down to build the houses that now roll out to the foot of those same mountains. Houses full of people just like me, with families they're just trying to provide the best lives they can and the farms and traditions that were displaced, are just gone. Things are rough all over.

From my upstairs bedroom window, I can see an oil fracking well in a field just behind a house in the next neighborhood. Not in my backyard, but not far enough away from it either. There's a metaphor there somewhere, just on the tip of my tongue… The point is that the world is changing for us all. "Progress" sometimes tramples as it tramps forward and that's just the way of it sometimes. But here's the thing: If I decide to join the anti-fracking movement (likely) and try to help ban fracking, my family's lives are *probably* not going to be in danger because of it. Most likely we won't be forced out of our homes and into the forests where we'll have to resort to picking berries and eating bark to survive. If fracking is proven to be the toxic health and environmental hazard that we fear it to be, then the oil companies will *probably* be forced to clean up their act, *eventually*, and shell out some compensation. *Probably.* Those are important distinctions.

But in Chiapas, they're standing up for themselves *knowing* their families will be threatened, but doing it anyway. Ya Basta. Enough is Enough. Their courage is inspiring people all over the world.

And that right there is part of the legacy of the Zapatista movement: It has become an inspiration for the downtrodden, the oppressed, the ignored, and the swindled the world over. Every movement that has happened since has been influenced by the Zapatista Movement.

Marcos said in his book ¡Ya Basta!, "Marcos is gay in San Francisco, black in South Africa, an Asian in Europe, a Chicano in San Ysidro, an anarchist in Spain...Marcos is all the exploited, marginalized, oppressed minorities resisting and saying `Enough'. He is every minority who is now beginning to speak and every majority that must shut up and listen. He is every untolerated group searching for a way to speak. Everything that makes power and the good consciences of those in power uncomfortable—this is Marcos."

That's another reason why we should care what happens in Chiapas. Because their struggle really is our struggle and vice versa. In an interview with *IPS Newswire*, Fabio Barbosa, an economist with the Autonomous University of Mexico said, "Exploration for oil has an impact on forests, water resources, and indigenous communities. The conflicts that already exist will be aggravated, but oil companies aren't stopped by social conflicts."

That's not necessarily true anymore. Take the fracking example. Fracking has been banned, or restricted with moratoriums, in Germany, France, Bulgaria, the Netherlands, Scotland and Wales, with other countries taking it under serious consideration. In the United States, several little towns around mine have banned fracking (though not yet mine. Not yet), a trend happening regionally across the country. Vermont and New York are the first to institute a complete ban statewide (which was later overturned by the state governments, but that's just a matter of resolve). So sometimes oil companies are stopped by social conflicts. Keep heart Chiapas.

We should also care because they are the one social experiment of their kind in the world, and there may be much that we can learn from their experiment. Unlike some of the other political movements in Latin America, they aren't advocates of communism, but neither are they completely free enterprise. They are close to, but still not completely a "third way" as has been adopted in Scandinavia, either. They are experimenting with a blend of modern economics and their traditional ways. Critics complain that we can't learn anything from them because conditions of the experiment are too unusual, too difficult to repeat anywhere else. But that strikes me as a particularly unimaginative response.

How's the experiment going, you ask? Well, after years of empty promises and 'death-by-bureaucratic-dialogue' the Zapatista took a slight hiatus from public view, much to the disappointment of many who had pinned their hopes on the movement's success and misinterpreted silence as surrender.

Just because they weren't making headlines didn't mean they weren't making strides. Chiapas remains the poorest of Mexico's 31 states with 75% of the population considered poor and a third living in extreme poverty – by *Mexico's* standards. That's pretty intense. At the same time many campesinos who were landless before the revolution now have land (course that land was seized and taken from other families, who originally took the land from____who originally took the land from____, who originally…to infinitum. The world has been cycles of land grabs since it began, and almost everybody's had a turn, but that's another discussion).

Tired of waiting for help from without, they decided to draw the help they needed from within. Zapatista's have taken their current territory and set up five caracoles (autonomous municipal jurisdictions) where they set about forming their own systems, independent of the Mexican government. At the entrance to the caracoles signs were placed that read, "You are entering Zapatista territory: Here the people rule and the government obeys."

The name caracole means snail, the symbol that has been chosen to represent their movement. As I understand it, this is because the humble little snail knows he moves at a different speed from those around him and by extraordinarily different means, but nonetheless moves patiently, with faith, to reach its destination. Its shell spirals both inward and outward, from the center of the heart. Outward and back, away from the more destructive aspects of capitalism, and towards a connection with their deepest roots. Inward as they experiment, evolve and explore new ideas. It also symbolizes their awareness that their journey will not be a quick one.

They've formed a two-tiered government: a regional government called the Council of Good Governance and then the governments of the five individual caracoles. The leaders are elected locally and each caracole governs themselves, including resolving conflicts and handling crimes or issues with drug trafficking, where it is said they have had surprisingly great success. A police force (possibly funded by roadside tourist dollars) stands at every entrance into their towns and they enforce a zero-tolerance policy, banishing or jailing every criminal.

Despite a preference for non-violent resistance, aside from a few isolated incidents, they maintain a standing army, who patrol their villages at night, armed primarily with discipline and sticks. They have set up their own health clinics, using a blend of traditional medicine shared from their grandmothers and western medicine shared by nurses and doctors who come to volunteer and teach, but then learn.

They've established schools in the same way, blends of tradition and modern. Much of their funding for these projects come from—you'll never guess where? Coffee cooperatives! (Again, shade grown and rainforest alliance coffees and chocolates make great gifts!)

They've accomplished all of this despite being continuously harassed and terrorized by paramilitary groups, driven from their homes and enduring the kind of "low-intensity conflict" discussed in Chapter 9. All throughout they steadfastly resisted, with or without media coverage, and occasionally surfaced for specific statements. Like at the end of the world.

Remember all the end of the world hoopla way back in December of 2012? December 21, 2012 was the last day of the last cycle of the Mayan calendar. Because the Maya were the only known Pre-Columbian American civilization to have a fully developed written system for math and science, because they used these to accomplish incredible engineering feats, because they studied the stars and seemed to make some sense of them, there are those who credit them not with being observant and making good use of their time, but with supernatural capabilities...like seeing into the future.

This belief was somehow combined with a supposed ancient Sumerian prediction about a probably fictional planet, called Niburu, that was supposed to collide with Earth in May of 2003. When that day came and went with no catastrophic BAM, the prediction's proponents said, "Oops! My bad. Miscalculated!" and after more creative calculating decided that the actual date was December 21, 2012. Coincidentally this was also the last date calculated in the Mayan calendar. Except it wasn't, because the calendar didn't end. It rolled over. That part was left out of the doomsday prediction.

The Long Count Calendar is designed on a vigesimal, a "modified base-20 system in which rotating digits represent powers of 20 days. Because the digits rotate, the calendar can "roll over" and repeat itself."xxxviii The date was significant, but not a prediction for the end of the world.

There's actually been nothing found in any of the thousands of Mayan tablets, ruins or works of art that suggest an end of the world. That didn't stop the media from stirring everyone up and posting apocalyptic headlines to the point that even those of us who thought it was all a bunch of hooey, still felt just the *teensiest* bit apprehensive as that day approached.

If you take a look at NASA's website leading up to December 21, 2012, you can actually read (and you should. It's pretty funny) their frustration at the theories traction compounding in their daily increasingly blatant sarcastic posts attempting to assure anyone who would listen that the world was not, in fact, ending.[xxxix]

You remember, right? There were end of the world parties and end of the world t-shirts for sale in commemoration. For my part, like I said, I had a teensy bit of apprehension, but mostly I'd concluded that perhaps the Mayans simply picked that day to stop calculating, assuming 2000 years was far enough and future Mayans could pick up where they left off and calculate on. I didn't know about the roll over at the time.

Meanwhile, the actual descendants of the Mayans who made that calendar seemed to expect the world to keep on spinning and had prepared a statement for the day. On December 21st, forty thousand Zapatistas, their faces covered in their signature bandana's and balaclavas, walked in such total silence you would easily have heard the rain that was falling on them as they marched—if not for all the shouts of encouragement coming from spectators.

They marched into the city centers of Palenque, Ocosingo, Altamirano, Las Margaritas, and San Cristobal De Las Casas, peacefully occupying these city centers for several hours. Their demonstrations were to celebrate the end of the calendar cycle, but was also in commemoration of the 19th anniversary of the revolutionary eruption in 1994 and the Christmas massacre in Acteal (see Chapter 9). They celebrated the successes of their movement and announced a six-point action plan for the years to come, which included continued friendships and partnerships with other groups who are also working towards better lives and representation for the poor and disenfranchised. They called once more for the government to honor the long unfulfilled terms of the San Andres Accords. In the meantime, they're doing their best to achieve the Accords goals on their own. At a commemoration for a fallen comrade, Subcommandante Marcos said:

"Rather than dedicating ourselves to training guerrillas, soldiers, and squadrons, we developed education and health promoters, who went about building the foundations of autonomy that today amaze the world. Instead of constructing barracks, improving our weapons, and building walls and trenches, we built schools, hospitals and health centers; improving our living conditions."

The commemoration was in honor of Josè Luis Solis López, a Zapatista teacher who used the name Galleano as an alias. Galleano was shot during an attack from the Central Agricultural Workers and Peasants-Historical (CIOAC-H), a group supported by right wing political groups. The Zapatista had detained one of CIOAC-H's leaders after he was discovered on Zapatista territory. In retaliation the group came in, destroyed a school, a health clinic and several other buildings and left Galleano dead and 15 others injured. "Who is Galleano?" Marcos called out to the crowd. "WE ARE ALL GALLEANO!" They called back to him.

At the same commemoration, Marcos also announced that he no longer existed, in fact, had never existed other than as a hologram for the media. But he was much more than that.

Someone had to know how 'the system' worked. Someone had to help the Indigenous communities understand the most effective ways to accomplish their goals, the sheer scope and capability of their adversaries. The seeming madness. And it does seem like madness: A system that requires enormous consumption of natural resources, through processes that poison the land, water and air, in exceptional, excessive amounts that changes the very climate of the planet; that leaves some starving while allowing others to throw away half the food they buy; with homes so crowded with crap they have reality shows about them; that compels its participants to buy the latest of everything in a frenzied, soul-depleting competition that results in no real winners? Madness.

It would be one thing if the people who always have to have more play only amongst themselves, but to create a system that only allows people to survive if they participate in the same game is sort of diabolical, isn't it? What would Gandal-Claus think?

I understand that many advances that have been made may only have been possible under some form of capitalism. If you ask me if I think the world has improved as a result of capitalism? Yes, it most certainly has and I agree that it would have been difficult to accomplish as much under a different system. Do I think it's time for something else? Yes, I think perhaps it is. Do I have an exact idea of what that looks like? Nope. No idea. But we won't find it unless we start experimenting with some new ideas.

That's part of what's happening in Chiapas. A people in search of a different way for themselves, and possibly finding some answers that might work for us all. Not all the answers, but perhaps a piece or two. A start.

Don't get me wrong. I don't think they've got themselves a little Utopia going on down there. They still have plenty of kinks to work out as well, and they're not exactly monks. In 2011, 17 tourists were kidnapped near Agua Azul as part of a confrontation between Zapatista sympathizers and the government-aligned farmers. The tourists were eventually released unharmed but one farmer was left dead and seven people were missing. They just disappeared.

Drug trafficking is yet another challenge facing the Zapatista. United States and Mexican efforts to curb drug trafficking by air and sea have forced drug cartels to transport by land so the drug cartels are now encroaching into the jungle, and more military and police are being sent into the area to combat the drug cartels. The Zapatistas have been accused of either being in cahoots with or outright being the drug cartels. I don't know about that. Either way Chiapas hasn't faced nearly the amount of drug-related violence as other parts of Mexico and there are fewer murders in the state of Chiapas than in many U.S. cities like Chicago, or New York, and certainly less than my home town of Memphis, Tennessee.

And people still die from curable diseases. But they've made tremendous progress. And nobody is giving up.

The Maya youth are taking the ground gained by their parents and grandparents and expanding it. And they aren't doing it by letting go of their traditional ways and joining the mainstream. They're embracing and reviving their cultures, especially through art and music.

Long an instrument, so to speak, of the oppressed, Hip Hop emerged during the 1970s Civil Rights Movement in the United States. You might even say it energized the movement and continued to give voice to the oppressed, through the 1990s.

The 90s are considered a spectacular time for Hip Hop's use as a form of social activism, with figures like Public Enemy, Tupac Shakur, and Hip Hop Metal blend, Rage Against the Machine. These groups used their music as vehicles to speak out against oppression, to encourage their listeners to question even their own norms. Tupac Shakur (named by his Black Panther mother after an 18th century Incan leader who rebelled against the Spanish), spoke out against domestic violence and disrespecting women, among other social concerns. Public Enemy spoke out about inequality, and in particular, the plight of the Black Man in America. Rage Against the Machine used their music to back several movements and address social issues globally. They wrote songs to spread awareness and used profits from their concerts to fund social organizations like U.N.I.T.E., Women Alive and…the Zapatista Front for National Liberation. Lead singer for Rage Against the Machine, Zack de la Rocha, visited Chiapas and helped write several songs on the Zapatista struggle, including "People of the Sun," "Wind Below," "Zapata's Blood," and "War Within a Breath."

Many critics say that American Hip Hop ain't what it used to be and the bravery in music that defined the 90s doesn't exist today. They say that record labels won't endorse conscious rap, that is, rap that has deeper messages than drinking gin and juice, driving expensive cars, wearing jewels, and shallow crap like that. That's not every modern rap artist, but there's no hiding the truth that rap is no longer the voice of the oppressed. At least not in main stream America. But Hip Hop is still living up to its legacy. You can find dedicated artists and warriors performing on social platforms like SunCloud, OurStage or YouTube. That's where you'll find current Zapatista supporters like Emcee Killa and Grim Reaperz, who released their video "Zapatista," a powerful track of inspiring images and lyrics, in 2015. Take a look.

Rap has also become a strong part of reviving and celebrating the culture of Chiapas and the Indigenous Mexico world. Maya rapper Pat Boy Rap Maya, encourages fellow natives to reclaim their culture. His name is taken from a Maya word that means, to create something new, and for his part of the world, he has. When he first started rapping, his village in the Yucatan Peninsula of Mexico had said he was wasting his time. Now others are following in his footsteps, and his own resume is three albums deep.

Balam Ajpu, is my current favorite. Originally from Guatemala, Balam Ajpu's Hip Hop is startling. The first song I heard began with the hoarse bellow of a howler monkey, which, as you might remember, sounds precisely like an aggressive jaguar in the middle of the night when it's over your palapa.

Then the music begins and it's a beautiful piece of music, but definitely not what you initially think of as hip hop. But keep listening. Native flutes, drums, and maracas invoke images of jungles and ancient palaces, then the spoken word merges and you can feel the power in the voices, deep in the center of your being, and you have no choice but to turn to the speaker (pun intended) with reverent attention. Sometimes rapped in Spanish, but most often in Tz'utujil, one of the 22 native languages of Guatemala and Chiapas. This is not Tupac's Hip Hop, but it's powerful and moving. Literally. I'm bid to dance before I realize what I'm doing.

Balam Apju, which means Jaguar Warriors, creates music that is an evolution of Hip Hop. In contrast to many other Hip Hop groups whose sound, while it may be good, is almost indistinguishable from U.S. groups or each other, Balam Apju has a sound distinctly their own, distinctly Maya, and it's powerful. Their first album, *Tributo a los 20 Narwals*, is strongly spiritual. Their plans for the next album are to focus on social and political issues. I wish I spoke Tz'utujil, but I don't have to. The power and the intention comes through the language barrier, no problem.

So what happens for Chiapas now? La Lucha Segue – the fight

continues.

Todos somos Marcos. Todos somos Moisès. Todos somos Americanos. Todos somos Mexicanos. Somos todos los pueblos de la tierra.

Chapter 17: Kidnapped!

"We must be willing to let go of the life we have planned, so as to have the life that is waiting for us."

Joseph Campbell

It was my last night in Chiapas and Francisco and I were swinging in our hammocks, swapping jokes after another day of touring the ruins. We'd spent all day seeing every last nook and cranny we could before the park closed, then came back to camp hot, dirty and tired and jumped into the pool.

It was still murky, but after way too many days without soap and shampoo, I was kind of murky myself. It was also blood boiling hot that day. The weather had taken a definitive turn and everyone and everything seemed to droop under the heat and humidity. Fallen fruit and vegetation in the jungle fermented, filling the hot hair with a pungent, stale-beer smell. Rare breezes from the cow field across the road wafted over a pungent smell of animal urine and rotting fruit.

Francisco had been hitting the pool every day and didn't appear to have any rashes or strange growths on him so I'd decided, *'Well what the heck. It's bloody hot!'*

I'd first tried it the day before. It had been the hottest day since I'd arrived. It was so hot it gave the Mississippi Delta a run for its 'most-miserable-climate-EVER-in-July' rating. We'd returned from a hike and I'd felt like my blood was boiling under my skin faster than it could be sweated out. We got to the pool and I jumped in with all of my clothes on. It felt divine. After a few minutes, the groundskeeper came up to us, pointed to a sign by the pool, then said something too fast for me to understand and I looked to Francisco. He smiled and nodded back to the man and said, "Si, gracias," then turned to me and asked, "¿Usted Entiende esto?" He said, asking if I'd understood what the man said.

"No, muy ràpido." I responded. (too fast).

Francisco laughed, "This you will love. He said the pool rule is that you have to wear a bathing suit. He said you need to put on a bathing suit to be in the pool."

I looked at him in disbelief, "Are you kidding me? My feet are literally sliding on the slimy scum growing on the bottom of this pool, but I've offended the dress code? And what about you?" I asked, indignantly. "You don't need one?"

"These are swim trunks, bella." he chuckled. "You see? I am always prepared."

Two older women lying in pool chairs started laughing. "The boys just want to see you in a bikini!" laughed a woman with a toned physique, a head full of silver hair and an easy going smile. "Do you have one?" she asked

"I do!" I replied. "You're American?" I asked, excited to hear pure English for the first time in forever.

"Minnesota." she answered. "You?"

"Colorado!" I said proudly.

"What on earth are *you* doing *here*?" she laughed. "Go get your swim suit and I'll buy a round of margaritas and you can tell me all about it!" she offered.

Susan and Theresa, were both yoga instructors from Minnesota (or so they said). They'd been best friends since they were kids and they'd been taking trips like this together all of their lives. Over several pitchers of margaritas they shared some of their wilder travel stories that had us alternately laughing in stitches or on the edges of our seats. I'd never met women like this before. I made a mental note that I'd found my role models.

Turned out they had actually been brave enough to rent a car which they were DRIVING around Chiapas. After hearing my tale of financial woe, they offered to give me a lift into town the next morning, let me try my credit card and bring me back right after.

In hindsight, accepting an offer that seemed too good to be true isn't usually the wisest choice, but I was so eager to see if my credit card worked, to put to rest the long anticipated question of whether or not I'd be spending the night sleeping in an airport chair or in a hotel bed, that I chanced it. We found an ATM and they dropped me off and said they had some business to attend to but they'd be back in an hour. For all I know, they were really drug lords, they seemed rather well-heeled for yoga instructors. Meeting them gave me a completely unrealistic vision of where I could take my yoga teaching. I've certainly never made enough money to go globetrotting. They also seemed fearless in a special forces kind of way.

The ATM was housed in a small, glass-fronted room with a cracked tile floor strewn with crushed cigarette butts and empty corn chip wrappers. It smelled like eau de ashtray and urine. I walked up to the ATM, surveying it nervously. I'd never used one before. Fortunately, there were instructions in both English and Spanish. Someone else came in the ATM room with me and I glanced over my shoulder to see if I was about to be mugged. I suspiciously eyed a short woman with long dark hair pulled back in a ponytail. She glanced and smiled politely, then opened a book while she waited.

I painstakingly followed the directions, grateful the girl waiting had a book to enjoy while she waited. When a thin metal door slid open and shuffled a stack of pesos my way, I almost jumped up and down, like I'd won the lottery, but decided that might appear suspicious, so I calmly took the money, folded some away in my money belt and folded the rest to put in my pocket.

The first thing I did was go to a nearby café and order la comida del dia, the food of the day. It may have been that, other than lunch at Agua Azul with Francisco, this was the first non-tunafish meal I'd had in a very long time, or it may very well have been that it was the absolute best thing I'd ever eaten.

It turned out to be a kind of chicken mole with chili peppers, mushrooms, beans, cocoa and rice. It was so good I wanted to audibly groan orgasmically with every bite, but I contained myself. I scraped my plate clean and washed it all down with a Negro Modelo.

My that my belly was now round like a pumpkin, what was next on the agenda for a lady of leisure like myself awaiting her ride back to camp? Why shopping, of course! I'm not a big shopper. Never having much money to spare I'd never really developed the habit, and I was pretty careful about what I did spend on, so I was in no danger of blowing my new gain frivolously. I had a pretty short list of wish items: A memento to capture the flavor of the experience, perhaps. A new outfit so I might actually have something I felt pretty in for my last couple of days. A token of gratitude for Francisco's friendship, especially since I knew he'd never allow me to pay him back for all the beers, transportation costs and park entrance fees.

I strolled down a street lined on either side with canvas tents filled with goods.

Many of the tents offered the same hand-made crafts, but with wildly differing costs for the same items. Some of the stores distinguished themselves by specializing in paintings or clothing or hand polished wood products, etc. I liked the kind looks of one proprietor who offered a variety of Chiapan handmade crafts and went into his tent. It was sort of a Chiapan General Store. A little of everything. There were beautiful carved wood bowls, cups, figurines, colorful shirts, pants, cloth purses, and basically anything else that could be made just down the street.

He had an authentic smile, and bright eyes. I exchanged a few polite pleasantries in Spanish, then I bought a pair of pants similar to ones I had seen a couple of other women wearing earlier that I had liked. They wrapped around almost like a skirt, but instead wrapped around and somehow formed two wide legs. They were brilliant white cotton embroidered on each hip with blue flowers. I also bought a beautiful, blue and white cloth bag with a weave similar to that of other local cloths I'd seen.

Then I moved on down the row of canvas kiosks. One kiosk was full of the most mesmerizing and whimsical toys made of wood and cloths. There were marionette's that hung, grinning from their handlebars; carved frogs and lizards that chirped when you rubbed their backs with a special wooden wand; and puzzle boxes with hidden compartments. I loved them, but I was so used to extreme frugality I couldn't justify them at the time. Wish I had.

Finally, I found a tent that was full of leather wallets, purses, vests, belts and leather bound journals. The workmanship was beautiful and the leather was soft and supple. The smell of rich leather filled the tent. I found a dark-leather bound journal engraved on the front with a wide branching tree that I felt had a decidedly masculine appeal. It had an inside pocket for stashing small mementos like ticket stubs or notes. I decided to buy it for Francisco as a token of how much I appreciated our friendship. I brought the journal up to my nose and smiled as I breathed in the rich, spicy suede aroma.

I met Susan and Theresa in front of the ATM kiosk and headed back to the campground, excitedly chattering about how unafraid I'd been, how exciting it was to shop and barter and how good the food was. I must have seemed like such a child to them. They were very good natured about it and shared some travel tips with me…one of which was warning me off of Francisco.

"It's a romantic culture," Susan warned, "he probably means no harm, but don't be disappointed if the relationship doesn't go anywhere."

I shook my head, "You've got the wrong idea." I said, "We're just friends."

Susan looked into the rearview mirror and locked her green eyes on my blues, "Are you sure I'm the one who's got the wrong idea?"

When we got back to the campground, I thanked them profusely for the ride and for the advice then headed back to my camp to show off my new clothes.

As I walked back to my palapa, Francisco was coming my way with Janez and Hasid.

"Hola, Doña!" he exclaimed. He turned to Hasid and Janez, "You guys go ahead. We'll catch up." When they were gone, his smile became anxious as he asked, "How did it go?"

I smiled, "How do you like my pants?" I said turning around, to model.

He smiled, dropping his head back and closing his eyes, "GRACIAS A DIOS!" he shouted to the sky in obvious relief. "It worked! I was afraid I was going to have to dip into my savings and escort you back to your own country!" he admitted.

I reached out and put my hand on his arm, "Would you really have done that?" I asked, deeply touched.

He stared at me, mildly surprised and asked, "What could I have done? Let you hitch hike all the way back to Villahermosa and sleep at the airport?" For a moment he looked embarrassed, then he shook his head and took me by my hand pulling me down the walkway. "Come on," he said, "One last tour of the park."

And then it was that night. There we were swinging in our hammocks, laughing at each other's jokes trying to one-up each other on adventure stories. I'd bought a round or three of beers and we were oblivious to the fireflies starting to sparkle and the frogs starting to croak, announcing the fall of dusk. The sky turned a pale blue, then slowly darkened. I thought about giving him the journal before we fell asleep, but I didn't want to break the fun vibe we had going. Then there was a pause in our conversation as we quietly watched the fireflies signaling each other in the jungle around us.

"Donna?" Francisco murmured.

"Yessss?" I drawled.

"I like you. You know that. ¿Verdad?" He asked in a soft voice.

My heart started racing. I had an idea of where he was going with this. My first thought was of Susan's warning.

"Absolutely," I answered, trying to sound nonchalant. "I like you, too."

Then Francisco got out of his hammock and came to stand over mine. He stood so close his legs touched mine as he looked down at me. I was painfully aware of the warmth where our legs touched, and I was speechless looking up into his eyes. Darkness was falling but there was still a enough light to see everything clearly, but it was the mystical light of dusk. Just enough light left that we could see the shine of each other's eyes.

"No," he said, "I mean, I *like* you." Then he reached his fingers towards me and grazed them against my cheek, then softly under my chin. "Much more than I was supposed to," he said almost in a whisper.

I sat frozen, yet electrified. My breath quickened. On the one hand, I wanted to...respond. I wanted to let him touch me. I wanted to feel his body, his lips pressed on mine. But there was the oath I'd taken. There was what Susan had said. There was the vast number of terrifying sexually transmittable miseries lurking in the world. There was the fact that I believed casual sex diminished the potential mystical power of sex when it happens between two people who really love each other. There was the fact that I was leaving the next day and he lived in Argentina and I in Colorado and there was no time to cultivate such love.

I took his hand and held it against my cheek, and looking into his eyes, whispered, "I can't. I'm sorry."

He sighed, "You don't like me in that way?"

I shook my head, "I do. But," I hesitated, "...this can't go anywhere and this is one place in my life where I have to be careful. I don't sleep with anyone I'm not deeply committed to, which isn't possible for us."

"It's just a kiss," he shrugged, smiling invitingly.

I laughed softly, "My fear is that it would turn into much more than a kiss."

"I don't want to say, goodbye," he said earnestly, fingers once more brushing lightly against my cheek.

"I don't either." I said, "But we will. You know the distance between our homes is too great and I've just gotten out of a relationship that I'm not sure is really over and ...." I faltered.

He put his hand on the back of my head and firmly, but gently pulled me towards him..and placed his lips against my forehead, "I will never forget you, Bella Donna." he said, then turned to his hammock..

"Nor will I forget you," I whispered, deep in turmoil.

I lay awake for what seemed like hours, wrestling with my various personality facets. There was the girl who wanted to carpe diem and reach eagerly for every wondrous experience that presented itself, to drink fully and deeply from the cup of life; this girl believed in magic and true love with a childlike devotion and was agonizing over whether this was a life-changing moment and true love might be lying in a hammock two feet away, but perhaps I was too suspicious or blind to see it. Then there was the girl who'd been on her own since she was sixteen and fully understood the potentially painful consequences of a wrong decision here. In the end, I decided to stay true to my oath and in my own hammock, believing that when true love arrived, I'd know it, and there would be no doubts. No hesitations.

The next morning, I awoke to find Francisco was already up and off somewhere, just as he had been every morning I'd woken up at the Maya Bell. I went and rinsed off at the showers for the last time, then packed up my pack and took my hammock back to the front desk. There was still no sign of Francisco, but I ran into Susan and Theresa again and they had generously offered to give me a ride to the bus station in Palenque, where I could get a direct bus back to Villahermosa. Susan asked where my special friend was and I told her he was gone when I woke up. She asked if anything had happened and I looked away and said, "No. But almost."

She laughed, in a knowing way I found irritating and said, "Yea, they can be very persuasive."

I didn't say anything. I didn't want to admit to either of us that Francisco may have been a Casanova. I couldn't believe that. I wanted to believe that he wasn't there that morning because it would be too painful to say goodbye. That's the way that I felt. I didn't necessarily think I was falling in love, but we had shared so much in such a short period. The friendship had formed deep, fast and intense. I didn't want to believe its main mojo was purely sexually motivated.

I decided to take the journal to the front office and leave it there for him in case he came back. I wrote a note telling him how much I enjoyed our time together and hinting a possible future trip to Argentina someday, because, who knows? I wrote my work address because I thought it might be more stable than my rental house address, then tore out a page, wrote his name in big letters and tucked it under the flap of the book. I handed it to the desk clerk asking in better-but-still-halting Spanish if he would see that Francisco got it. He smiled sympathetically and assured me he would.

I saw Susan and Theresa waiting by their car and started walking over. Susan had an angry, clinched-jaw expression and I wondered why. Until I came around a bend and ran smack dab into Francisco. He was talking with a newly arrived mochila (girl backpacker). There was a palpable awkwardness to this meeting that surprised me, as though I'd just caught him cheating on me. He obviously felt something, too, because he looked down in a way, I thought, as though he'd been caught doing something awful, a quite weird reaction given that nothing had happened between us. Nothing sexual anyway. The girl seemed especially embarrassed and stuttered out a hello in a European accent.

Francisco, gallant as ever, excused himself from the girl, and we stood facing each other with this nonsensical, bizarre sense of betrayal hanging in the air. It was weird, I felt jealous and hurt that it seemed he was moving on so quickly, but why shouldn't he? After all, we hadn't so much as shared a kiss. He was still in adventure mode and life was short. I silently thanked God we hadn't gone farther, while also understanding I had no right to feel the way that I did.

"That wasn't as it appeared," he started.

I rolled my eyes, and shook my head, "You don't owe me anything. You know, you have every right. You're still on the adventure. I'm heading back, nothing happened between us. It makes perfect sense that…" I faltered.

He put his hand on my arm and moved his head so he could look me deeply in the eyes, "It's not like that." He said.

To my own surprise, a tear rolled down my cheek and I felt the choking sensations of an approaching sob. I quickly wiped the tear away, then motioned towards Susan and Theresa, "I have to go. Susan and Theresa are giving me a ride to the bus station in Palenque."

He looked pained. He threw his arms around me and hugged me and I felt more tears run down my face, which I found infuriating. I pushed him away.

"It wasn't like that, Donna. This has been…so special. Extraordinario," he said, taking both of my hands in his. "I will *never* forget you."

My shoulders dropped, and I looked back into his eyes. I could feel he meant what he said.

I smiled and whispered, "Yes it has." I was so relieved that I could take this memory back with me, beautiful and unmarred.

I took a deep breath and shook myself, "I have to go. My bus in Palenque leaves in fifteen minutes. I left something for you at the front desk, okay?" I reached over and wrapped my arms around him, wanting to melt into him as he wrapped his strong arms around me. "I am so glad to have met you," I wept. I forced myself to pull away, then I hurried down the walk way towards the car. I looked back and Francisco was still standing there watching me, a look of grief on his face.

When I got to the car, Susan stopped and put a hand on my shoulder, "Hey," she said. "I was wrong. It wasn't like I thought. Okay?"

I smiled through tears and nodded, "I know."

They dropped me off in the town of Palenque where we exchanged addresses and promises to stay in touch and tour the world together, though we've never connected since. My bus left Palenque within five minutes after they dropped me off and went directly to Villahermosa with only a couple of stops. Much faster than the bus I rode at the beginning of my trip. I was lucky and got a seat by the window. A middle-aged woman in a long black skirt and beautifully embroidered white blouse took the seat next to mine. I smiled and said, "Buenas Dias," but then spent the rest of the ride looking out the window, thinking about my adventure and wondering if I made the right call.

The bus arrived in Villahermosa just as the sun was disappearing behind the tips of the tallest Ceiba trees, the last of its rays spraying through their branchless trunks, just under the umbrella of their broad canopies. The station swarmed with people, and the shouts of drivers calling passengers to their buses filled the air. Absolute chaos. This setting that had been so frightening to me just recently, greeted a different woman returning. One who wasn't afraid and felt more sure of herself, more optimistic about the people around her...and who spoke more of the language than when she'd ridden the bus out. I stood beside the bus waiting for my backpack, marveling at how I'd felt the first time I'd stood beside the bus near Palenque, when I felt so small and vulnerable. Then, I suspected everyone I saw was secretly thinking of robbing me. But now I saw a man with a good heart and a family to care for, just doing his job. He handed me my backpack and I handed him a few pesos and said, "Gracias," as casually as if this was what and how I did things every day.

The setting sun reminded me of the admonition to stay off the streets of Villahermosa after sunset so I shouldered my pack and headed to the front entrance to catch a taxi. A taxi pulled to the curb just a little ways in front of me and I hurried towards it, but then I heard someone behind me shouting.

"¡Oye! ¿Que pasa?" an angry woman shouted, and somehow, I intuitively knew it was directed at me. I turned to see a small, pretty woman with long curly black hair and eyes lined with dark liner, glaring at me.

I shouted back, "¿Que? What?" She started speaking angrily, and too fast for me to understand, until she pointed over her shoulder at the long line I hadn't noticed when I walked out. A long line of people all glaring at me. My eyes grew wide with obvious surprise and I said, "Oh. ¡Lo Siento! (I'm sorry.)" I shouted. "¡Escupa! (excuse me)." And began walking to the back of the line.

The woman's face immediately transformed from a snarl to kindness and she laughed good naturedly, as did many other people in the line. My face was bright red. As I walked, I noticed a few still had snarls on their face, but they no longer frightened me. When I looked directly at them, smiled genuinely and nodded, they dropped their snarl and smiled back. I'd cracked the code!

As I stood in line, the sun dripped below the horizon, setting the sky on fire with brilliant pinks, yellows, oranges and reds streaking across the sky, while in the opposite direction, it was morphing through different stages of blue and stars were emerging on the lower end of the sky. The falling dusk pressed out the last vapors of day.

I considered how close I really was to the Best Western, where'd I'd called from Palenque to make a reservation. A fitting place, I thought, to stay my final night. And they had a shuttle to the airport. Effortless trip finale. I was really looking forward to a little pampering.

The line waiting for taxis was moving painfully slow. It was only a few blocks to the hotel and it looked like it might take an hour to get a cab with the long line. *Why am I in line at all*, I asked myself, *I know my way to the hotel?*

I thought of the *Lonely Planet* Thorn Tree Forum person who'd said, no matter what, take a cab if it's after sunset.

I looked to the sky and its stark contrast gazing from east to west, deducing whether this would be considered after sunset or not. One thing was for sure, it wasn't getting any earlier, nor did the line appear to be getting any shorter. With my new found confidence I decided to hell with it, I was sure I was so close to my hotel I should almost be able to see it. I could make it before full dark fell, I concluded.

I lurched forward, throwing the pack fully onto my hip bones, and resolutely walked out of the line. The gap quickly closed behind me, and I set off down the sidewalk. I turned left and found myself on a street that was completely empty except for a man sitting on a bench talking on a cell phone. Amazing. When I'd walked this way a week ago, there'd barely been room to get me and my pack through the clog of people.

I liked the peace of it. It gave me a chance to really see the buildings on either side of the street, some of which were covered with beautiful murals of rural life. The man on the phone finished his call and stood up slipping the phone into his pocket and turned to walk in my direction. He had curly black and gray hair, a dark mustache and a paunch belly hanging over spindly legs. He seemed to be in a fabulous mood as he shouted out, "Palenque! Palenque!" He weaved slightly from side to side, obviously inebriated. Somehow he knew that I was coming from or going to Palenque. That must be the main reason gringos are credited with coming to Villahermosa. I smiled and nodded, feeling a sense of traveler's pride I didn't really deserve, as if I'd just come back from leading Livingston through the Congo.

My approacher said something else that I didn't understand and I smiled, but waved him away with a "No gracias," meaning "no thank you, I don't need a guide/drugs/tour or anything else you might be selling." He correctly deduced I didn't have a full grasp of the language, because he said something else, waved for me to stop as he took a phone out of his pocket, and well, I didn't want to be rude, so I stopped. He held up one finger, motioning me to wait as he spoke into the phone.

As he came closer, I could see his bloodshot eyes and smell the booze easily as he stopped less than two feet from me, a little too close for comfort, but again, I didn't want to appear rude. He smiled in a way that made me distinctly uncomfortable and said, "Soy tu Amigo! (I am your friend)." He slurred when he spoke and his glassy eyes conveyed something other than friendship. The hair on the back of my neck stood up. Words of advice: anyone who announces themselves as your friend, probably isn't. As soon as he said that I knew I'd made a mistake in stopping. I just didn't know how big of a mistake.

I smiled, trying to convey kindness and once again said, "No gracias." As I turned to move passed him, I waved my hand as Francisco had taught me to do with assertive vendors, but when I did this, he shot out his hand and quickly locked strong fingers around my wrist. He moved quicker than I would have expected for someone I had been certain was too inebriated to hardly walk.

His fingers closed around my arm in a painful vice grip that I couldn't pull away from and now he was saying something to me in a low growl with a crystal clear demeanor. He wasn't drunk. He wasn't drunk at all. He glanced up the road where a van had just turned the corner and gave them a wave. Turning back to me he growled something menacingly low, without the slightest trace of slurring. I pulled at my arm but he held it fast as though I'd barely moved. For a moment I just stood frozen in shock and confusion. The van was boxed in by cars at a red light but that wouldn't be for long. I knew I had to get away before that van reached us.

I frantically looked around me, searching for anything or anyone that could help. I spotted a small crowd coming up the road, perhaps others braving the roads when faced with the extremely long taxi queue. Among them I saw a family with a mother, a father and four children. I looked into the eyes of the mother and she met my gaze. Somehow she grasped immediately what was happening. I saw the concern in her eyes. She said something to her family.

The light changed in the other direction and the van started pulling towards us, only a few blocks away now. From the other direction, the family approached us and with complete nonchalance kept walking straight into us as though we weren't taking up the middle of the side walk. Three of the children wrapped themselves around me and kept walking with me without the slightest pause. The villain was distracted enough to relax his grip so I yanked and twisted my arm free and, just like that, I had been scooped away by the small children, and then the older child, mother and father closed in behind us, blocking us off from the booze-smelling villain. I heard someone, I'm not sure who, actually say, "Disculpe, por favor (excuse me, please)."

It was surreal. We all just kept walking, as if nothing was happening. We just walked away, leaving the man standing dumbfounded on the sidewalk.

The van stopped and the side door slid open. The boozy villain jumped inside and they drove off. I kept walking with the family so shaken I could barely speak. I'd just been kidnapped,

Yes, it was for less than five minutes, but still. That could have gone very, very wrong for me. This family saw what was going on and they could have crossed the street so as not to get involved, but they didn't. They walked right into us and scooped me away as if I were gum accidentally stuck to the bottom of one of their shoes. I stumbled with them, grasping for the right words. I was chanting, "Muchas gracias. Muchas gracias. Muchas gracias." Without turning to look at them, but loud enough that they heard. The mother squeezed my arm and I took her hand and squeezed it trying to convey the depth of my emotion, once again relying on body language to communicate for what I had no words.

The mother smiled and nodded. We kept walking fast, as if we weren't out of the woods yet. "¿Adonde Va?" She asked (Where are you going?)" That one I now knew, so I answered, "Best Western."

She nodded as we approached the next block and she pointed to the familiar sign, the entrance, just half a block away. I looked over my shoulder and there was no sign of the van, nor the sinister man. The family continued walking quickly away, "Vaya con Dios (Go with God)." The mother said.

"Tu tambien. Vaya con Dios. Muchas Gracias (You too. Go with God. Thank you so much)." I said, then turned and ran to the hotel, stumbling up the steps and rushing through the doors, panting hard. Safe.

I was ecstatic to see the familiar face of José, the same clerk who seemed to always be on duty when I was here before. He smiled an enthusiastic welcome to me, "Bienvenida de vuelta, Ms. -----. ¿Como fue su viaje?" (Welcome back! How was your trip?)

I appreciated his enthusiasm at seeing me, especially as my appearance hadn't improved after many days in the jungle without a real shower.

"¡Buenas noche, Josè! ¡Bien, muchas gracias!" I wanted to hug him! I flipped through my book as he checked me in looking for something about toiletries, then I asked, "Disculpe Josè, ¿Hay champu in la cuarta? Mina fue robado en la selva (Excuse me Jose, Is there shampoo in the room? Mine was stolen in the jungle.")

Josè burst out laughing and nodded with an expression of 'that explains a lot,' "Si, claro." He said, still laughing.

He picked up the phone and said something too quickly for me to completely understand, though I did catch a few words I recognized from the list of toiletries I'd just read in the guide book, like jabon, champu, acondicionador, and cepillo de pelo (soap, shampoo, conditioner and hair brush). I must have smelled to high heaven. My scary encounter followed by a run with a heavy pack on my back probably didn't help much.

While he was checking me in I saw a beautiful white blouse in the window of the hotel gift shop and thought it would go really well with the pants I'd purchased in Palenque the day before so I asked Josè to add them to my bill. He nodded with a smile and handed me my room card. I rushed to my room, threw my pack on the floor and took a very long, a very hot, bath before dinner. When I came down to dinner, Josè smiled and nodded approvingly at my transformed appearance, except for my clunky yoga-mama-Buddha-sandals, which seemed a bit at odds with the rest of my outfit. Tevas don't go with everything.

The maître d pulled my chair out for me when he showed me to my table. The Chardonnay was crisp and cold and the dinner was a deliciously hot and creamy pasta alfredo. As I rose to leave, I left a generous tip on the table.

The next morning the hotel shuttle took me back to the airport without the slightest hint of adventure and I tried to deeply soak in the sights of the jungle along the ride. I felt so different, like a different person had crawled into my skin. Not quite three weeks had passed, yet so much had profoundly changed in me. I thought about the beautiful people I'd met, the people who went out of their way and took risks to help me when they could have just passed me and my haphazard-situations by. It was none of their business, after all, what happened to one silly little white girl in over her head. But they didn't. And I wondered why not?

I thought of the woman in the church in Villahermosa at the beginning of my trip. I thought about the cross worn by so many people I'd encountered, and the knowledge that many people here were devoutly Catholic, although a bit of Chiapas' own blend of Catholicism, but a faith in God nonetheless. I wondered if it was their religious culture that brought out the best in them or was it something else in their culture. Or was Gandal-Claus…was it God looking out for little ole me once again?

Then I thought about Jorge, the taxi driver at the beginning of my trip, about Jose at the Best Western, about the amazing girl at the Bus ticket counter, about all of the wonderful people I had encountered, and I thought about who I had been in those situations. Incapable of communicating effectively with words, I'd had to resort to showing my vulnerability, desperately trying to connect through eye contact, gestures, and body posturing. In such a state I was fully authentic because I wasn't adept enough at any of those forms of communication to cloak anything about myself. I did something I'd been told never to do: I showed them exactly who I was in the moment. I stood before them a raw, sometimes frightened, sometimes goofy, flawed human being who desperately needed their help. I reached out and they met my authenticity with their own, innate and beautiful natures.

I wondered how often travelers who come to the United States encounter similarly kind people. I hoped often. I vowed to be that kind of person given the slightest opportunity.

That night I was lying on my bed, in my own home, safely back in Colorado, looking at pictures from my trip, marveling, pondering, and appreciating, when the phone rang. It was my ex asking if he could come over and talk. I was tired and confused, but I also had butterflies in my stomach, so I said yes. It's been twelve years and we've been together ever since.

A year later, almost to the day I left the Maya Bell, I was sitting in my office and the office manager came in and dropped my mail on my desk. Amongst a stack of miscellaneous letters and trade journals there was an advertisement in Spanish for a beautiful beachside resort in Argentina. Handwritten across the bottom of the flyer were only two words, in Spanish: "Te Recuerdo." *I remember you.*

If you liked what you read, please let Amazon know by taking a sec to review it, even if only a word or two...and please feel free to

share it with your friends. Lots of them! If you have a comment about anything in the book you'd like to share with me, or would like to be added to a mailing list so you'll be the first to know about future releases, email me at yogamamasbuddhasandals@gmail.com. I will only send you notice of new work, not a daily blog, or advertising or any other time-sucking, in-box clogging, word clutter. Again, Thank you for reading my story.

ABOUT THE AUTHOR

Donna Stewart was born in Memphis, Tennessee but she grew up, in every sense of the words, in Colorado. She has a bachelor's in Political Science and Creative Writing and studied psychology in graduate school...and life. She lives with her amazing family in Colorado.

Acknowledgements

No book is ever really written by only one person and I owe a lot to those who've helped me write mine: Special thanks go to my amazing husband, Darren, for acting as my sounding board, editor, and primary literary support team. And for the amazing feat of patience as I let this book flood over into other areas of our lives. Thank you to my wonderful daughter, Nila, for all of her patience while I was writing this book and sometimes didn't have as much time to play. She is also the photographer for the cover shot, demonstrating that, at just barely 8-years-old, she's got strong talent for photography. Thank you to Terry Bacon, for repeating over and over and over to "Get Published!" And for teaching me how it's done. Thank you to Chuck Thompson for your own amazing works and for taking a few minutes of your time for little ole me. Thank you to Steve Meyers for convincing me I had a way with words. Thank you to Bruce Spining for your insight and encouragement. Thank you to Terry Hobbs, for inspiring me and helping me smooth out the rougher edges (and catch many, many misspellings, grammatical errors and verbal inconsistencies!). Thank you, Chris McCoy, for convincing me that others might actually enjoy reading my crazy stories. Thank you to Anna Price and Dennis Johnson, for taking me out of the woods, teaching me how to comb out my hair when I need to, but remain wild on the inside. Thank you for sharing your love of literature and theater and for reassuring me of their importance in the world. Thank you for being there. Without you, I would never have survived. Dennis, thank you for that time you called the letters I wrote to you, when I was away in San Luis for the summer, "marvelous writing." All of your words have always meant way more than you know. Thank you to my mother, for the gift of a beautiful and powerful faith in God.

ENDNOTES

[i] http://mexicolesstraveled.com/comalcalco.htm

[ii] http://www.mexconnect.com/articles/1241-did-you-know-mayan-pyramid-in-tabasco-mexico-has-possible-roman-links

[iii] Winik, Lyric Wallwork. Meltdown. Forbes Magazine. http://www.forbes.com/forbes-life-magazine/1999/0308/043.html

[iv] http://borgenproject.org/poverty-in-mexico/

[v] http://flag.blackened.net/revolt/mexico/reports/back94.html

[vi] http://cronkitenewsonline.com/2014/07/central-american-minors-pushed-north-by-poverty-violence-and-hopes-for-refuge/

[vii] http://cronkitenewsonline.com/2014/07/central-american-minors-pushed-north-by-poverty-violence-and-hopes-for-refuge/

[viii] http://www.huffingtonpost.com/2012/08/21/food-waste-americans-throw-away-food-study_n_1819340.html

[ix] http://www.pbs.org/frontlineworld/fellows/mexico0803/3.html

[x] Higgins, Nicholas. Understanding the Chiapan Rebellion. Modernist Visions and the Invisible Chiapan Indian. University of Texas press. 2004.

[xi] Higgins, Nicholas P. Understanding the Chiapas Rebellion. 2004.

[xii] Chompsky, Noam. !Ya Basta! Ten Years of Zapatista Uprising. Writings of Subcomandante Insurgente Marcos. AK Press, Edinburgh, Scotland. 2004

[xiii] Useconomy.about.com/od/tradepolicy/p/NAFTA_Problems.htm

[xiv] https://www.jacobinmag.com/2016/04/zapatistas-ezln-san-andres-marcos-chiapas/

[xv] http://schoolsforchiapas.org/wp-content/uploads/2014/03/Understanding-the-Acteal-Massacre.pdf
The Politics of Massacre: Acteal, Low Intensity Warfare and NGOs by George Caffentzis, January, 1998

[xvi] http://schoolsforchiapas.org/wp-content/uploads/2014/03/Understanding-the-Acteal-Massacre.pdf
The Politics of Massacre: Acteal, Low Intensity Warfare and NGOs by George Caffentzis, January, 1998

[xvii] Benjamin, Thomas. "A Time of Requonquest: History, the Maya Revival, and the Zapatista Rebellion in Chiapas." American Historical Review. April 2000.

[xviii] http://www.livescience.com/5759-rare-vegetarian-spider-discovered.html

[xix] Fair World Project. Maya Vinic: Moving from Tragedy to Triumph. http://fairworldproject.org/voices-of-fair-trade/maya-vinic-moving-from-tragedy-to-triumph/

[xx] Whc.unesco.org/en/list/411/

[xxi] Phillips, Tony. "Why the World Didn't End Yesterday." http://science.nasa.gov/science-news/science-at-nasa/2012/14dec_yesterday/

[xxii] Halperin, Maurice. The Rise and Decline of Fidel Castro: An Essay in Contemporary History. University of California Press, Berkeley. 1972

[xxiii]Schele, Elaine Day. May 2012. The Untold Story of Alberto Ruz L'Huillier and his Archaeological Excavations at Palenque, Mèxico: a micro-and macro historical approach. UT Electronic Theses and Dissertations. Citable URI: http://hdl.handle.net/2152/22254

[xxiv] Phillips, J.D. Guiteras Is Slain In Battle In Cuba. The New York Times. May 9, 1935. P. 1, 11.

[xxv] Le Riverend, J. En Memoria de Alberto Ruz L'Huillier. Revista de la Biblioteca Jose Marti. XXI (70):165-170.

[xxvi] Coe, Michael. Breaking the Maya Code. Revised. Thames & Hudson, New York, N.Y. 1999.

[xxvii] Schele, Elaine Day. May 2012. The Untold Story of Alberto Ruz L'Huillier and his Archaeological Excavations at Palenque, Mèxico: a micro-and macro historical approach. UT Electronic Theses and Dissertations. Citable URI: http://hdl.handle.net/2152/22254

[xxviii] Barnett, Tracy L. Subcoyote Alberto: Father of Latin America's Green Movement. The Huffington Post. May 25, 2011.

[xxix] (Ruz and Mason 1953:96)

[xxx] Jade in Mesoamerica. The Met. http://www.metmuseum.org/toah/hd/jade2/hd_jade2.htm

[xxxi] Genesis 2, verse 15.

[xxxii]http://www.ipsnews.net/2016/03/rural-community-fights-a-second-dam-and-a-new-expropriation-of-land/

[xxxiii] http://business.financialpost.com/news/energy/mexico-opens-up-huge-oil-reserves-to-foreign-production-offering-massive-potential-and-big-risk

[xxxiv]http://www.ipsnews.net/2016/03/rural-community-fights-a-second-dam-and-a-new-expropriation-of-land/

[xxxv] Inter Press Service News Agency. Rural Community Fights a Second Dam and a New Expropriation of Land. http://www.ipsnews.net/2016/03/rural-community-fights-a-second-dam-and-a-new-expropriation-of-land/

[xxxvi] SIPAZ, The International Service for Peace. https://sipazen.wordpress.com/2015/11/19/chiapas-ejidatarios-from-chicoasen-initiate-hunger-strike-against-chicoasen-ii-dam-project/

[xxxvii] Sachs, Jeffrey. "The End of Poverty: Economic Possibilities of our Time." Penguin books. 2006

[xxxviii] Phillips, Tony. "Why the World Didn't End Yesterday." Dec. 22, 2012. http://science.nasa.gov/science-news/science-at-nasa/2012/14dec_yesterday/

[xxxix] "Beyond 2012: Why the World Didn't End." December 22, 2012. http://www.nasa.gov/topics/earth/features/2012.html

CPSIA information can be obtained
at www.ICGtesting.com
Printed in the USA
FSHW01n1121220518
48559FS